The Turns

A. E. W. Mason

Alpha Editions

This edition published in 2024

ISBN : 9789362518491

Design and Setting By
Alpha Editions
www.alphaedis.com
Email - info@alphaedis.com

Contents

CHAPTER I

THE SWINGING OF A CHANDELIER

At the first glance it looked as if the midnight chimes of a clock in an old city of the Midlands might most fitly ring in this history. But we live in a very small island, and its inhabitants have for so long been wanderers upon the face of the earth that one can hardly search amongst them for the beginnings of either people or events without slipping unexpectedly over the edge of England. So it is in this instance. For, although it was in England that Captain Rames, Mr. Benoliel, Cynthia, the little naturalized Frenchman, and the rest of them met and struggled more or less inefficiently to express themselves; although, too, Ludsey, the old city, was during a period the pivot of their lives; for the beginnings of their relationship one with another, it is necessary to go further afield, and back by some few years. One must turn toward a lonely estancia in the south-west of Argentina, where, on a hot, still night of summer, a heavy chandelier touched by no human hand swung gently to and fro.

This queer thing happened in the dining-room of the house, and between half-past ten and eleven o'clock. It was half-way through January, and Mr. and Mrs. Daventry were still seated at the table over a late supper. For Robert Daventry had on that day begun the harvesting of his eight leagues of wheat, and there had been little rest for any one upon the estancia since daybreak. He sat now taking his ease opposite his wife, with a cup of black coffee in front of him and a cigar between his lips, a big, broad, sunburnt man with a beard growing gray and a thick crop of brown hair upon his head; loose-limbed still, and still getting, when he stood up, the value of every inch of his six feet two. As he lounged at the table he debated with his wife in a curious gentle voice a question which, played with once, had begun of late years to insist upon an answer.

"We are both over fifty, Joan," he said. "And we have made our money."

"We have also made our friends, Robert," replied his wife. She was a short, stoutish woman, quick with her hands, practical in her speech. Capacity was written broad upon her like a label, and, for all her husband's bulk, she was the better man of the two, even at the first casual glance. There was a noticeable suggestion of softness and amiability in Robert Daventry. It was hardly, perhaps, to be localized in any feature. Rather he diffused it about him like an atmosphere. One would have wondered how it came about that in a country so stern as Argentina he had prospered so exceedingly had his wife not been present to explain his prosperity. It was so evident that she drove the cart and that he ran between the shafts--evident, that is, to others than Robert Daventry. She had been clever enough and fond enough to conceal from him their exact relationship. So now it was with an air of pleading that she replied to him:

"We have not only made our friends, Robert. We have made them here. If we go, we lose them."

"Yes," he answered. "But it wouldn't be as if we had to start quite fresh again. I have old ties with Warwickshire. Thirty years won't have broken them all."

Joan Daventry answered slowly:

"Thirty years. That's a long time, Robert."

"And yet," said Robert Daventry with a wistfulness in his voice which almost weakened her into a consent against which her judgment no less than her inclinations fought. "And yet there's a house on the London road which I might have passed yesterday--it's so vivid to me now. A white house set back from the highway behind a great wall of old red brick. Above the coping of the wall you can see the rows of level windows and the roof of a wing a story lower than the rest of the house. And if the gates are open you catch a glimpse of great cedar trees on a wide lawn--a lawn of fine grass like emeralds."

His eyes turned back upon his boyhood, and the thought of his county set his heart aching. Long white roads, rising and dipping between high elms, with a yard or two of turf on either side for a horse to canter on; cottages, real cottages, not shapeless buildings of corrugated iron standing gauntly up against the sky-line at the edge of a round of burnt, bare plain, but cottages rich with phlox and deep in trees--the pictures were flung before his eyes by the lantern of his memories as if upon a white sheet. But, above all, it was the thought of the greenery of Warwickshire which caught at his throat; the woods flecked with sunlight, the lawns like emeralds.

He glanced at a thermometer which hung against the wall. Here, even at eleven o'clock of the night, it marked this January ninety-seven degrees of heat. The mosquitoes trumpeted and drummed against the gauze curtains which covered the open windows; and outside the windows the night was black and hot like velvet.

Robert Daventry drew his handkerchief across his forehead and with his elbow on the table leaned his face upon his hand. His wife looked at him quickly and with solicitude.

"You are tired to-night, Robert," she said gently. "That's why you want to give the estancia up."

Robert Daventry shook his head and corrected her.

"No, Joan. But I am more tired to-night and very likely that's the explanation." Then he laughed at a recollection. "Do you remember when the squadron came to Montevideo two years ago? There was a dinner at the legation at Buenos Ayres. I sat next to the commodore, and he asked me how old I was. When I told him that I was just fifty, he replied: 'Ah, now you will begin to find life very interesting. For you will notice every year that you are able to do a little less than you did the year before.' Well, I am beginning, my dear, to find life interesting from the commodore's point of view."

Joan did not answer him at once, and the couple sat for awhile in silence, with their thoughts estranged.

For Joan Daventry shrank, with all her soul, from that coveted white house on the London road. Old ties could be resumed, was Robert's thought. He was forgetful that the ties were his, and his alone. She had no share in them and she had come to a time of life when the making of new friends is a weariness and a labor. With infinite toil and self-denial they had carved out their niche here in the Argentine Republic. They spent the winter in their house in Buenos Ayres, the summer upon the Daventry estancia. Their life was an ordered, comfortable progression of the months. For both of them, to her thinking, the time for new adventures had long gone by. They had had their full proportion of them in their youth. And so while Robert Daventry dreamed of a green future Joan was busily remembering.

"When we first came here to settle," she said slowly, as she counted up all that had been done in these twenty-seven years, "we drove for two days. If the house on the London road is vivid to you, that drive is as clear to me. Our heaviest luggage was our hopes;" and Robert Daventry smiled across the table.

"I have not forgotten that either," he said; and there was a whole world of love in his voice.

"When we reached here we found a tin house with three rooms and nothing else, not a tree, hardly a track. Now there's an avenue half a mile long, there are plantations, there's a real brick house for the plantations to shelter. There are wells, there's a garden, there's a village at the end of the avenue, there's even a railway station to-day. These things are our doing, Robert;" and her voice was lifted up with pride.

"I know," replied her husband. "But I ask myself whether the time has not come to hand them on."

Once more the look of solicitude shone in his wife's eyes.

"I could leave the estancia," she said doubtfully, "though it would almost break my heart to do it. But suppose we did. What would become of you in England? I have a fear," and she leaned forward across the table.

"Why a fear?" he asked.

"Because I think that people who have lived hard, like you and me, run a great risk if they retire just when they feel that they are beginning to grow old. A real risk of life, I mean. I think such as you and I would be killed off by inactivity rather than by any disease."

She did not deny that something was wrong in their present situation. But she had a different conception of what that something was; and she had a different remedy.

"We should find life too dull?" he exclaimed. "Too lonely, Joan?" and he struck the table with his hand; "I find it lonely here;" and at that she uttered a low cry:

"Oh, my dear, and what of me?" and the wistfulness of her voice struck him to silence, a remorseful silence. After all, his days were full.

"There's our other plan," she suggested gently.

"Yes. To be sure! There's our other plan," he said. He leaned back in his chair, his face upturned toward the ceiling, and a thoughtful look in his eyes.

"We have talked it over, haven't we? But we have played with it all the time. It would be so big an experiment."

He ended the sentence abruptly. The look of thought passed from his face. It became curious, perplexed. Then he cried with a start of dismay:

"You see, Joan, even my eyes are beginning to play tricks with me. I could swear that the chandelier is swinging to and fro above our heads."

Joan looked anxiously at her husband, and then up toward the ceiling. At once surprise drove the anxiety from her face and thoughts.

"But it *is* swinging," she exclaimed. Both of them stared at the chandelier. There was not a doubt about the phenomenon possible. Not a breath of wind stirred in the garden, not a sound was audible overhead. Yet very gently the chandelier, with its lighted globes, oscillated above their heads. Robert Daventry rose to his feet and touched it.

"Yes, it is swinging," he said. He stopped it, and held it quite still. Then he resumed his seat.

"Very well, Joan," he said with a new briskness in his voice, "we will make the experiment. Come! When we go to Buenos Ayres in the winter! We will try the other plan. Even if it fails it will be worth making."

Joan's face lighted up.

"If it fails, then we'll go home," she said.

No doubt the relief which Robert Daventry felt in the proof that his eyes were not failing him led him thus briskly to fall in with the scheme which both approached with timidity; and so the swinging of the chandelier had its share in bringing them to their decision. But the chandelier had not done with them. For hardly had Robert Daventry ceased to speak when it began again to swing backward and forward before their eyes. So it swung for exactly five minutes and then of its own accord it stopped.

"That's very strange," said Robert Daventry. He looked at the clock upon the mantel-shelf. It was five minutes past eleven.

"It's unaccountable," he continued. But he was able to account for it the next day. For a local paper brought to them the news that at ten minutes to eleven o'clock on the evening before, seven hundred miles away on the other side of the great barrier of the Andes, an earthquake had set the shores of the Pacific heaving like a sea, and Valparaiso, that city of earthquakes, had tumbled into ruins.

CHAPTER II

OF AN EARTHQUAKE AND JAMES CHALLONER

The experiences of James Challoner on that day of ruin at Valparaiso were various, but none of them were pleasant. It was his twenty-eighth birthday and up to two o'clock in the afternoon he was, as for the last six weeks he had been, a clerk in the great house of R. C. Royle & Sons. There was no sort of business in Chile which R. C. Royle & Sons were not prepared to undertake and carry through with efficiency, from a colossal deal in nitrates to the homeward freight of your portmanteau. It was, to be sure, upon the latter class of work that James Challoner was asked to concentrate his abilities. But advancement was a principle of the house, and in the vast ramifications of its business, opportunities of advancement came quickly. James Challoner, who for the best part of five years had been drifting unsuccessfully up and down the Pacific Coast, between Callao and Concepcion, was consequently accounted a lucky man to have secured employment in that house at all.

"If he can only keep it!" said his friends, shrugging their shoulders, and his young wife, in the little house up the hill, bent over her child and whispered the same words. But in her mouth they were a prayer.

At two o'clock, then, upon his birthday, James Challoner returned from his luncheon to the office, but as he took his seat he was summoned to the manager's room. He walked down the long room between the tables on which samples of produce were exhibited, then past the cashier's brass-fenced desks where the banking business was done, to a little compartment partitioned off in a corner. There Wallace Bourdon, a young partner in control of this branch of the firm, sat in a tilted chair, with his knees against a table, awaiting him.

"Mr. Challoner, it is within your knowledge, I suppose, that we are negotiating with the Government at Santiago for the construction of a new railway in the north."

Challoner shook his head.

"That's not in my department, sir," he said.

"Quite true," said Wallace Bourdon. He opened a drawer of the table and threw half a dozen letters down on the top of it under Challoner's eyes. "These letters are copies of our proposals. There are two firms competing with us to which these copies would be valuable. They were found in your desk while you were out at luncheon. What were they doing there?"

James Challoner stared at the letters and pulled at his moustache.

"I can't think, sir. They must have been put there," he said, and then with a cry of indignation: "I must have an enemy in the office."

"Well, that's hard," said Wallace Bourdon sympathetically. "For he seems to have got back on you good and strong. You can draw your money from the cashier, Mr. Challoner, and clear out of this house just as soon as you can find it convenient;" and Wallace Bourdon dropped the legs of his chair onto the floor.

James Challoner took his money and went out into the town. He sat moodily on a high stool at a bar for an hour or so. Then some men of his acquaintance joined him, and from moody he became blusterful and boisterous. But both the moodiness and the bluster were phases of the one deep-seated feeling--a reluctance to go up the hill and meet his wife. It was seven o'clock before he had gained the necessary courage, and when he did face his wife he followed the usual practice of his kind and blurted out aggressively the news of his dismissal.

"I was lowering myself by going into the office at all as a clerk," he cried. "I told you so when you urged me to do it. Upon my word it almost serves me right, Doris. I have never known any good come from a man's lowering himself. He is bound to make enemies amongst his new associates. Jealousy is a despicable thing, but there's a deal of it floating about in the world, and one's a fool to shut one's eyes to it. However, we can't let the business rest there. My honor's impugned. That's the truth of it, Doris. I lie under a dishonorable charge. There's a stigma on our child's name, and it must be removed."

He drew a chair briskly up to the table, pulled a piece of note-paper toward him, and dipped his pen in the ink.

"Let me see, now! Who can my enemy be? Who is it that hates me? Can't you think of some one?" and in an instant he pushed the blotting pad from him. "You might say something, Doris. You just stand and look and never open your mouth."

That was James Challoner's trouble, and the cause of his uneasiness. His wife neither buoyed him up with high-sounding phrases, nor afforded him the opportunity by any reproach to work himself into a fine heat of indignation. She had given him one dreadful look, her whole countenance a quivering cry of dismay made visible, and thereafter she had just stood with no word on her lips, her great eyes disconcertingly fixed upon his face and her mind quite hidden. She went out from the room and left him sitting in great discomfort. He detested her habit of silence, but he feared still more the thought of him which it might conceal, and he dared not break it with acrimonies. When she returned again into the room it was to say:

"Dinner is ready."

"Well, we must dine," said Challoner.

"It is fortunate that after all I didn't hire that servant at once," said Doris.

"Yes, that was lucky. We can't afford a servant now," said James Challoner.

Fear lest his wife should "lower herself" did not trouble him at all. During dinner he talked in self-defence, flurriedly, about his enemy, pointing vaguely to this man or to that, and watching keenly for some droop of disdain about Doris's lips. But she gave no sign, and at the back of all his thought was the wounding question:

"What does she think of me?"

He smoked his pipe outside the door after dinner, with the lighted streets of the town spread out below him. The house stood apart, high up on the great amphitheatre of hills above Valparaiso; and on the opposite side of the road the ground fell steeply. The great bay lay open beneath his eyes to the distant tip of its northern horn; no inland pool could have slept more quietly than did the Pacific on that summer night; still water and mirrored stars, it widened out in the warm dusk to the sky's rim. A huge black steamer lay out beyond the edge of the jetty, with the great lights blazing from its saloon windows and the little lights steady on its masts. From the close-built streets at the water's edge there rose a pleasant murmur of many voices. No warnings were being given. Valparaiso, like any other tropical city, was taking its ease in the cool of the evening.

At ten o'clock James Challoner, having nothing better to do and no money to spend, went indoors. He locked the front door and with a definite relief found that his wife had already gone to bed. He stood in the empty, barely furnished sitting-room, and his thoughts were swept back to the morning at Southampton, five years ago, when Doris had crept on board the steamer which was to take them to South America. He remembered bitterly the buoyant hopes with which that runaway marriage had begun and Doris's fears that her flight had been already discovered and that an attempt at the last moment might be made to stop her.

"It has been a bad mistake for me," he said, as all the wonderful things which he might have done, had he not been hampered with a wife, glittered in his mind. The truth, however, was not to be grasped by him unless he would face truthfully the history of his marriage, and that he was not constituted to do. It was a story common enough: A young man with no will and caressing manners, who was hastily packed off to South America, with a few hundred pounds in his pocket, to avoid exposure in his own country, and a young girl too staunch to her beliefs--these were the characters, and, given them, the story tells itself. "Yes, it has all been a very bad mistake for me," thought James Challoner, and switching off the lights he betook himself to bed. A door in the inner wall of his bedroom opened into the room where his wife and child slept. He listened for a moment with his ear against the panel. All was silent in that room.

"She can sleep," he grumbled, finding even a grievance here. But he did not sleep for long. For, just at the moment when the chandelier began to swing in Mr. Daventry's dining-room, he was shaken out of his slumber. He lay for a few seconds in the vague and pleasant space between wakefulness and dreams, playing with the fancy that he was in a cabin on a ship at sea. But the fancy passed, and he was beset by a stranger illusion. He happened to be lying upon his side, with his face turned toward the outer wall of his bedroom; and as he lay he saw quite distinctly the wall gently and noiselessly split open. It split open high up and near to the ceiling, and it let through the stars and a strip of sky. Then the wall closed neatly together again, brick fitting with brick, so that not a chink was left. The room once more was black, the stars shut out.

Challoner was still pondering upon this remarkable phenomenon when a third sensation shook him altogether out of his lethargy. He was violently jolted. This could be no illusion. It was as if some one, crouching beneath the bed, had suddenly risen on hands and knees and struck the mattress with his shoulders. Challoner sprang out of bed, tottered, and clung to the bedpost for support. The room was rocking like a tree in a gale and underneath his feet the boards strained and heaved. It was his first experience of an earthquake, but he had no doubt that he was undergoing it, and fear made his hands grip the iron post of the bed so that his palms were bruised. His chief terror was the floor. The feel of it moving unstably beneath his feet, the sound of its boards cracking loosened his knees. At any moment it might burst upward and explode. At some moment and very soon it must. He had no fear that it would collapse and gape open; it would surely burst like a shell; and in his fear of that explosion the rocking of the walls was of no account.

He tried to think, and instinct reminded him of civilized man's chief necessities.

"My shoes, my money."

He groped along the bed for the switch of the light, but light did not answer to the summons. In the darkness he stooped, found his shoes, and slipped them on. His few dollars, drawn that afternoon from the cashier of R. C. Royle & Sons, were in the drawer of a night-table by his bed. He found them. There was a cupboard in the inner wall. He lurched across to it, and, tearing a long overcoat from a hook, slipped it on and dropped the money in his pocket. Close by the cupboard was the door of his wife's bedroom. He remembered her now, and flung the door open.

"Doris," he cried, and no answer was returned to him.

"Doris," he cried again, and this time the wail of his child answered him from her cot.

He crossed to the bed. He leaned over it and put out his hand to shake his wife by the shoulder out of her deep sleep. And with a shock he became aware that she was leaning upon her elbow in the darkness. She was wide-awake all the time.

"Quick!" he cried, in a sudden exasperation. "There is an earthquake. The house is falling."

She replied in a strange, quiet voice:

"I know."

She made no beginning of a movement. She was awake, had been, perhaps, longer awake than he himself; she knew the swift peril which had befallen them; yet she remained propped on her elbow in the darkness, passively expectant. Or was she dazed? Even at that moment the question flashed through Challoner's mind and brought him a queer relief. But it was answered in a moment.

"I called to you twice," he said; and his wife answered:

"I heard;" and there was again no hint of bewilderment in her voice. It was the voice of a woman who had all her wits about her; not of one who was stunned.

Meanwhile the earth rumbled beneath them and the room shook. Challoner felt for a candle by the bedside, struck a match, and lighted it. His wife watched him quietly. Her dark eyes shone in the candle-light, inscrutably veiling her thoughts.

"Quick!" he cried. "Get up. There's no time to lose." He lifted the child out of the cot, still wrapped in her bedclothes.

"Come."

His wife rose, as it seemed to him, with incredible slowness. He could have screamed in his terror. As he stumbled across the floor to the door, she opened a wardrobe and, taking out a cloak, drew it about her shoulders. In the door-way he turned and saw her.

"Good God!" he cried, and the question in his mind leaped to his lips and was uttered. "Do you want to kill us all?"

"I had to find a cloak."

"A cloak!" he cried contemptuously. He himself had tarried to slip on his overcoat, but, no doubt, that was different. Certainly his wife made no rejoinder. "To be buried under this house for the sake of a cloak," he cried, his lips so chattering with terror that he could hardly pronounce the words.

"Go first," she said; and he ran out of the doorway. She followed him, leaving the door open behind her, and the candle burning in the room. They were still in the passage when an appalling roar deafened their ears. The lighted candle shot up into the air and was extinguished, and in the darkness the splitting of timber, the overthrow and the wreckage of furniture, rent the air and ceased. Of a sudden the throats of the fugitives were choked with dust. The fear which had so terrified him was justified. The floor had exploded, like artillery, in the room he had this moment quitted. His terror became a panic. He would have killed his wife had she stood in his way. He rushed downstairs, inarticulately crying. He fumbled in the darkness for the bolt of the front door, sobbing and cursing. He found it, flung the door open, and leaped out into the open air. He ran across the road, and as he ran a great stone fell with a crash, from the archway of the door, and the walls of the passage clashed together behind him. With a loud clatter of thunder the whole house crumbled down into a smoking heap of bricks. Challoner turned. He was quite alone with the child in his arms. And for a little while he stood very still.

But he was no longer in darkness. About many of the villas on the hillside the flames were creeping, and their inhabitants were racing upward to the open heights, or searching desperately among the ruins for those whom the earthquake had entrapped. While lower down by the water's edge the city was ablaze and over all the bay the sky was red. The ground still shook beneath Challoner's feet, and the child in his arms began to cry. He laid it down against the low wall of the path and crept cautiously back to the ruins of his house.

"Doris," he called, and again, "Doris."

His voice was low, but there was more of awe than grief audible in the cry. "Doris," he called a third time, but in a louder and more urgent tone. A few bricks, hanging to a fragment of wall dislodged themselves and clattered down upon the heap of ruin. But no other answer came. He stooped suddenly where the archway of the entrance door had been. The great stone had fallen with so much force that one end had sunk into the ground; the other, however, rested upon a fragment of the stone pillar of the door; and so the stone lay under a pile of bricks titled at an angle. Through the space left by the angle a woman's hand and arm protruded. It was not pinned down by the stone. It pointed with limp fingers toward Challoner, and beside it a trickle of blood ran out. Challoner knelt and touched the hand.

"Doris," he said.

Her voice had not answered to his, and now there was no response in her fingers to his touch. The arm moved quite easily. The walls of the passage had borne her down and crushed her. Challoner remembered with a shiver the crash and clatter of them as they had knocked together just behind his heels. His wife had been killed in that downfall. She could not have survived.

Challoner rose again to his feet.

"She was awake," he said, and he talked aloud to himself. "She should have hurried. She could have escaped had she hurried;" and the picture of her leaning upon her elbow in her bed in the dark troubled his soul. There is no terror like the terror which comes from the shaking of the earth and the overthrow of its houses. Yet she, a woman--so ran his thoughts--had endured it. Her hand pointing, from beneath the stones, accused him for all the limpness of its fingers. She had welcomed it.

The child wailed from the other side of the road. Challoner crossed to it. He stood and looked at it doubtfully. Still in doubt, he looked away. From the blazing town rose a babel of cries, a roar of flames, a crash of buildings falling in, and every now and then, quite distinct from the confusion, a shrill, clear scream would leap into the air like a thin fountain of water. But the sea was calm; the great ship, with every cord of its rigging strung black against the glowing sky, lay without a movement. Boats were plying between it and the shore. Challoner could see the tiny specks of them on the red water.

"There's no tidal wave," he said in a dull voice. "That's extraordinary;" and then he picked up his daughter in his arms, and climbed higher up the hill to await the dawn.

CHAPTER III

CHALLONER'S PILGRIMAGE

There were two more shocks that night, the first at five minutes past one, the second half an hour before sunrise. James Challoner sat in the centre of the most open space he could find, his overcoat drawn close about him and his daughter clasped tightly to his breast. But it was almost unconsciously that he held her so. His brain was dazed, and the only image at all clear in his mind was that of his dead wife's hand protruding beneath the great stone and directing against him its mute accusation. But, even so, it was the limp look of the fingers which chiefly troubled him, and that only troubled him from time to time. For the greater part of the interval before daybreak he sat watching the roofs of the buildings below him burst in tongues of fire and topple down with a clatter of slates in bright showers of sparks, much as a child sits open-mouthed at the fireworks. Now he huddled his coat close about him, now some spire of flame towering skyward more terribly beautiful than the rest, drew a cry from his lips; and now again, looking out over the quiet pond of the bay, he asked dully, "Why is there no tidal wave?"

Morning came at last over the hill behind him, gray and extraordinarily cold. All about him he saw people, huddled like himself upon the slopes, men, women, and children, shivering in their night-attire and their bare feet bloody from the stones. All at once Challoner was aware that he was hungry. His little daughter reached out her arms and wailed. Hunger, too, as the sun rose, mastered the fears of the refugees upon the hill-side. One by one, group by group, they rose stiffly and straggled down to the ruined ways by the water-side. Challoner went with the rest; and half-way down they all began to hurry, beset by the same fear. There would not be food enough for all. The thought seemed to sweep like a wind across the face of the hill, and the hurry became savage.

Along the open esplanade families were squatting side by side. A few of the more fortunate had somehow secured and erected tents; and others were crowded into storage sheds. But the most of them were sitting in the open waiting desolately for they knew not what. And already in that town, though the earthquake was barely six hours old, catastrophe had made its sharp division between the sheep and the goats. For whereas upon the esplanade men and women, and amongst them many unexpected figures, were already organizing succor for the outcasts, amongst the smoking ruins the marauders were already at work, robbing, murdering. There was no longer any law in Valparaiso.

Challoner made his way to the esplanade. A man whom he knew, the agent of a steamship company, hurried past him. Challoner stopped him.

"Where can I get food?" he asked.

Challoner was a strongly built, tall man, and the agent answered roughly.

"You? You will have to wait. You are able to;" and then he caught sight of the child in Challoner's arms, still wrapped about with her bedclothes. His voice changed to friendliness.

"Yours?" he asked.

Challoner nodded.

"Where's its mother?"

Challoner answered simply:

"Dead."

The agent took out a piece of paper and a pencil from his pocket. "Sorry," he said. "Of course, that alters the case." He wrote a line upon the paper and gave it to Challoner. Then he pointed to a tin shed, around which a crowd was already collecting.

"We are distributing a little food there. You'll be given your share, for you have a child to look after. But I should advise you to look slippy;" and the agent hurried off.

Challoner did look slippy. Because of his child he got food for himself as well as for his child; and as he sat on the ground, in the shadow of a low wall, after his meal, that fact set him thinking. There is much loving kindness for children in South America. From east to west it runs across the continent, just as from east to west human life is cheap, provided that it is grown up. You might, anywhere in those days, and, in some places you may still, slay your neighbor and avoid anything like excessive inconvenience as a result of your slaying. But if you kick a boy into the gutter because he refuses to desist from whistling, to your distraction, outside your office window, you are liable to be fined heavily, and you may be sent to prison. For you have hurt the *dignidad del hombre*. Challoner was aware generally of the consideration for children which prevailed. But now it was brought very practically home to him in the particular. His little daughter Doris was a definite asset to him. He looked down upon her with new eyes as she slept on the ground at his side, with a chubby hand thrown across his knee. She was no longer a nuisance. She was as good as money--better, indeed, since money could not buy food to-day in Valparaiso. And there had been a moment when he had stood, up there before the ruins of his house, doubting whether he should leave her behind or no. James Challoner was quite chilled by the thought of the mistake he had almost made, and the fool he had almost been.

Doris moved her head in her sleep.

"Precious one," he said affectionately; and he proceeded in his turn to sleep.

He woke up in time to see two great Chilian cruisers sweep round the point into the bay, and a stoutly built, square captain, whom he could have mistaken for an Englishman, come ashore with his sailors, to take command of the town. He obtained shelter in a hut for that night, and during the hours of darkness he thought out his own immediate problem.

Valparaiso was not, and for some months would not be. Even when it should be rebuilt there would be no work for him, since--in his thoughts he clung to euphemisms--his enemies had ruined his good name. Therefore he must get away and he had his daughter at his hand to assist him.

He obtained, through his good Samaritan, the agent, a rough suit for himself and some clothing for his child and a parcel of food. He slung the parcel over his shoulders, lifted his child in his arms, and walked out that afternoon from Valparaiso up the great post-road toward the Andes. He was strong and his girl inherited of his strength. It was summer, a summer of no rain. He tramped along the valleys of Chile, and his daughter was his passport and franked his way. He secured a night's shelter at a farm-house here, food and a trifle of money there, a ride for Doris upon a mule one day, a lift for both of them in a cart the next. The valley narrowed, the green floor of it became stones, the trees thinned, the great barrier of the cordilleras closed in about James Challoner and towered higher and higher above his head. The road wound sharply upward, now backward, and forward in a desolate, wild country of gray rock splashed with orange and yellow and deep red. He started early one morning and stood on the top of the Cumbre Pass, thirteen thousand feet above the sea, by mid-day. On the very summit he was overtaken by the post and driven down at a gallop to Las Cuevas. From Las Cuevas he walked to Punta del Inca. And at Punta del Inca he took his ease for a week, with the great snow-mass of Aconcagua showing in a gap of the hills across the valley.

It was the season of the baths at Punta del Inca. The hotel was full and James Challoner prospered, as from the beginning he had thought that he would. He had reckoned upon Punta del Inca on that night in Valparaiso when he had determined upon his journey. He sat by the natural bridge, with his little daughter in his arms, a travel-stained and patient figure, and amongst those gigantic hills he told his moving story to such as passed and would listen. He went up to the hotel at night, and under the lights of the veranda he told it again. Amongst the many qualities which he misused was a vivid gift of narrative, and he possessed, at this time at all events, a gentle voice with an admirable note of emotion. Thus all was in his favor. The beauty and peace of the scenery, his manner, the prettiness of his child--even the story which he had to tell. But it was not quite the story which would have been told at Valparaiso where, to be sure, he had, as we know, enemies.

"Why did you come to South America?" some curious soul would ask.

"I was a younger son," he would answer; and then, with a charming modesty for the benefit of any English who might be present, "I am of the Dorsetshire Challoners. These old properties.... Land isn't what it was.... An estate mortgaged to the hilt. How could any one take an allowance that must be wrung from it at the cost of the very laborers? No, I thought I would make my own way in the new lands."

He spoke without any arrogance of virtue, any contempt for other younger sons who had not his own compunction, any consciousness of heroism. He went on to tell the romantic story of his marriage and elopement.

"I made my way," he continued, "at least I was making it. My wife, of course, helped me--" and perhaps here his voice would falter ever so slightly, he would turn his face aside and whisper to the stars, yet so that the whisper was audible to people nearer than the stars--"My God, how she helped me! We had dug out our little corner in Valparaiso. There was just room in it for a wife and a child and myself. And then the earthquake came and ruined all."

He made no complaint; he stated the simple facts; he was reticent concerning his wife's death. But by his reticence he managed to wring from it the last ounce of profit; he did not, for instance, describe how he had found her leaning upon her elbow in the darkness, with the walls of her room tottering about her. James Challoner had not forgiven her for that. She had made it so plain that she preferred for her child and herself an appalling death beneath the bricks than the slower decline into misery which awaited them. He tried to omit that remembrance from his mind, as he certainly did from his story.

A collection was made for him to send him on his way. He accepted it with dignity.

"I do not ask for your names," he said. "It would be the merest pretence. I cannot promise to pay you back. I take it as from one man to another." And so with his pocket full he journeyed downward to the vineyards of Mendoza.

At Mendoza he took the train and in a night and a day came to Buenos Ayres. It was in the cool of the evening that he stepped out upon the platform. He was in no doubt what he should do. He had stopped in Buenos Ayres for a month on his way out from England; and he had thought out his plan very carefully during his last night in Valparaiso. He took a train for Barracas, and in the train he tied an old bootlace about his daughter's arm. He left the train before it crossed the bridge, and walked up a hill where great houses stand back behind walls and gardens much as one may see them in Clapham. Some way up the hill he stopped in front of one of these houses.

It was noticeable amongst the houses, because a curious turnstile was let into the garden wall. The turnstile supported a small circular platform partitioned off with screens. James Challoner placed his child upon the platform, rang the bell, and turned the stile. The platform revolved, the child disappeared from view within the garden, and the screens were so arranged that those who received the child within could not see James Challoner outside.

James Challoner went back into the middle of the road, yawned, and stretched his arms above his head. To-day you may cross the Andes from Valparaiso to Buenos Ayres in forty-eight hours. James Challoner had taken four months. He thought of his journey with a chuckle. His daughter had made his way easy.

"Nine hundred miles and I've done 'em on eiderdown," he said. "That's the only bit of comfort I've ever got out of my marriage."

He had left his child in a foundling hospital kept by some wealthy old ladies. He had tied a bootlace round her arm, rather because it was the conventional thing to do, than with any intention of reclaiming her. He was now a free man. He lit his pipe and stuck his hands in his pockets. With a pleasant sense of lightness, he strolled down to exploit his freedom in the bright streets of Buenos Ayres.

CHAPTER IV

CYNTHIA'S BIRTHDAY

Cynthia woke on the eighth of January to the knowledge that a thrilling day for her had just begun. She looked out beneath the sun blinds across the Daventry estancia. Not a hand-breadth of cloud was visible. The brown earth baked under a blinding sun and the sky fitted down-upon it like a cap of brass. Inside the room, however, there was neither glare nor heat; and Cynthia stood with her expectations of the day fluttering about her like a shower of rose leaves. She was seventeen this morning, and the pride of it set her heart dancing. There would be letters downstairs from her friends, she hoped. There was a string of pearls, she knew. It had been bought that winter in Buenos Ayres with so elaborate a secrecy, and after so much furtive discussion as to whether it was good enough, that she could not but know of it. Moreover, there was a most important telegram to be despatched immediately after breakfast; a telegram of so much consequence that no hand but hers must write it out and send it off. So Cynthia was quick this morning. She dressed herself in a cool white frock, her white shoes and stockings, and ran lightly down the stairs into that room where years before a chandelier had of its own accord swung to and fro.

Valparaiso had long since been rebuilt, but Robert and Joan Daventry still kept house in Buenos Ayres through the winter, and made the estancia their summer home. The years, however, had brought their changes. Robert and Joan were frankly an old couple nowadays; a young Englishman was sitting at the breakfast table; he undertook the whole burden of management; and, finally, there was Cynthia. The "other plan," so often debated and so often shelved, had been adopted, after all; the experiment from which Robert Daventry had so shrunk had been risked; and Cynthia was the triumphant flower of it.

She greeted the old couple tenderly, shook hands with Richard Walton, the young manager, and received his good wishes with a pretty assumption of great dignity. But her eyes strayed to the table, where her place was piled high with parcels and letters, and her dignity vanished in her delight.

"I have many friends," she cried, with a sort of wonder in her voice very taking to those who looked on her while she spoke. For she could not but have friends, it seemed. So frank a wish to please and so sweet a modesty were linked to so much beauty. It was not the beauty of Argentina, though a rhapsodist might have maintained that some of its sunlight was held prisoner in the heavy ripples of her hair. But the hair was light brown in color, where the gold did not shine, and the rose was in her cheeks. A broad forehead, eyebrows thick and brown, curving across a fair skin above great eyes of a deep blue set rather wide apart, gave to her face a curious distinction. And her eyes looked out from so dark a wealth of lashes that they seemed unfathomable with mysteries--until she spoke. Then kindliness and a fresh joy in life lit them with soft fires. For the rest, she was neither short nor remarkable for height, the nose and the nostrils delicate, the chin small, but a definite chin. As for her mouth, it was not a rosebud, nor again was it a letter-box. It suited her and she could afford to smile. One granted her, at a glance, health and a look of race.

She began to open her letters and her presents. "Yes, I have many friends," she repeated.

"It may be surprising," said Robert Daventry. "But it seems to be true. In fact, I am not quite sure that I have not some small token about me that Joan and I don't dislike you altogether."

He fumbled first in one pocket, then in another.

"Really?" cried Cynthia. She leaned toward him, all eagerness and curiosity. Her lips were parted in a smile. She followed the movements of his hands with an air of suspense. She knew very well that half the pleasure of the givers would be spoilt if she betrayed any knowledge of the gift.

"What can it be?" Her whole attitude asked, while Robert Daventry slapped himself and looked under the table in a great fluster lest he should have mislaid the present. His concern was sheer farce; she, with a subtle skill of comedy, played her little part of happy impatience.

"Ah!" cried Robert Daventry at last. "It is not lost;" and he took out from his breast pocket a narrow case of green leather and from the white satin lining of the case the expected string of pearls. She stood up while Robert Daventry clasped it about her throat, and, as she took her seat again, she said in a low voice:

"You are both extraordinarily kind to me. I often wonder what would have become of me but for you--where I should be now."

For a moment both of the old people looked startled. Then Robert Daventry hastened to protest.

"My dear," he cried in a flurry, "you are, after all, of my flesh and blood. And flesh and blood has its claims."

Joan's quiet voice came to his help:

"Besides, the debt is not all on one side, Cynthia. We were not very contented until you came to us, were we Robert?"

"No, we weren't," he replied with relief, like a man floundering who finds solid ground under his feet. "We had lived hard and had done a great deal of work, and we were beginning to ask ourselves why. The heat and the ardor were over, you see. Our lives were cooling down. We had come to a time when one is apt to sit at night over the fire and wonder regretfully, now that no change is possible, whether we hadn't aimed at the wrong things and got less than we might have got out of our lives. We had piled up, and were still piling up, a great deal more money than we had any use for. We had made Daventry out of a plain as bare as the palm of my hand, and we had no one very dear to us to whom we could leave it. There didn't seem to be much use in things. Next week was going to be like this week, and the week after like next week, and life altogether nothing more than a succession of dull things. We were very nearly abandoning the estancia and retiring to England when my brother died."

"And left me to you," said Cynthia.

Robert Daventry nodded.

"And then our discontent vanished," said he.

Cynthia shook her head.

"I don't remember very much of those days, but I remember enough to be sure that I gave you a good deal of trouble." She spoke lightly to hide the emotion which the kindness of these friends had stirred in her.

Joan Daventry smiled.

"Yes, you gave us trouble, Cynthia," she said. "We are frightened by it still, at times. We are growing old and there is no other young spirit in the house, and it is possible that you might find your life rather dull, just as we did before you came to us."

"Dull?" cried Cynthia. "With you two dear people?" She held a hand lovingly to each, and now was hiding nothing of what she felt. "Besides, I have my friends. I meet them in Buenos Ayres. They come here to visit me. You gave them to me, as you have given me everything. Look at the number of them!" and she proudly pointed to her letters. She read them through and she breakfasted, and at the end of the meal gathered them in her hands.

"I must send some telegrams," she said. "I will drive to the railway station."

"Now?" Joan Daventry asked anxiously. "Can't they be sent later, in the afternoon, Cynthia?"

"No, mother," Cynthia replied. "Some might wait, but there's one which must go off now."

Joan Daventry looked at Richard Walton. The blinds were down and the window closed; so that the room was dark and cool. But a glance at her manager's face told her sufficiently what the heat was like outside. He had been abroad since daybreak and he was the color of a ripe mulberry. Joan Daventry looked to him for assistance. But, though his eyes were fixed with a momentary intentness upon Cynthia, he did not give it. He spoke on another subject.

"If you go, Miss Cynthia, I hope you will leave at home the pearls you are wearing round your throat. We are cutting the corn to-day and there are a good many men about of whom I know nothing at all. More hands came in last night than we had use for. It's all right, of course, but I shouldn't wear those pearls."

"Of course not," said Cynthia. "I will put them away."

"And you will take a man with you," said Robert Daventry. Neither he nor Joan had been brought up in cotton-wool; nor did they ever think to cloister Cynthia. She was left her liberty; and so half an hour afterward, with a big straw hat shading her face from the sun, she drove in her cart along the avenue to the railway station. She sent off the messages of thanks and then wrote out the important telegram which was to mark the day for her. She wrote it out without an alteration. For her thoughts had run fastidiously on the wording of it all through breakfast-time. She addressed it to:

CAPTAIN RAMES, R. N.,

S.S. Perhaps,

Tilbury Docks,

London.

And she handed it to the operator with a certain trepidation like one who does some daring and irrevocable deed. The operator, however, was quite unmoved. The important message to which so much consideration had been given, wore to him quite a commonplace look. It amounted, indeed, to no more than this:

"Every heart-felt wish for a triumphant journey, from an unknown friend in South America."

Thus, the very words were conventional and the sentiment no great matter to make a fuss about. But this was not Cynthia's point of view.

She had spoken the truth at the breakfast table when she had told Joan and Robert Daventry that she did not find her life dull. But they were old people, and, in spite of her many friends, she was, to be sure, much alone with them. She was reticent of her feelings in their presence, not through any habit of concealment, but from modesty and the disparity of years. On the other side it was Joan's theory that youth should be trusted rather than pried upon. Cynthia was thus thrown back a good deal upon herself, and if she did not find life dull, it was, perhaps, because with life she had very little to do. She was seventeen, a girl of clear eyes and health and silver thoughts; and romance had its way with her. All that loving care could imagine for the clean and delicate training of mind and body had been lavished on her; and little by little she had fashioned for herself a wonderland of dreams and beautiful things. The only ugly thing about it was the iron turnstile in the wall by which you gained admittance. But that could not be helped. Its ugliness was recognized. The turnstile had been there from the beginning--why, Cynthia could not have told you. It was indeed itself the beginning. It was there in her dreams and her fancies, offering admission to somewhere, before the somewhere was explored, and found to be the wonderland.

In this world, then, she moved amidst a very goodly company. She was careful about her company, choosing it from the world at large. She claimed the best of all the nations for her friends, yet with a pretty shyness which often enough set her blushing and laughing at her own pretension. She had a test. Unless you answered to it, there was no admission, the turnstile did not revolve. Coronets went for nothing, even brave deeds did not suffice. He who entered--and, by the way, it must regretfully be admitted that "he" does accurately represent the sex of those who were allowed to enter. For it had never occurred to Cynthia at all to let another woman into her world. She was modest, but her modesty had its limits. He who entered, then, must have given proofs that he was possessed with a definite idea, that his life moved to the tune of it.

The population of Cynthia's private enclosure was consequently strictly limited; and, since she only knew her heroes through the newspaper and books, some even of those who were admitted came in under false pretences, and had summarily to be ejected. She was thus on the lookout for recruits. Captain Rames was the latest of them, and Cynthia knew less of him even than of the others. She had seen a blurred portrait of him in a daily paper; she knew that he was an officer in the navy, aged thirty-four, and it seemed to her that he had passed her test. For, this very afternoon, in command of a Dundee whaler, he was off southward into seas where no ship yet had sailed.

The clerk stamped her telegram and took it behind the partition into his office. Cynthia climbed back into her cart.

"I will drive back across the farm," she said. "I want to see the reaping."

At the end of the short, wide street of one-storied huts and houses she turned through a gate in a wire fence onto a wide plain of brown grass. A mile across the plain, separated by no fence or hedge, the glistening acres of wheat began, and at the edge Cynthia could see little men seated on reaping-machines drawn by little horses like toys. She drove toward them thinking of the telegram, and, with a blush under her straw hat, of its reception. As a matter of fact, Captain Rames was rather busy that day, and anonymous telegrams did not receive from him the attention which was no doubt their due. In three hours' time, she thought, Captain Rames might be wondering what his unknown friend was like, with a heart full of gratitude for her unknown friendship. Meanwhile, she was driving nearer and nearer to the little toys at the edge of the wheat-field. The little toys were growing larger and larger. Cynthia came out of her rose-mist.

"There are some new machines," she said, with interest, to the man who was with her. He was an old half-breed who had long been on the estate.

"Yes, Senorita," he answered. He pointed to one longer than the rest and drawn by six horses. "It does everything. It cuts, it ties in sheaves."

The whirring of the machinery came louder and louder to their ears. The young horse which she was driving cocked its ears and became restive. She gave the reins to the servant.

"I will walk forward," she said. "You can wait here." She descended to the ground. She walked forward toward the edge of the wheat. There realities awaited her.

CHAPTER V

THE REAPER

The great reaping-machine came swaying over the uneven ground toward her, along the edge of those glistening acres. A huge arm of iron rose and fell, catching up the swathes of wheat and flinging them into the machine, whence they rolled out tied. Six horses harnessed behind pushed it and a man, perched upon a tiny saddle, steered and controlled it. The machine was about twenty paces from her when it came suddenly to a stop. The driver leaped down from his seat. It seemed to Cynthia that the mechanism must have gone wrong. She expected to see him bend over a joint or a spring. But he did not stoop. The moment his feet touched the ground, he ran straight toward her and very swiftly.

He ran with his head down, and his shoulders bent. It was a heavy rush rather than a run. Cynthia recoiled. The words of Richard Walton sprang into her mind, and her hand rose instinctively to her throat. Could she have forgotten after all to remove the string of pearls? But she had removed it. And still the man was running toward her. The fear that she wore the pearls, and the proof that she did not, had followed so immediately upon his rush that he had as yet covered only half the ground between them. It was herself he aimed at then. She cast a rapid glance toward her cart. The Gaucho was leaning down over the opposite side, and talking to some one who stood by the wheel. A cry would not bring him to her side in time. She turned, with half a mind to run. But, though her white skirt reached only to her ankles, it would still impede her. She turned back and with a beating heart faced him. And a few feet from her he stopped.

He looked at her, drew a great breath, and cried "Ah!" like a man who has reached his goal.

"What do you want?" asked Cynthia, and in spite of her efforts her voice shook.

A South American harvest finds no use for the weak. The man who stood opposite to her was broad and powerful, with a heavy, coarse face, burnt to the color of brick by the sun. The sweat streaked it, and the dirt of many a day clung to it, and it was seamed by exposure. He was of the men who move from estancia to estancia while the harvest lasts, working from sunrise to dark, living upon *mate* tea and roasted sheep, and earning a pound a day, and thereafter lying soddened in some den until the last centavo has been squandered. A battered black hat was pressed low upon his clotted hair; a month's growth of beard straggled over his chin and cheeks. And his eyes were evil. That, more than any other quality of the man, Cynthia noticed. Their quick glance held her. She was terrified.

"What do you want?" she asked a second time, and her voice wavered still more audibly.

She stood in front of him, her lovely brows, under the big brim of her straw hat, troubled, and her great eyes wide and alert with fear. She was in the poise for flight like a startled deer, yet did not dare to turn to fly. And in the man, as he looked at her, there came a change.

He did not answer her question. But very slowly he smiled, and the smile was spiteful. He nodded his head at her; a malicious contentment overspread his face; and from head to heel his eyes inspected her. They approved her beauty and the simple daintiness of her clothes; they took note of her slenderness of hand and foot; they remarked the lines and supple youth of her figure; and through her white frock they seemed to make sure of the roundness of her limbs. Cynthia grew suddenly hot with shame. This man was appraising her--nothing less. Appraising her as if for a market! Her fear dropped from her. She cried a third time, but with spirit:

"What do you want of me?" and if her voice shook now, it was with a quiver of indignation.

She heard the thud of a horse's hoofs behind her. The reaper heard it, too. Without a word, and without any hurry, he turned away from her and slouched back to his machine. Cynthia's cart the next moment was driven up to her side. She climbed into it and took the reins. The encounter had shaken her more than she had thought. She was trembling, and she drove over the ground quickly, until she saw the slate roof of the house, flashing like silver, from a clump of dark trees quite near.

Then she reined in her horse and turned round. Far away at the edge of the wheat, the man and the machine and the six horses stood out black like a little toy. The clank and rattle of the iron came to her ears through the still air, faintly, like the mechanism of a toy. But Cynthia shivered as she looked back.

"Who is he?" she asked of the old Gaucho. He shrugged his shoulders.

"I do not know him, Señorita. I do not think he was here last year. They come in herds and go in herds when the corn is stacked."

Up and down, along the glistening line, the man drove his horses and manipulated his machine. He stopped no more. With each journey a wide band of wheat went down. Thus he had been working, balanced in his saddle, since daybreak. So, with but a two hours' rest, he would go under the burning afternoon sun until darkness came and bade him stop. To the Gaucho he was one of a herd of men who did the like; for a few weeks here; then for another few weeks on another estancia further down the line. But for Cynthia this man stood strangely out from the herd. He had stopped her, and she did not know why. She sat and watched his slow, obstinate progression. The persistence, the physical strength of the man daunted her. There was something of nature's own relentlessness in his capacity to endure and work. She magnified him, and was, at the same time, interested and alarmed. For of this she was sure. He had not stopped her merely because she was a girl, and alone. He had stopped her because she was herself. She remembered his smile, his nods of the head, his malice. He had a personal feeling, a personal animosity. She could not understand it, yet she was sure.

"How long will he stay?" she asked.

"A month," said the Gaucho.

"He was not here last year?"

"I do not recognize him."

"Why, then--" she began and did not finish the question. It was in her mind to ask, "Why does he hate me?" But she was aware at once that the Gaucho could not answer it. "And he will stay a month?" she asked again, uneasily.

"Yes, unless the Señorita wishes him to go. It will be, of course, as the Señorita wishes."

Cynthia nodded her head. There was a way out of the trouble, to be sure. But, on the other hand, she would have to say why she wished the man to go. At the recital of her story Mr. and Mrs. Daventry would be excited and alarmed. She herself would henceforth be surrounded with precautions. She determined to say nothing at all about her adventure. She would be careful during this month where she roamed. The man would be at work and it would be easy to avoid him. She gathered the reins again in her hands and drove to the house.

CHAPTER VI

A VISITOR AT THE ESTANCIA

Cynthia accordingly held her tongue. Nevertheless, that evening Richard Walton said to her across the dinner table:

"So you were, after all, molested by one of the hands, Miss Cynthia."

"Molested!" cried Robert Daventry indignantly.

Cynthia's face flamed.

"Who told you?" she asked of Richard Walton.

"Pedro."

Cynthia had not thought of the Gaucho. He had seemed so entirely uninterested, so utterly unalarmed.

"'Molested' is too strong a word," she said hastily. She now meant to make as light of the encounter as she possibly could. "It was very likely my fault. I got out of the trap and walked toward the wheat. It may be that the man fancied I wished to speak to him."

"What did he do?"

The question came from Joan Daventry.

"He sprang from his seat, ran to me, and stopped in front of me. That was all."

"Quite all?"

Cynthia nodded.

"He just stood and stared at me until Pedro drove up."

"Did he say nothing?"

"Not a word."

In spite of her resolve to treat the adventure lightly, Cynthia's voice grew troubled as she answered the questions. For she answered them with her eyes upon Joan Daventry's face, and she saw the perplexity there deepen into disquietude and misgiving. She turned toward Robert Daventry. Upon his face uneasiness was still more evident. He was plainly agitated. He sat listening in suspense. His indignation had gone.

Cynthia's fear revived under the stimulation of their anxiety. She continued slowly:

"But although he did me no harm, although he threatened none, there was something strange. He saw me at once. He ran so very quickly to me the moment I was within reach. He seemed almost to be looking out for me."

Joan sank back into her chair with a gesture of helplessness, which was all the more alarming because it was so singularly out of keeping with her character. Her eyes sought her husband's and sought them in dismay. Cynthia noticed both the gesture and the look. They kindled a vague terror in the girl. The wide brown plain was as a picture before her. She saw the great wheat-field glistening in the heat, a wind-wheel in a corner above a well, and this man with the evil eyes and the face of malice looking her over from head to foot.

"Yes," she said. "He seemed to be expecting me, and there was something else. He seemed to hate me;" and Robert Daventry with a cry sprang sharply to his feet.

Joan raised a quick warning hand. But the cry had been uttered; and with a sob Cynthia buried her face in her hands.

"I am frightened now," she said. "You frighten me."

Robert Daventry stood over her, clumsily remorseful, and laid his great hand on her shoulder.

"There's nothing to fear, Cynthia," he began. "Joan and I--" he broke off abruptly at a second warning from his wife. "We will pack that man off about his business to-morrow."

"Yes," said Mrs. Daventry. She had mastered her agitation, and now affected carelessness. "We can't really have Cynthia's birthday spoilt in this way."

"No, of course not," cried Robert Daventry, seizing upon this explanation of his distress. But he could not leave it in its simplicity. "It's abominable that Cynthia should have her birthday spoilt. She has only one a year, poor girl. That's what's troubling us, Cynthia. Nothing else. But it's enough to upset us, isn't it? To think that you should actually have your birthday spoilt--by one of my men, too."

So he went on, like a commentator on an ancient text, expanding the explanation, underlining it, and forcing upon Cynthia's intelligence its complete improbability. Even in the midst of her fears she could not but look with amusement toward Joan; and the two women exchanged the smile of their sex at the perennial clumsiness of man.

"He shall go first thing to-morrow morning," cried Mr. Daventry; and Richard Walton quietly rejoined:

"He has gone already. I paid him off this morning."

Mr. Daventry ceased abruptly from his vociferations.

"Thank you, Walton," he said. "Then that's ended," and he sat down.

But he had hardly taken his seat when the door opened and the parlor-maid brought to him upon a salver a folded slip of dirty paper.

"A man came with this to the door, sir. He is waiting for an answer."

Robert Daventry unfolded the slip and read the message written within it. He did not lift his eyes when he had read. He sat staring at the paper like a statue. And he sat amidst a deep silence. The cloud which had but now been lifted, had gathered once more above the heads of that small company. Though Robert Daventry did not speak, his long silence spoke for him; and though he schooled his face to composure, it was plain that he schooled it. A vague disquiet held the others at the table. Not one of them but had a conviction that this dirty, insignificant, scrap of writing announced a catastrophe.

Joan was the first to move. She walked round the table and stood behind her husband. He did not hear the rustle of her gown; and he was not aware that she leaned over him to read the message until the pressure of her hand upon his shoulder reminded him that she was his ally.

"You had better see the man, Robert," she said. "He calls late, but probably he needs help."

Thus she sought to pass the message off.

"Very well, I will," said Robert. He turned to the parlor-maid. "Bring him to my study when I ring the bell."

"I will come with you," said Joan, as the servant went out from the room.

Richard Walton rose from his chair.

"Perhaps you would like me, too?"

"No, I don't think that's necessary," replied Joan Daventry. "But perhaps you would stay within sound of the bell. We don't know who this man is or what he wants. If we ring again, you would know that we needed your advice."

"Certainly, I will be upon the lookout," said Walton, and he went from the room and crossed to the servants' quarters. There he would hear the bell at once should it ring for him. Joan meanwhile turned with a smile to Cynthia.

"We will leave you here for a few minutes," she said, and the composure of her voice almost reassured the girl; would, indeed, have quite reassured her but for Robert Daventry. She saw that his hands trembled so that the paper shook in them, even as her hands had trembled this morning when she climbed up by the edge of the wheat into her cart.

"Yes, wait here, Cynthia," said Robert Daventry, as he got to his feet; and Cynthia noticed that while he spoke to her he altogether avoided the glance of her eyes. The old couple went out of the room together, leaving her alone, and carefully latched the door behind them. In the hall for a moment they stood resting from their pretence. A broken word or two burst from Robert Daventry:

"What shall we do, Joan? This is what we have dreaded always."

Joan raised her finger to her lips.

"Hush! Speak lower. What I said was true. We don't know who he is, or what he wants. He may not be the man who stopped her in the field at all."

Robert Daventry shook his head. It was rather his nature to run to meet misfortune if he saw its shadow in his way.

"What shall we do?" he repeated. "Money will send him away," said Joan.

"And bring him back again," replied Robert hopelessly. "Sooner or later Cynthia will know;" and Joan threw up her head at his words.

"No," she said vigorously. "No."

At her left hand a door stood open upon a dark room. This was the smoking-room. She entered the room and crossed it to the opposite wall. Then she opened a second door, and advancing into this inner room, felt for the switch in the darkness and turned on the light. Bookcases, filled for the most part with books on agriculture, lined the room, a round table, littered with papers, occupied the centre, in the recess of a window stood a writing-desk. This was Robert Daventry's study. Her husband followed her, and saw that her finger was already on the bell.

"Let us decide what we are to do," he said, "before you ring."

Joan shook her head.

"We can't. We must be guided by what the man knows, and by what he wants. Only we admit nothing," she declared resolutely; and she pressed the bell. It rang in the passage by the kitchen, but Cynthia, left alone in the dining-room, heard it too.

The moment she heard it, Cynthia rose from her chair, and ran silently to the door. She unlatched it without a sound, and drew it toward her until it was just wide enough open for her to see out. There she stood grasping the door-knob, and in a moment a heavy foot sounded in the hall. Cynthia set her eyes to the chink. She saw first a maid-servant cross the hall, and pass into the smoking-room, and after the maid a man. The man was the reaper who had leapt from his machine and rushed toward her that morning. The maid-servant came back alone and crossed the hall again to the servants' quarters. A door was shut loudly--the door of Robert Daventry's study--and then another door opened noiselessly, and opened wide--the door of the dining-room. Cynthia came out into the hall. All the color had gone from her face, her eyes were wide with terror. The man meant her harm--not a doubt of it. He had some power to inflict the harm--that was sure. Otherwise why was he admitted, why were her friends in such concern?

Cynthia was quite alone in the hall now. Voices sounded faintly from the kitchen and in the room behind her a clock ticked. But there were no other sounds. She crossed to the threshold of the smoking-room and looked in. At the other end a bright bar of light on the floor held her eyes. The light came from the study. Cynthia watched it for a moment irresolute. But the temptation grew. She was sure that beyond that bright bar of light, behind that closed door, here in this far-away corner of Argentina, good and evil were at grips for her. A sense of loneliness suddenly possessed her, she longed for the neighborly noises of a city. And while she stood she heard her own name pronounced by Robert Daventry, and at once a harsh, strange voice rose in a laugh, loud and arrogant. She looked about her in a panic. She must fly, or she must know the truth, the whole of it, the worst of it. She stole swiftly and noiselessly into the room. Close by that bar of light a big, low chair stood against the wall. Cynthia crouched in the chair, her frock a blur of misty white in the darkness. There she remained, very still and quiet; and every word spoken in the study came clearly to her ears.

CHAPTER VII

BOTH SIDES OF THE DOOR

Within the room the three people were standing, the reaper upon one side of the table, Joan and Robert Daventry close together upon the other. The reaper was still laughing.

"Cynthia!" he cried, repeating contemptuously the name which Robert Daventry had used. "There's no Cynthia. There's a very pretty little girl I saw this morning in the corn. But her pretty little name is Doris Challoner. And, taking all in all, it's the better name of the two."

He spoke with an easy and most disquieting assurance, but Joan had enough of that quality to meet with him in the gate. She had always been a good fighter; she had stood by her husband often enough in the early days of the estancia, when his nerve would have failed him but for her; and she was for putting up to-night the best fight of her whole long, active life. Money, to her thinking, they could make again, old as they were, if the need came. But they could not open their hearts to a second Cynthia, even if they could find one.

"Nonsense," she answered boldly. "Her name is Cynthia Daventry."

"Where was she born, then?" asked the reaper.

"In Patagonia."

"Never in this world," cried the man. "She was born in Concepcion, and that's her farthest south."

Joan shrugged her shoulders.

"We ought to know. She is my husband's niece."

A grin overspread the reaper's face.

"And is that so?" he asked, in a mock surprise. "I wasn't aware of it."

"Well, you are now," said Joan.

"Yes, and the news alters our relations altogether, doesn't it?" he said pleasantly.

He tossed his battered hat upon the table, pulled out a chair, and sat down in it at his ease, his legs stretched out, his hands deep in his pockets. He nodded familiarly to Joan.

"How do you do, sis?" He turned his face toward Mr. Daventry, "You have got a nice little place, brother Robert. Shows what honest work can do if persevered with day after day for a great number of consecutive years. Quite a nice little place. You haven't, by any chance, got a nice little cigar, too, have you, Robert, for your long-lost brother?"

Robert Daventry's face grew red, and the veins swelled upon his forehead. He was a man quickly moved to passion, and quick, too, the passion exhausted, to swing back into doubts and hesitations. He blew either hot or cold, and, sooner or later, he was sure to blow cold. Now, however, his temper was up, and he brought his great fist down with violence upon the table.

"What do you mean by your insolence?" he shouted "Stand up!"

Joan laid a hand upon the old man's arm to restrain him. The reaper, for his part, never budged from his attitude.

"You have got a nerve," he said. "You tell me a pack of lies--that's all right, you've got money. But when I take you at your word, it's 'insolence' and 'stand up.' How's that, if you please?" He sat and laughed for a little in contemptuous jerks. "Your niece, indeed! The girl's my daughter."

Neither Joan nor Robert believed him for a moment. They thought of Cynthia, and compared that image at their hearts with the actual man who sprawled on the chair in front of them. Robert counted him up, his heavy features, his grime-engrained, spoilt hands, the whole degraded, unkempt look of him. Cynthia's father! The claim was preposterous.

"Her father!" cried Robert Daventry, leaning across the table. "Look at yourself in the glass!"

The sneer stung the reaper to a fury. He sprang to his feet, and from habit his hand slipped to the knife at the back of his waistband. But he mastered himself in a second or two. He was there for other ends than violence, and he withdrew his hand.

"I sha'n't forget that," he said, in a perfectly quiet voice, which contrasted in the strangest way with the convulsion of his face. "You got home there. Right home;" and he sat down again.

Joan interposed before her husband could say another word, and used soft words. The man was not Cynthia's father to be sure, but he knew something of the girl's history. That was certain--and he knew more than either Joan or Robert knew themselves. If she was to fight her battle with success, she must know what he knew.

"You could not expect us to accept your mere statement," she said.

"No, that's reasonable," said the reaper, and he began his story. But the insult rankled in his breast and as he spoke he kept turning a murderous eye on the man who had inflicted it.

He told the story of the earthquake at Valparaiso, and the flight of James Challoner across the Andes. It was a story told with a wealth of detail, and difficult altogether to discredit. Neither Joan nor Robert did altogether discredit it. It might be true or it might not. This man might have obtained it from James Challoner, or might somehow have come across it by himself. But they were still convinced he could not be James Challoner himself.

"We shall want more proof than that," said Joan calmly, and Robert nodded his head. Neither of them had felt more confidence than at this moment since the crumpled slip of paper had been brought into the dining-room.

But outside the door Cynthia huddled in the great chair with her ear to the door, listened with a growing terror. She had never doubted until this hour that she was the daughter of Robert Daventry's brother. She had been secure in that belief. Now the security was going. She clutched the arms of her chair, feeling the whole world slipping from beneath her feet--even as it had slipped at Valparaiso. For certain memories, quite clear in her mind, were being explained to her. An open hill-side at night, a strange red light upon the world, the crash of houses, little flames creeping, and ships quietly at anchor on the smoothest of seas--that was one picture in her memories which had often puzzled her, which would puzzle her no longer if she believed the story which was being told on the other side of the door. She remembered, too, a long journey amongst mountains, and a bridge over a deep and narrow torrent, and many people with kind faces who spoke to her.

"Of course, it isn't certain," she pleaded to herself desperately; and the husky voice behind the door began again:

"I travelled down to Buenos Ayres by train. I had little money, and no prospects, and a child on my hands. I couldn't make a home for her. So I went straight to the foundling hospital. It stands back in a garden, and is kept by some wealthy sisters. There's a turnstile in the brick wall of the garden, a little iron turnstile--but you know it well, both of you;" and he broke off with a laugh.

Inside the study Joan and Robert Daventry, still remained unconvinced. Outside Cynthia was persuaded.

"It's true then," she whispered to herself. "It's quite true;" and she wrung her hands in the darkness, and her voice broke in a sob. She had no longer any shadow of doubt. The turnstile in the brick wall was for her the overwhelming proof.

Examined in a court of law by the rules of evidence, it might seem flimsy enough. To Cynthia, it was complete corroboration of the testimony of her memories. The turnstile in the brick wall--the one ugly thing in her imagined wonderland of heroes--the turnstile which had always been there before the land was--how had it come there, she asked herself? And she was in no doubt as to the answer. The turnstile was a memory too. It was the turnstile of a foundling hospital, where her father had left her and gone his way. No wonder, she reflected bitterly, it was the one ugly thing in her world of fancies.

She leaned back, shivering, with her hands covering her face. She was humiliated, but she was still more terrified. Shame cut deep, but fear touched the very nerves of her heart. The man who had this morning rushed at her was her father, and she remembered the malice of his smile, and the evil, covetous look of him as he appraised her. She grew hot, now, as she thought upon it.

"What harm does he mean?" she asked; and suddenly she sat forward on the edge of her chair, quivering from head to foot like a spring some touch had released. For her father's voice rose again:

"I tied a bootlace round the child's arm. I can't say that I ever thought to come back for her. But there's a convention in these things, isn't there?" he added with a grin. "I have been a conservative all my life, and now I have found the advantage of it."

"How?" asked Joan. "Even if your story were true, your daughter wouldn't be wearing a bootlace or even the mark of it round her arm now."

"No, from the look of her she'd be more likely to be wearing a diamond bangle, bless her! But all the same the bootlace helps."

"How?"

Again the implacable question was uttered by Joan. She must know all that this man had upon his side by way of argument. That was her first necessity.

"How does the bootlace help?"

"It helps because the child wearing that bootlace was received by the same old ladies who allowed you a few months afterward to adopt her--that's how. Don't you leave those old ladies out of your reckoning, Mrs. Daventry, or you will run up against a snag. I went back to the foundling a year ago and claimed my daughter."

"You did?" cried Joan. She was startled. For a moment, too, she was disconcerted. She knew nothing of any such visit. But the statement was so easily capable of proof that the reaper would hardly have made it, had it not been true. And she was quick to see how strong a presumption such a visit would create, that he was the girl's father. Then she sprang to the weak point in the statement.

"If it were true that Cynthia was your daughter, and that you claimed her a year ago, how is it that you wait until a chance meeting in a field brings you face to face?"

"There's no chance about it, believe me," James Challoner returned. For it was he. The delicate manners had been rubbed off him, the gentle voice, which had charmed so many dollars from reluctant pockets long ago at Punta del Inca, had thickened and grown husky, the well-knit figure had spread to heaviness. But this was James Challoner, after fourteen years had told their tale. "The old ladies lied to me. Yes, actually lied to me," and he spread out his hands in indignation. "Lied to a father about his daughter! They were religious people too!"

"If they did lie," Robert Daventry burst in, "they did the best thing they ever did in all their good lives."

James Challoner waved Robert Daventry and his outburst aside. He kept his eyes fixed upon Joan's face.

"Yes, they lied to me," he said. "I gave them the day and the month and the year, when I placed Doris on the turnstile. They pretended to make inquiries, and they lied to me. They told me she was dead. Ah!" and he suddenly leaned forward and pointed an accusing finger at Joan, "You are glad to hear that. Yes, I thought you would be."

Try as she did, Joan had not been able to keep a flash of joy out of her face.

"It's a matter of indifference to me," she replied, "since Cynthia is not your child."

She still clung obstinately to that belief. He might have heard the story from James Challoner, and James Challoner might be dead. Any hypothesis was possible in her eyes, except the one which was true. She would not have it that this man was Cynthia's father.

"Oh, it is a matter of indifference to you!" said Challoner ironically. "I will tell you something that won't be. Those old ladies lied just as clumsily as I have ever seen it done. Poor old souls, they were rattled out of their senses at the thought of the sin they were committing. A child could have seen they were lying--as I did who am no child. And I began to cast about for a reason for the lie. It wasn't very difficult to find it. Some one had adopted her, some one they didn't want me to discover, some one rich, then, I reckoned, who could give the girl a position."

At the word "rich" Robert and Joan exchanged a glance. So much were they disconcerted by Challoner's knowledge and assurance that now they hoped rather than feared that blackmail was the end he had in view.

"So I began to make inquiries," continued Challoner. "I found out who were the patrons, who took most interest in the institution, and amongst them who had adopted a child. I came upon you in the end." And again he began to laugh. "Those poor innocent old women had actually given me the date when you took Doris away as the date of the child's death. It took me a little time to find out all about you; and when I had found out I had no money. So I had to work my way along until I reached you. But I have reached you," he exclaimed, lolling back in his chair, "and, by George, the very first day I am at work here, out the girl comes to meet me. Why, I recognized her in a second;" and Joan slipped in, as she thought, under his guard. With a thrill of delight she believed that he had made a mistake, and a mistake which would discredit every word of his story.

"Recognized her!" she repeated scornfully. "And the last time, when, on your own showing, you saw her she was three years old!"

Challoner, however, merely smiled at her.

"If you had a family at your back, old lady, you wouldn't be so high," he said; and once more Robert Daventry interposed.

"Speak respectfully to my wife," he cried.

"What, are you butting in again?" asked Challoner, with a look of surprise. "You didn't do any good, you know, the last time you interfered."

Once more Joan was called upon to restrain her husband. She saw the man convicted of a lie, and she did not mean to lose the advantage of that conviction.

"How did you recognize her?" she asked, smiling in her turn. "How did you recognize in the girl of seventeen the child of three?"

"I'll tell you," said Challoner confidently. "And, by the way, she's not seventeen to-day. It might interest you to know that. She's seventeen and a half. She was born on the seventeenth of July."

"Keep to the point," said Joan.

"Certainly, I will," replied Challoner, "though it's by no means necessary to substantiate my authority--yes," and his voice suddenly rang out loud upon the word, so that Cynthia in the darkness on the other side of the door shivered as if she had been struck, "yes, my authority. I don't say that she's like what she was when she was three. I don't even say she's like her mother. She isn't. She's a Challoner--and in the Challoner's home, by Wareham in

Dorsetshire, there are some pictures worth looking at. I sat opposite one of them at the dinner table all through my boyhood, and whenever I was at home afterward--until I came out here. It was the portrait of my great-great-grandmother, painted by Romney, when she was a girl; and I tell you the girl who came stepping so prettily across the field this morning, in her white frock and big straw hat, might have stepped right out of that picture frame. That's how I recognized her."

He ended on a note of triumph, and for the first time Joan's confidence failed her altogether. Again, it was not, of course, a conclusive piece of evidence, gauged by any laws of reasoning, but just as Challoner's description of the turnstile had convinced Cynthia outside the door because of the particular illumination it lent to an obscure fancy, so this detail of the picture did more to convince Joan Daventry than the rest of the story. Some portions of that story she knew to be true: the bootlace, the abandonment of the child. But what she had obstinately been combating was the contention that it was true of this man who sat before her. He might have learnt it all from the real father; he might now be seeking to make his profit out of the knowledge. That had been her hope. But it failed her now. For the particular detail of the girl's resemblance, now that she was seventeen, to the Romney portrait in the Challoners' dining-room he could not have learned from another. It did suggest that the man in front of her was the Challoner he claimed to be. Of course the detail might have been invented. But it did not sound to her invented; and, so far as her knowledge could test it, the rest of his story was true. She looked him over again with new eyes.

"But you can't prove that," she said. "Even if it were true, you couldn't prove it."

"Should I need to?" asked Challoner. "After I had put those old ladies from the Foundling into the witness-box, should I need to, Mrs. Daventry? Would they stick to their lie? Any tenth-rate attorney could turn 'em inside out as easy as an old glove, if they tried to. But they wouldn't try--and you know it as well as I do."

Challoner had put his finger on the danger-spot of the Daventrys' position. Those two old ladies would have suffered much heart-searching before they told their lie, and not a little remorse afterward. Questioned upon their oaths they would speak the truth, and the whole truth. Of that Joan felt sure.

"There are men, too, in Buenos Ayres who knew me when I was in Chile," Challoner continued; and then once more Robert Daventry interposed.

"But you wouldn't be mad enough to go to law with us," he cried, and Challoner laughed.

"Oh, yes, I would, and I would put you into the witness-box, too. A pretty figure you would cut, with your Patagonian brother, eh? I wouldn't bring my action here, of course, in this district. You've got your local syndic in your pocket, I grant you. But the law runs in Buenos Ayres nowadays, and don't you forget it."

Robert Daventry turned aside to hide his discomfiture, and walked once or twice across the room. He had no doubt that this man was James Challoner and Cynthia's father. His story was too circumstantial to be disputed. Moreover, neither he nor Joan could publicly dispute it. There had been no brother in Patagonia. He turned abruptly to Challoner: "How much do you want?"

Joan moved quickly to his side with a cry of protest. Money it might be necessary to pay, but it must be asked for, not offered. To offer it was to admit the claim.

"What are you saying, Robert?" she cried.

Robert turned to her quietly.

"It must come to that in the end. Why not now and have done with it? How much?"

A smile of triumph broadened over Challoner's face. Outside the door Cynthia leaned forward, her hands clasped over her heart in an agony of suspense. Why didn't he answer? Why was he so long?

The answer came at length:

"I want my daughter, nothing else. She is not of age. I have a right to her; I'll take her away with me to-night."

Cynthia crouched back in her chair, clasping its arms tightly with her hands, and making herself very small. To Joan and Robert Daventry the demand was incredible, even though their ears had heard it. Challoner could not mean it. It was an expedient to raise the price. But Cynthia had caught a note of malice in his voice which brought back before her eyes the malice of his looks as he had stood before her in the field. He meant to take her away, and that night. She glanced toward the door. To leave her home, to be swallowed up in the darkness with this stranger for her companion! She clung to the chair in a panic of terror. Then she heard Robert Daventry repeating the words in a daze:

"You want to take her away? Cynthia?" And as though the meaning of Challoner's demand for the first time broke in on him, "Never!" he cried violently.

"I want to take her away to-night;" and now the malice in Challoner's voice was audible to Joan too. She stared at him over the table. He sat nodding his head at her with little quick movements, his eyes very bright, and a horrid smile about his mouth. She remembered what Cynthia herself had said: "He seemed to hate me."

"You grudge her her happiness, her life with us!" she exclaimed; and Challoner beat his fist upon the table in a sudden anger.

"Is it strange?" he cried. "All these years here she has been sitting soft and walking daintily. What have I been doing? 'Look at yourself in a glass'--That's what you said," and he turned to Robert Daventry. "I told you I'd remember it, and I do. A fine life I have had of it for fourteen years. Mate tea and enough work a day to throw a trades-unionist into hysterics! No wonder I've lost my looks."

All the bitterness of his fourteen years of degradation seemed to be concentrated in his words. The easy good-humor with which he had begun had vanished. He was a man venomous with grievances. He was still the old James Challoner in this; he had enemies, only now the enemies were not a few to be searched for through a list, but all who had a sixpence in their pockets. Joan herself was frightened. She realized the mistake which she and her husband had made in their eagerness to disbelieve the story of this man. She understood now that when she had thought of Cynthia and compared her with the reaper, she had been thinking only of the flower and had omitted her own assiduous cultivation of the plant. She recognized now that the look of race which fourteen years of luxury had refined in the girl, fourteen years of degradation might well have obliterated in the man.

"I have had enough of it," cried James Challoner. "It's now her turn."

"But we offer you freedom from that life," said Joan, and her voice began to plead.

"I want my daughter," Challoner retorted implacably.

"But you can't make a home for her," said Robert Daventry.

Challoner chuckled and his voice lost its violence.

"You must take me for a softy," he said with a drawl of amusement. "I mean her to make a home for me, where I can do a bit of sitting soft and recover my good looks."

"But she can't make a home for you," said Joan.

"Oh, yes she can."

"How?"

Cynthia outside the door waited in a despairing bewilderment. The changed tones of those whom she had looked upon as her parents assured her that the reaper had authority and rights, could claim her, could take her away. But how, she asked herself, was she to make a home for him? She had learned no profession, practised no art. The tears rose to her eyes and flowed down her cheeks; and the answer came.

"She's a rare one for looks," said Challoner. His eyes narrowed to slits and his face became mean and despicable to look upon. "You'll not find her equal strolling under the lamps of Buenos Ayres."

Joan flinched and uttered a cry. The movement was that of one who has been slapped in the face. Cynthia felt her heart stand still within her breast. She had lived in Buenos Ayres, where knowledge comes quickly to women. She was neither ignorant nor a fool. She understood, and once more her eyes went to the door. It was all quiet in the hall. A few quick steps and she would be out of the house. She rose from her chair. For the dark night, which a minute before had so appalled her, now appealed to her as a friend and refuge. But as she turned, she heard Robert Daventry say in a choking voice:

"Go! or I'll have you thrown out;" and the bell rang violently.

"Oh, is that the game?" replied Challoner.

Daventry strode round the room.

"Not a word! Go! I loathe you."

And the door was wrenched violently open. Cynthia had just time to drop into her chair. She heard her father's voice close to her, and no longer through the panels of a door. She cowered down, covering her face with her hands, and drawing in her feet.

"All right, I'll go," said Challoner. "I can afford to go. For I have the law on my side."

"The law! Try it!"

"I will."

Challoner was standing in the doorway now. He was looking back into the study. But he had only to turn his head to see that blur of misty white in the chair, only to bend down and draw the trembling hands from the girl's face to find his daughter in his grasp. Cynthia lay holding her breath, ready at a touch of him to swoon.

"She's my daughter. All your money won't get over that. Just wait and see. I'll come back with the law at my side, and take her away--yes--if I have to tie her hand and foot to take her."

He flung out across the smoking-room, looking neither to the right nor to the left. Joan and Robert Daventry followed quickly behind him, afraid lest he should force his way into the dining-room where they had left Cynthia. Not one of them saw the girl huddled in the great chair in the dark room. Richard Walton came into the hall.

"I'll see you off the premises," he said to Challoner, and a moment afterward the front door slammed.

With the slamming of that door Cynthia seemed to swim back into life; and all at once there came upon her a great longing for comfort and kind words. She was hurt and humiliated as she had never thought to be. It seemed to her that she was tainted, and she was terribly afraid. She took a swift step toward the door, and there Joan's voice speaking in a whisper arrested her.

Joan was standing with her husband by the dining-room, and seeking to compose her agitation before she entered it. Her voice was still shaking from her encounter.

"Not a word to Cynthia," she said. "We sha'n't let her go, Robert," and her voice was very wistful, and appealed for confirmation of her words. "So there's no need to trouble her--as this story would trouble her."

"No, we'll not say a word to her," replied Robert. He made an effort to be hearty, but it quite failed to hide his distress. "We shall find a way out somehow when we think it all over. No, we'll not breathe a word, my dear. Cynthia's birthday mustn't be spoilt," and, thoroughly miserable, the old couple went into the dining-room and closed the door behind them.

Cynthia made up her mind. Since they wished her not to know, since it would add so much to their distress if they learned that she did know, she would keep her knowledge to herself. It seemed to her then a small return to make to them for their devotion, but it was to cost her much more than she imagined. She would wait, schooling herself to patience, hiding her fears. But she could not face her friends to-night and keep her secret. For that she had not the strength. She ran swiftly and silently up to her room and flung herself upon her bed and buried her face in the pillows. There she lay trembling until the thought came to her that Joan would not retire without coming to ask why she had gone upstairs so early. She undressed and was hardly in bed before Joan knocked on the door.

"I had a headache," said Cynthia. "It is the heat, no doubt. I shall be myself in the morning."

"You are sure? You wouldn't like the doctor?" Joan asked anxiously.

"Oh, no!" exclaimed Cynthia.

Joan put her hand to the switch of the light, and Cynthia started up in bed with a wild gesture.

"Don't turn the light out, please, mother," she cried; and the next moment feared that Joan would have heard the terror underneath her words. But Joan herself was occupied. She kissed Cynthia and left her alone with the light burning in her room.

CHAPTER VIII

THE FLIGHT

But though the light burned in her room, Cynthia did not sleep till daybreak. For the first few hours there was a strange bustle about the passages of the house, for which she did not seek at all to find a cause. She welcomed it for its companionship. Familiar voices informed her that her friends were awake about her, and she was comforted. She tried to fall asleep before the noise should cease, but gradually the estancia sank into silence, and she was still awake. Then began her hours of terror. Her window was open, and every flutter of the night air which shook the curtains was her father's coarse, strong hand upon the sill. If she closed her eyes for a moment, his dark and evil face was already bending over her, as she lay helpless in her bed. If she heard a wardrobe crack it was he stepping clumsily about the room. Half the night she spent crouching up in her bed, her eyes wild with fear, her heart racing and stopping, while she listened for the sound of his footsteps outside the house. And heard them; did a twig snap on a tree in the garden, she heard them. There was he, prowling about the walls, watching, perhaps, for just her light to be put out before he slipped in through a window to take her away. If she heard no sounds, then he was already in the house, creeping along the corridor toward her door. From the moment when this particular fear seized hold upon her, her eyes were fixed in an agony of suspense upon the long mirror in her room. The door was at her right hand, set in the wall against which the head of her bed was placed. A high screen stood by the side of the bed and hid it from her altogether. But across the room the long mirror faced her, and by looking at its bright surface she could see whether the door opened or not. It was a white door, with a round brass handle, and, continually, she was very sure that she saw the handle turn. In her frantic imaginings her father's very semblance changed. Gross though he was, still more she distorted him, making his likeness fit with the knowledge which she had of him. He meant to drag her away, and batten on what she had of youth and freshness and good looks; and this, out of malice almost as much as for profit, and to punish her for the happiness of her life. He swelled into some grotesque and corpulent thing of evil with a fat, loathsome face and gripping hands.

The night was a night of disillusionment for Cynthia. Romance was stunned in her. All her pretty dreams, wherein she shyly walked with the bright ones of the earth, were rent and blown to space like gossamer. She seemed separated from them by a generation of years. She looked back upon them with derision. A fine heroine she was to be if that door opened. She was to walk--yes--but under the gas-lamps, and not shyly, and with any who would. That was the plan deliberately conceived for her and conceived by her own father. The mere thought of it seemed to sully her, to make her unworthy. She remembered that only that morning she had sent a telegram to Captain Rames, with a thrill of excitement, as though she were doing a remarkable thing. She had actually dared. She sat up, and in the bitterness of her heart laughed at the great significance she had set upon herself. Her father had a different view of her importance, and from head to foot she ached with the pain of her humiliation.

Thus through the long hours she swung between terror and abasement, each one mastering her in turn. Once she started up with a despairing cry as she imagined her father driving her out into the street with blows.

Could she make her living honestly if she ran away from him, she wondered miserably, bethinking that at the worst she must kill herself? At another moment she would recall with a pang of contempt her enchanted garden and scorch its flowers with her ridicule. She would walk in that garden no more. It was closed. She had been an impostor in it always. It was a place of falsities. There was but one true, real thing in it all--the turnstile in the wall which gave admission to its precincts. Yes, that was true, and the turnstile, with all it meant of shame and indifference, became to her a new epitome of life.

Gradually the night wore through. A finger of gray light slipped through the curtains, and was laid upon the ceiling of the room. Birds began to sing in the garden. Cynthia turned out her light and fell asleep at last. She slept late and woke to just such another day of heat as yesterday. She lay for a moment, happily convinced that all which had occurred last night had occurred only in a dream. But she looked into the mirror across the room and saw the door, and the truth was made known to her. These things had happened.

Certainly the door was still closed, the night had passed. But other nights would follow, and through the closed door, not her father, but fear and shame had passed to bear her company. She came down to breakfast pale and heavy-eyed, and found Joan and Robert Daventry already at the table. She was afraid lest they should remark the alteration in her looks, and she set herself to counterfeit an air of gaiety. It was not very successful, but Joan and Robert Daventry were making precisely the same pretence, with still poorer results. They could not meet her eyes any more than she theirs; and they were trying for the sake of her happiness to hide from her a catastrophe, her knowledge of which for the sake of their happiness she was trying to hide from them. Thus they all talked with great speed about things of no importance, and laughed noisily whether laughter was appropriate or not, until Robert Daventry suddenly turned to Cynthia and blurted out with an affected blitheness:

"I hope, my dear, that you haven't made many absolutely unalterable arrangements for the summer." And Cynthia turned as white as the table-cloth and looked suddenly down to hide the terror in her eyes. They were going to give her up, then! That was her first despairing thought. No doubt it could not be helped. They were compelled to.

"No," she answered faintly. "No arrangements that cannot be altered. I was going to stay for a week with--" and as she compared the summer which she had planned with that which awaited her, she stopped, lest the choking of her voice should betray her.

"That's well," continued Robert, "for you have a journey to make, Cynthia. I have had a telegram this morning from England. I bought some property in Warwickshire a few years ago. We thought you would not, perhaps, want to live all your life in the Argentine after we had gone. So we bought it for you. But it appears there's some sort of lawyer's trouble over the title."

"We have known there was some trouble," Joan hastened to explain, "for quite a long time. But until this telegram arrived we did not think it very serious."

"Now we know what it is," continued Robert, "and I am afraid that we must go to England and attend to it. Luckily, we have Walton now to look after the estancia." And since Cynthia made no reply, but still looked upon the cloth, he continued in some perplexity: "I hope, my dear, you won't be disappointed. Joan and I, indeed, were inclined to be confident that you would enjoy the trip."

"And, of course, I shall," cried Cynthia; and now she raised her head and gazed at her friends with shining eyes. She had not dared to yield her face to their scrutiny in the first revulsion of her feelings. Even now the room whirled about her. "I shall be delighted to go with you. When shall we start?"

"Yes, that's the point," said Mr. Daventry, uncomfortably. "The telegram is very urgent, and there's a boat sailing from Buenos Ayres to-morrow. I am afraid, Cynthia, that we must catch it. There's certain to be no difficulty about cabins just at this time of the year, and, in fact, I have already telegraphed to retain them. So you see we must leave Daventry by the night train. Can you be ready?"

"Of course," said Cynthia.

The color came back again into her pale cheeks and made them rosy, and the smile returned to her lips. No telegram had come. The bustle in the corridors during the early hours of the evening was explained to her. Over night, Robert and Joan had made up their minds to an instant flight, and had set about their preparations. Cynthia drew her breath again. She resumed life and some part of her faith in life. The world was not peopled with James Challoners, as, in the shock of her horror, she had almost been persuaded. Here were two who, for her sake, were abandoning their home and the place which their labors had made for them in the country of their adoption. Her great trouble during that day of hurried preparation was to avoid blurting out to her two friends her gratitude and her knowledge.

They travelled by night and, reaching Buenos Ayres in the morning, drove straight along the docks to their ship. Once on board, Cynthia noticed that Joan made this and that excuse about the arrangement of her cabin to keep her from the deck until the steamer had warped out into the basin. Then she gave a sigh of relief and sat down in a chair.

"You won't mind, dear, will you?" she said. "We shall probably be kept some time in England. But you will soon make friends. Robert was speaking about it last night. He said it was a good hunting country, and that we could get you some fine horses and--" and suddenly she felt Cynthia's arms about her neck, and the girl's tears upon her cheeks.

"My dear, my dear, you are too kind to me!" cried Cynthia. "I don't mind about the horses, if only you'll keep me with you."

"Of course, of course," said Mrs. Daventry. "What should we do without you ourselves."

The screw was churning up the mud of the River Plate, the flat banks dotted with low trees were slipping past the port-holes.

"Let us go out and get the steward to arrange our chairs on deck," said Mrs. Daventry. She put Cynthia's outburst down, not to any guess at the true reason of their flight, but to a young girl's moment of emotion.

The steamer put into Montevideo, and Santos, and Rio, and glided northward along the woods and white sands of Brazil. It passed one morning into the narrows of the Cape Verde Islands, and there was dressed from stem to stern with flags.

Cynthia asked the reason of the first officer, who was leaning beside her on the rail, and for answer he pointed northward to a small black ship which was coming down toward them, and handed to her his binocular.

"That's the *Perhaps*, bound for the South," he said; and he saw the girl's face flush red.

She put the glasses to her eyes, and gazed for a long while at the boat. The *Perhaps* was a full-rigged ship, with auxiliary steam, broad in the beam, with strong, rounded bows. She had the trade-wind behind her, and came lumbering down the channel with every sail set upon her yards.

"But she's so small," cried Cynthia.

"She has to be small," replied the first officer. "Length's no use for her work. Look at us! We should crack like a filbert in the ice-pack. She won't."

"But she's out for three years," said Cynthia.

"There'll be a relief ship with fresh stores, no doubt. And there are not many of them on board, twenty-nine all told."

Cynthia looked again, and held the glasses to her eyes until the boats drew level. She could make out small figures upon the bridge and deck; she saw answering signals break out in answer to their own good wishes; and then the name in new gold letters came out upon the black stern beneath the counter.

"Thank you," she said as she handed back the glasses. But her eyes were still fixed upon that full-rigged ship lumbering heavily to the unknown South.

"I am very glad to have seen the *Perhaps*," she said slowly.

The first officer looked at her curiously. There was a quiver of emotion in her voice.

"Perhaps you have friends on board," he said. "If you have, I envy them."

"No," she said slowly. "I know no one on board. But I am glad to have seen the ship, for I was interested in it in a part of my life which is now over."

The first officer was about to smile. Here was a remarkably pretty girl of seventeen or so, talking about a part of her life which was over! But the big, dark-blue eyes swept round and rested gravely on his face, and he bowed to her with a fitting solemnity.

Cynthia exaggerated, no doubt, taking herself seriously as young girls will. But the shock of that last night in the estancia had wrought a revolution in her thoughts. Though James Challoner no longer seemed to grip her hand, she walked in the chill shadow of his presence. Nor did that shadow quite lift even when she had landed in England.

They travelled into Warwickshire, and so came to that white house behind the old wall of red brick on the London road which Robert Daventry had once coveted for himself and had afterward bought for Cynthia. The Daventrys made it their home now. Though Cynthia never read a word about it in the papers, that disputed title took a long while in the settling. Robert Daventry resumed the old ties. Joan, with Cynthia at her side, found the making of new ones not the laborious business she had feared, and Cynthia had her horses and as many friends as she had room for in her life. But the shadow was still about her. James Challoner might have found the means to follow them to England. At any corner of a lane she might discover his gross and sinister figure upon the path. A few miles away, the ancient city of Ludsey lifted high its old steeples and its modern chimneys. She was always secretly upon her guard in its climbing streets. There was always in her life a mirror facing a closed door, and at her heart a great fear lest she should see the door open.

CHAPTER IX

ROBERT DAVENTRY EXPLAINS

Thus the greater part of three years passed, but toward the end of the third the influenza became virulent throughout that country. It was a winter of sharp frosts and sudden thaws. One week the lanes were deep in snow and the fields white squares ruled off by the hedges; the next the whole country-side ran water. The epidemic was at its worst in November, and during that month it attacked Joan Daventry. She was now a woman of seventy, and the activity of her life had worn out her heart. She died within a week of her seizure, and from that time Robert Daventry's strength steadily declined. It may have been that the loss of Joan loosened his hold on life, or, again it may have been, as Dr. Hill declared, that he caught a chill at the graveside which he could not shake off. But, whatever the cause, he ailed through November, and in the beginning of the following month, while sitting on the bench at Ludsey, he was seized with a great faintness. He was driven back to the white house, and took to his bed; and on the next day the snow fell again.

Ten days after he had fallen sick, Dr. Hill came from the bedroom and found Cynthia waiting as ever for his news. He was an oldish man, and quite at home in that house. He slipped his arm through hers and said in a grave and gentle voice:

"Your father wants you, my dear. He has something to say to you."

Cynthia looked at him anxiously.

"Won't it tire him too much to talk?"

"He will not, I think, be tired for very long. You had better go to him at once, for his mind is quite clear now. I will come back to-morrow morning, unless you telephone to me before then that you want me. It is now, I am afraid, a matter of waiting."

He drove away from the door. Cynthia walked back along the passages to the room where the old man lay in a great four-poster bed. The afternoon was closing in, and the room was not yet lit. But there was light enough for her to appreciate all that Dr. Hill had meant. Robert Daventry had grown so frail, his hands and face were so very nearly transparent.

"I have a good deal to tell you, Cynthia," he said feebly, and his lips tried to smile. "So listen to me carefully."

The nurse went out of the room. Cynthia sat down by the bed and took the old man's hand in hers. She made no pretence that another opportunity would come.

"You will be very well off, my dear, I am thankful to say," he continued. "There's the estancia, about which I will say a word to you later, and a little more than four hundred thousand pounds in the stocks. It's practically all coming to you. Of course, the profit on the estancia varies with the season, and may in bad years mean nothing; but on the average, I reckon you ought to have about twenty-five thousand a year. That leaves out this house and the little farm which goes with it. They are yours already. I have made Hill one of my executors--he'll be rather a figurehead, I expect--and Isaac Benoliel, of Culver, the other. They are both friends and neighbors of yours, and understanding people. I have tied up half the money on you and your children. If you haven't any children you will bequeath it as you like. But I am hoping very much that you will have them. I once asked a woman what she looked back upon as the happiest time of her life, and she said the evenings when she and her husband used to sit alone together before their first child was born. I think that was a wise saying, Cynthia. It struck me very much at the time, and has never since seemed to me less true than it did then. And, you know, everybody can't expect quite the same luck as Joan and I had in finding you." He pressed her hand with such strength as he had, and lay for a little while silent, husbanding his strength.

"I was advised by my lawyer," he resumed, "to tie my whole fortune up. But I talked it over with Joan and we were afraid that it might perhaps occur to you afterward that we didn't completely trust you."

"Oh, father, I should never have thought that," Cynthia protested gently.

The old man shook his head.

"One can never be quite certain that queer, stinging ideas won't come," he said. "And we both were anxious that you should be sure always that we had no fear of the way in which you would manage your life. So you will be completely mistress of half your fortune," and he hesitated for a moment, "when you come of age. But I would like you, when you are in doubt, to consult Isaac Benoliel. I have a great faith in him."

"I, too," said Cynthia. "I will consult him."

A look of relief came into Robert Daventry's face.

"I am glad of that," he said. "There are people, of course, who are prejudiced against him. He is a Jew, and he's new, and he has that queer sort of indefinable position which attracts criticism. But I think you will find him a valuable friend."

Daventry's voice had weakened to a whisper, and he lay back upon his pillows with his eyes closed. Cynthia moved, but the pressure of his hand retained her. She sat and waited, speaking no word and holding back the tears which smarted in her eyes. Robert Daventry spoke again.

"There's some medicine," he said. "Hill gave it me to keep me going. It's in a glass."

Cynthia lifted a glass filled with some grayish liquid, and held it to the old man's lips. He drank, and resumed:

"I have written down during the last day or two the heads of what I wanted to say on a paper."

Cynthia found a slip of paper on the table by the bedside.

"Just read."

There were some words written one below the other on the paper in a straggling hand. Cynthia read them out.

"Money."

"I have said all I have to say, I think, about that."

"Diana Royle," Cynthia read next. But she read the name slowly, so slowly that Robert Daventry noticed her deliberation.

"I don't think you can see, Cynthia," he said. "It's getting dark."

"Oh, yes, father, I can see quite clearly," she replied. "What of Mrs. Royle?"

"You know her," said Robert. "You like her, too, I think, don't you?" Cynthia did not reply, but Daventry had not asked the question in the tone of one needing a reply. "You will want some one to live with you until you get married, which, by the way, you don't seem to be in a hurry to do, my dear. The young fellows round here don't seem to have made much impression. Oh! I am not bustling you, my dear. Only--only--don't leave it too long, Cynthia," he said, and his hand sought hers again.

Cynthia stirred uneasily. It was the way of men, to want to marry every girl off as soon as possible, she knew. It was a form of vanity. But she wished to give no promise.

"You will probably go to London, I don't want you to mope down here all the time. There's no reason that you should. You can have your house in town. But you will want some one with you, and I thought my cousin, Diana Royle, would be the most suitable person."

Cynthia raised her head as if she was about to speak. But she did not, and Daventry said:

"I wrote to her about it."

"Oh," said Cynthia slowly. "You have already written?"

"Yes, and she consented at once. You see her husband left her badly off when he died. So it will be an advantage to her. And though she is older than you are, she is not so much older that you won't be in sympathy with one another."

Cynthia nodded her head.

"I see," she said. "Yes, of course, I know her very well." But a note of reserve was audible, or rather would have been audible to any other in that room. But Robert Daventry was altogether occupied in the effort to master his overmastering weakness. There was more which he wished to say; there was something which he must say.

"Then that's settled," he whispered; and with his eyes he asked for his cordial. Cynthia once more supported him, and held the glass to his lips.

"Now, what comes next?" he asked, and Cynthia looked at the paper.

"The estancia," she said.

"Yes," said Daventry, and a smile suddenly illumined his face and made it young. "The estancia! You have the right to dispose of it, Cynthia. For one never knows what changes may come. But I don't want you to let it go unless there is some great necessity. It brings in, generally, a good income, and now that Walton looks after it, it gives very little trouble. Walton is a good man. I should give him an interest in it, if I were you, and as time goes on increase his interest. Keep him and keep it. I want you very much to do that. I am proud of the Daventry estancia, for one thing. For another, the best part of Joan's life and of mine was spent there. There, too, we first brought you when you came to us. There's yet another reason," and he stopped, and thought. "Yes, there's yet another reason why I care for it so much--but--" and he shook his head and gave up the effort to interpret it: "it's not very clear in my mind just now. I only know it's there--a strong reason."

He was speaking with a depth of tenderness in his voice for which Cynthia was hardly prepared. Always he had seemed to her to look upon the estancia as a business proposition rather than as the soil in which his heart was rooted. Always, too, he had seemed so contented to live in England, and he had taken his part with so much zest in the local administration of the county. She was as puzzled now by this note of yearning--for it was no less than yearning--as by the reason which he could not interpret. It was all made plain to her in after years, but by another than Robert Daventry.

"I want you very much to keep the estancia, Cynthia."

"Of course I will keep it," she said, and again she made no pretence that the day was distant when it would be hers to keep. Her heart was heavy with grief, it went out in love to this dear friend of hers; she was young and the cry was loud in her bosom, "What will I do without you?" but her lips did not utter it. He would be quite sure of her love without her protests. There was comprehension enough, and to spare, between them to make her certain of that. And, since he wanted her to listen, she put aside her distress and the thought of the loneliness which awaited her and obeyed him.

"I would even be glad"--and the old man hesitated with the timidity of one asking a heavy favor.--"Yes, I would be glad if you would go back there--oh, not often--but just once or twice to see that all was going on well."

Cynthia's hand trembled for a moment. She looked at him with a sudden terror in her eyes. But he was lying now upon his side with his face to the window, and seeing things not to be seen through its panes. It cost Cynthia a great deal to make the promise he sought from her. She shrank from a return to the estancia with every fibre of her body. But she made it. He besought her in so wistful a voice.

"Yes, I will go back, father."

"Thank you," he said gently.

Outside the window the snow lay white and deep upon the slate roofs of the outbuildings, and was piled upon the black branches of the trees. Overhead was a gray sky of winter. But for the glimmer of the snow it would almost have been dark. A smile shone again on the old man's face.

"Perhaps Walton's cutting the corn to-day! Think of it!" he said, with a great longing, and before Cynthia's eyes there rose immediately the vision of a great glistening field of standing wheat and a reaping-machine like a black toy outlined against it. They remained thus in silence for a little while. Cynthia was thinking.

"After all, he may not be in the Argentine.... I may not meet him.... He will have no power over me.... There is no reason why I should be afraid."

And then, as though in answer to these arguments, Robert Daventry said:

"You can go back now, Cynthia, without fear."

The girl looked at him with startled eyes. Had she spoken aloud, she asked herself? Had she betrayed her secret just at this last moment? But her eyes fell upon the slip of paper in her hand, and there she saw written plainly under the word "estancia" the name "James Challoner."

Robert Daventry looked toward a bureau which stood by the window.

"The little drawer on the left. No, the one above that. There's a cutting from a newspaper."

Cynthia found in the drawer half a column of a Spanish newspaper. The name was on the top of the column. It was a paper published in Buenos Ayres. She brought the cutting back to the bed and placed it between his fingers.

"Yes, that's it," he said, and he lay back upon his pillows, and gathered his strength. "I have got to tell you now something which we have always kept a secret from you."

"There is no need to tell it," said Cynthia.

Robert Daventry stared at her.

"If you do know it," he said slowly, "we have made the cruellest mistake we could possibly have made. You can't know it!"

"It's about James Challoner--my father?" asked Cynthia, and Robert Daventry shut his eyes with a look of great distress upon his face.

"How long have you known?" he asked.

"From the night when he came to the estancia," she answered. And she told how she had slipped into the smoking-room and how, huddled in the great chair, she had heard all that James Challoner proposed for her. The shadow deepened upon Daventry's face as he listened, and when she had ended he asked with deep regret:

"Why didn't you tell us this, Cynthia?"

"Because, just outside the smoking-room door in the hall, you both decided not to tell me--not to breathe a word of--of my father's visit. You thought the knowledge would trouble and frighten me. You thought it would hurt. Well, I was as certain that you would be greatly distressed to know that already I had the knowledge. So I held my tongue."

"And it did trouble you?"

"Yes."

"A great deal?"

"Yes," Cynthia admitted. "I was frightened. I did not know what power he might have. I knew you had fled from him for my sake."

"And since you have been here--during these three years--you have still been troubled, still frightened lest he should come and claim you with the law at his side?"

Though the old man could hardly speak above a whisper, he was strangely insistent in his questioning. The words came unevenly, with breaks between, and now and then a weak gasp for breath. Cynthia replied quite simply:

"Yes, here, too, I have thought that he might come. I used to be frightened at night. I used to hear him in the house."

And with every word she spoke the compunction and distress deepened in Daventry's mind.

"What a pity!" he said. "Neither of us guessed, not even Joan, who was quicker than I to notice things. And we thought we knew all about you, Cynthia!" A faint smile lit up his face. "How little, after all, we did know! For we could have spared you all this trouble. Read." And opening his hand he let her take from it the newspaper slip. She uttered a cry as she read the first lines.

"It's true," said Daventry, from the bed.

Cynthia carried the cutting over to the window and read by the fading light. It gave the account of an inquest held at a small town twenty-five miles up the line from the Daventry estancia on the body of an Englishman who had been stabbed to the heart by a Gaucho in a drunken quarrel at a tavern. There was a witness who had worked with the Englishman, and could identify him. He called himself James Challoner, and, when he was drunk, he would boast of his family. Cynthia looked at the date of the paper. It was almost three years old. James Challoner had been killed within a week of his dismissal by Robert Daventry. Cynthia let the slip of paper fall from her fingers, and stood by the window until Robert Daventry called her to his side.

"You held your tongue so as not to distress us," he whispered. "We held ours so as not to frighten you. And so because we were careful of your happiness, and you of ours, you have gone through years of anxiety and terror. Needless anxiety! Terror without a cause! I am so sorry. It seems so pitiful. It seems rather grim to me, Cynthia."

Cynthia answered quietly:

"That's the way things happen." And when she had spoken, Robert Daventry, with an effort, raised himself upon his elbow and peered into her face.

"You oughtn't to be able to say that, Cynthia," he said remorsefully. "You oughtn't to be able to think it. It's not the proper philosophy for twenty. I am afraid, my dear, that trouble has gone deep." He fell back and in a moment a little whimsical smile flickered upon his face. "I don't think I'll tell Joan about this," he said. "She wouldn't like it. She wouldn't forgive herself for not having noticed that you were troubled."

"After all, it was my fault," said Cynthia. "For I hid in the room. However, it's all over now."

But Daventry was not prepared to accept her word. Some flash of insight forbade him.

"It has left its mark, my dear," he insisted, and in broken sentences he dwelt upon his theme. His mind began to wander after a little, but through his wanderings there ran the thread of this idea:

"Joan was always so careful.... Even when you were quite a little girl ... we were never to laugh at you.... 'Children and dogs' she used to say, 'you must never laugh at them. Little things warp children for life.' ... Do you remember when you used to write plays and perform them to us at Christmas, in a toy theatre, with small figures in tin slides?... Joan was always careful that we should take them seriously, and not laugh at the wrong place. I never did want to laugh at the wrong place. I thought you wrote very good plays, Cynthia. I used to say you were a genius. But Joan wouldn't have it. 'No!' she said, 'All children are born dramatists, but they forget the trick of it afterward.' ... I suppose she knew. She was a very clever woman--" and so he drifted off gradually into sleep. Cynthia stayed by his side while the twilight faded and the darkness came; and the light of the fire danced ever more brightly upon the ceiling of the room. The wind set from the west, and as the hours passed the chimes from the great clock in Ludsey Church tower came softly and faintly into the room. But they did not disturb the old man's rest. He went floating out on a calm tide of sleep to his death, and Cynthia sat by his side wondering in the intervals of her grief at the strange arrangement of life which ordained that the efforts of people to secure the happiness of others should only cause needless terrors and vain miseries.

CHAPTER X

MR. BENOLIEL

"There are no ladies," Captain Rames said indignantly, as he took his seat in Mr. Benoliel's dining-room.

His neighbor, a florid and handsome man, a little past the prime of life, glanced at the name on the visiting-card which marked Captain Rames's place, and smiled sympathetically.

"I can quite understand," he returned with a pleasant pomposity, "that to a sailor who has been three years in the Antarctic the deficiency is a very lamentable business. But there are some elements of consolation. Amongst the twelve men seated at this round table of mahogany, you will hardly see one who has not made some stir in the world. Upon your right, for instance, you will see Mr. Winthrop, that long and sallow person. He is a political resident in one of the native States of Rajputana, and his work, in six volumes, on the Indian bangle, is, I believe, supposed to be the last word upon the subject. A little nearer to you you will see a youth, though he is not so young as he looks. He is M. Poileaux, and the only aviator who has not yet fallen into the sea. When he does, he will come here no more. I myself am a surgeon whose name, I believe, is not unknown."

And with a large white hand the famous Sir James Burrell discreetly pointed out others of note to his companion.

Captain Rames glanced indifferently round the table. A few of the twelve were in black coats, and amongst those few was Mr. Benoliel. It was the night of a court ball, and most of the guests were in some uniform or another, or shone in the gold of the privy councillor.

"They are, no doubt, men of vast importance," replied Captain Rames bluntly. "But leaving you out of account, Sir James, I could dispense with the lot of them. When I dine in Grosvenor Square, in June, I do ask that there should be a petticoat on one side of me, at all events."

The surgeon laughed good-humoredly. He studied his neighbor with a quick observing eye. Captain Rames was of the middle height with a squareness of build, which his gold epaulets exaggerated at this moment, and he was square, too, of face. His hair was thick and curved over from the side, parting in a dark turbulent comb, his forehead was broad, his eyes keen and very steady. Vigor rather than refinement was the mark of him; he had more character than intellect, more capacity than knowledge; thus Sir James Burrell defined him.

"I have played the comforter," he said, "at so many bedsides that I should feel my vanity touched if I failed to console you," he returned. "Let me bring to your attention the menu. I am confident that it will appeal to you."

"Yes, that's all right," Rames admitted, as he leaned forward and glanced at the card. "But why should it particularly appeal to me?"

Sir James Burrell shrugged his shoulders.

"My profession brings me into touch with interesting people. I take my pleasure in observing them. And I have always noticed that the men who cheerfully endure the greatest hardships are also the first to demand the best of the luxuries, when they are within reach."

"Well, it's true," said Captain Rames. "I can make a shift with pemmican, but I honestly like a good dinner. It's the contrast, I suppose."

Sir James shook his head.

"It goes deeper than that," said he. "Your pale saints are no doubt profitable to the painters of glass windows, but I doubt if the world owes so very much to them. The great things are really done by the people who have a good deal of the animal in them; and animals like good dinners."

Captain Rames was mollified, and his face took on a jovial look.

"I am animal enough," he said, "to purr when my back is scratched."

But Sir James Burrell was mounted on a hobby and hardly heeded the interruption.

"I could quote historical instances, but I need go no further than this room. Do you see the man sitting next to our host, and upon his right?"

Captain Rames saw a small thin man in the dress of a privy councillor, a man with a peaked, fleshless face, in which a pair of small eyes twinkled alertly. A scanty crop of gray hair covered the back of his skull, and left markedly visible the height and the narrowness of his forehead. Captain Rames leaned forward with a new interest.

"Yes, and I recognize his face," he said. "Surely that is Henry Smale."

"Exactly," returned Sir James. "He is in the cabinet, and, quite apart from politics, he is, upon scientific grounds, a man of great distinction."

"But, surely, he disproves your theory. He looks an ascetic."

"And is nothing of the kind," interrupted Sir James. "I admit that his look of asceticism has been a great asset to him in his career. But the public has quite misjudged him. He is a voluptuary, with the face of a monk--the most useful combination for public life in this country which you could possibly imagine.

If he dines alone at his club, he will not dine under a guinea; and he has the animal weaknesses up to the brim of him. For instance, he is as jealous as a dog. Filch from him the smallest of his prerogatives, and he will turn upon you bitterly. Yet he has done great things, and initiated bold policies. Why? Because he has enough of the animal in him to do great things." And upon that Sir James broke off.

The butler was standing at the elbow of Captain Rames, with a jug of champagne in one hand and a decanter of red wine in the other. He bent down and offered Captain Rames his choice. Sir James Burrell intervened.

"By the way," he said, "have you any wish to stand particularly well with your host?"

"I am now beginning to think that I have," replied Captain Rames.

"Then I should choose his Burgundy. He has his fancies, like the rest of us, and to prefer his Nuits-St.-George to champagne is one way to his esteem."

Captain Rames took the hint, and, as he raised his glass to his lips, Mr. Benoliel smiled to him across the table.

"I will ask your opinion upon that wine, Captain Rames," he said, and so turned again to Henry Smale.

"You see, he noticed at once," said Sir James.

Captain Rames had noticed something too. At the mention of his name, Henry Smale had looked up with interest. He was even now obviously asking a question of Mr. Benoliel about him. Rames began to take more careful stock of his host. Mr. Benoliel was a tall, high-shouldered man, with a dark thin face in which delicacy seemed to predominate over strength. His hair was black, and a little black moustache drew a pencil line along his upper lip. His fingers were long and extraordinarily restless. It was difficult to make a guess at his age. A first glance would put him in the forties. But when Mr. Benoliel showed his eyes--which was not always, for he had a trick of looking out between lids half-closed--it seemed that he must have lived for centuries; so much of fatigue and so much of patience were suddenly revealed.

"I wonder why he asked me to dine here," said Harry Rames.

"You were certain to dine here," replied Sir James.

"I met him but the once by the purest accident."

"You were certain to meet him," said Sir James. "All famous people meet him. All famous people dine here once. But he is not really a snob. For, quite a number of them are never invited twice."

"He can be a good friend?"

"Of that I cannot speak," said Sir James.

The courses followed one after the other, and Harry Rames found his eyes continually wandering back across the silver and bright flowers to the exotic figure of his host. He took his share in the conversation about him, but a movement of Mr. Benoliel would check him in his speech or cause him to listen with an absent ear. He watched the play of his delicate fingers upon the table-cloth, the continual restlessness of his body. Mr. Benoliel was of his race; there was in his aspect a queer mixture of the financier and the dilettante, the shrewd business man and the sensuous appreciator of art. There was a touch, too, of the feminine in him.

"I told you that you would not be bored," said Sir James Burrell toward the end of the dinner. "You are not the first man who has fallen under the spell of Mr. Benoliel."

Harry Rames laughed.

"I am under no spell, I assure you," he said frankly. "I was wondering whether he was likely to be of use to me."

"It is very likely," returned Sir James. "He has been of use to many. He plays at omniscience. To anticipate a wish before it is expressed, to serve an ambition before it has been revealed--that is one of our host's little vanities. He may have asked you here with no other object than to gratify it."

Harry Rames glanced quickly at his companion.

"Is that so?" he asked eagerly. Then his face fell. "But I am not even a friend of his."

"I do not think that matters," said the surgeon. "He likes to pose as Providence, and the posture will be more dramatic if it is assumed toward an acquaintance rather than a friend."

"He is a sham, then," said Rames bluntly.

"By no means," Sir James replied suavely. "Let us say, rather, that he is an artist."

Captain Rames turned with a furrowed brow to his companion.

"I am no great hand at subtleties," he said. "Will you tell me what you know of Mr. Benoliel? I am a beginner in the world, and he may be of importance to me."

Sir James Burrell smiled. He was in his element. To supply a character much as some author of the seventeenth century might have done, was a foible which continually tempted him. He was not always successful. Paradox allured him into difficulties, cheap epigrams at times blazed before him, and would not be quiet until he had uttered them. But often he managed to hit off, with some happiness, at all events, the externals of the person whom he described. He drank his wine now slowly and set down his glass. Then, twisting the delicate stem with the finger-tips of his large and handsome hand, he began:

"He is a Jew, of course, and an Oriental. But from what quarter of the Orient, who shall say? You may give him any birthplace, from the Levant to Casa Blanca, and no one will contradict you. Some hold him to be a charlatan, as you are inclined to do. But he is an accepted personage, not blown into notice and out of it by the favor of a season, but a permanency. How he became so, I cannot tell you. He is very busy all day, although when the darkness comes it would be difficult to point to any one thing which he has done. He is always at the top table at public dinners, and very near to the chairman. But he never proposes a toast or responds to one. If he writes a letter to the *Times*, it appears in leaded type. If you want secret information on any subject, he can get it for you. If you want help, he will find the man who can give it. He is a power in the city. He is a power in politics, and the motor-cars of prime-ministers stand at his door at ten o'clock in the morning. Yet he was never in the House, and has never made a speech on any platform. It is believed by many that he might achieve greatness if he chose. But he never chooses. He has the air at a discussion of being able to say the last word on any subject, but he does not say it. He seems, indeed, to stand high in the world on a pedestal which has no legs to it. That is how I describe him. For the rest, he is rich, and I have never heard him utter an opinion which was not derived from others or altogether banal. But, listen! He is going to speak to us."

"However, I can recommend the old brandy," was all that Mr. Benoliel had at that moment to say.

"There, what did I tell you!" said Sir James, triumphant at the success of his diagnosis.

"Well, if his talk is banal his brandy isn't, God bless him," said Captain Rames. "But I interrupted you."

"He has been guilty of one weakness," Sir James resumed. "He married into an old family of great poverty and the marriage lasted for six months. His wife lives handsomely in Eton Square--But I see that I am going to lose you, for our host is beckoning to you."

Captain Rames obeyed the summons with alacrity and walked round the table.

"I see that you are going on to Buckingham Palace," said Mr. Benoliel. "So I thought that I would interrupt your conversation with Sir James Burrell. For I want to introduce you to Mr. Smale."

Mr. Smale held out his hand. At a sign from Benoliel, the butler brought up a chair and placed it between Smale and his host.

"Sit down," said Benoliel, and Captain Rames obeyed.

"Benoliel tells me," said Smale, "that you are thinking of Parliament."

Captain Rames was startled. He could not remember that in his one brief conversation with his host he had even mentioned his ambition.

"I inferred it from a casual word or two you let drop," said Benoliel with a smile.

"Well, it's true," said Rames. "I should like to stand on your side very much, Mr. Smale, if I could find a seat to contest."

Henry Smale nodded.

"That, no doubt, could be arranged. You would be a strong candidate. You bring a reputation and some breath of romance to favor you. But--" and he pursed up his lips as if in doubt and looked at Captain Rames with a searching eye. Rames was disconcerted. He had been back in England for some six months, and during those six months he had been much sought after. At this period of his life, doubts of him had been rarely expressed behind his back, and never to his face. Young ladies whom he did not know had clamored for his autograph, young ladies whom he did know had approached him with a winning humility; established beauty had smiled at him; established fame had welcomed him as an equal. The calm scrutiny of Henry Smale was a displeasing splash of cold water.

"Of course," he said, with a diffidence which he did not feel, "I might be a failure."

And Henry Smale replied promptly:

"That's just it. You might be a failure. Meanwhile you are a great success, and have the chance of standing quite alone in your career. For what you set out to do is not yet done. You leave the laurel for another to snatch."

"That is quite true, Mr. Smale," Harry Rames replied. "But I have considered it. I am not yielding to an impulse. I have counted the risk!"

He spoke with a nice adjustment of firmness and modesty. Henry Smale rose from his chair.

"Very well," he said. "Will you come down to the House at four o'clock to-morrow afternoon? I will introduce you to Hanley, the chief whip."

Captain Rames flushed with pleasure.

"Thank you, I shall be delighted," he cried, rising in his turn; and as the two men shook hands, Mr. Benoliel said gently:

"I was thinking of Ludsey. It has no candidate on your side, Smale."

CHAPTER XI

A MAN ON THE MAKE

A week later, and much about the same hour, Captain Rames was driven along the Mall in St. James's Park. Friday had come round again, and the light did not burn in the clock-tower at Westminster. But the windows of the admiralty blazed upon the horse-guards' parade, and its great doors stood open for a glittering company. It was the night of official dinners and receptions in honor of the king's birthday. Soldiers in scarlet, sailors in blue, ministers and privy councillors in gold, and ladies in their shimmering gowns thronged with the smaller fry in black coats up the shallow steps into a hall decorated with Union Jacks. There was a thrill of expectancy in the air that evening. Rumors were rife that the government was inclined to advise a dissolution. Members' wives were speculating whether they must go back to the constituencies and tread the ways of deference; their husbands how soon the time would come when they must exchange the erect dignity of the member for the supple curves of the candidate; and curious eyes dwelt, as if in hope of answer upon a sturdy white-haired man with a blunt, good-humored face, who, wearing a uniform with epaulets, left you in doubt whether he was a fireman or an admiral. He was, however, the Prime-Minister, and he stood in the hall amongst his friends, bearing the world lightly according to his wont. He stepped forward and shook hands with Rames as he passed, and so turned again to his friends. He was heard to say, "I have to-day achieved the ambition of my life;" and curious ears eager to glean a hint were inclined toward him.

"To-day?" one of the group exclaimed. "You have been Prime-Minister for three years."

The Prime-Minister laughed.

"That's nothing," he said. "To become Prime-Minister was merely to take a step on the way. But to-night I wear for the first time the uniform of an Elder Brother of the Trinity, and that means that I need never wear knee-breeches again as long as I live."

The curious ears were disappointed; Harry Rames shook hands with the First Lord of the Admiralty, passed on, and in the second room was touched on the elbow by Isaac Benoliel.

"I have been asked by a young friend of mine to bring you to her, and I beg you to come at once, for she is in her most imperious mood," said Mr. Benoliel in a voice of whimsical entreaty.

"We will go to her as fast as we can," said Captain Rames.

He had now been three months in England, and the shy warmth of many welcomes had made him thoroughly aware that he was a momentous personage to young ladies. He was human enough to enjoy his importance, and he followed Mr. Benoliel with alacrity toward a side of the room where Cynthia Daventry sat talking to a young man in the office of the Board of Trade. Rames noticed the clear and delicate profile of her face and the distinction which set her apart; he noticed, too, that, although she did not once look his way, the young gentleman in the Civil Service uniform was summarily dismissed.

"Cynthia, this is Captain Rames," said Isaac Benoliel, and however imperious a mood Cynthia might have shown to him, she had reserved none of it for Captain Rames. Her eyes swept over him swiftly with the shy and eager look to which he had grown accustomed: she gave him her hand.

"I am very glad to meet you," she said impulsively, "because--" and she halted suddenly upon the word, with the color like a rose in her cheeks, "I suppose that you are tired of congratulations."

Captain Rames expanded: he laughed genially, a fastidious critic might have said too noisily.

"By no means," he exclaimed. "Indeed, Miss Daventry, you may lay it on with a trowel."

"I am not prepared to do that," answered Cynthia, and though she spoke lightly, her voice was guarded, and even in the eager eyes there was a constant watchfulness.

Eight months had passed since Cynthia had sat by the bedside of Robert Daventry and listened to his instructions. She had taken Diana Royle to live with her as he had bidden, though she had taken her reluctantly. She had spent nearly all that time at the white house upon the London road, in spite of Mrs. Royle's repeated suggestion that Beaulieu, or preferably Cap D'Ail in the south of France would be more satisfactory places for wintering. Diana Royle was glad to be relieved from her genteel penury in Sussex Gardens, Kensington, but she had no liking for the country. Cynthia, however, was deaf to her hints. She lived for a while in solitude, broken only by the companionship of the few neighbors with whom she was most intimate. The swift deaths of the two old people who had so long lived for her and in her, left her desolate and inclined ever regretfully to search back across her life for occasions in which she had failed of kindness toward them, or hurt them by forgetfulness. She was young, however, and with no taint of morbidness. The sense of desolation passed, and Diana Royle began to urge a new plan.

"You ought to take a house in town for the season, Cynthia. I know of one in an excellent position, which would just suit you. It's in Curzon Street, and the right end of the street, one of those nice, flat-fronted houses, old outside and tiled bath-rooms inside. I happened, I think, to see an advertisement of it to-day."

Mrs. Royle handed the newspaper to Cynthia, looked it over.

"We might think of it," she said.

"I am sure neither Mr. nor Mrs. Daventry would have wished you to bury yourself always in the country."

"That's true," said Cynthia. "My father looked forward to my taking a house in town."

"I don't think you could do better than this, dear," said Diana Royle. "I know the house quite well by sight."

"Well, we'll think of it," said Cynthia.

Mrs. Royle suppressed a shrug of irritation.

"You will find the house will be snapped up, dear, if you take too long thinking of it," she said with asperity.

Cynthia looked at her with innocent eyes.

"But I expect there will be other houses in London, won't there?" she asked.

She had no wish to be churlish, she understood how deeply her companion longed for the paved roadways and the streets. And in her own heart, too, she was beginning to turn to the unknown world of London with an expectancy of adventure, which drew her and thrilled her, even while she hesitated.

"I don't understand you, Cynthia," Diana Royle cried in exasperation. "Are you afraid?"

The question was intended merely as a gibe, but Cynthia turned to her with startled eyes, and Mrs. Royle knew that she had chanced upon a truth.

"Of what are you afraid?" she asked curiously, and Cynthia answered while she looked into the fire:

"I once lay all night staring into a great bright mirror which revealed to me a shut door. I was in terror lest the door should open. I dreaded what might come through. I seem still to be looking into the great mirror, and with the same kind of fear. Only now the door opens upon the world, and not on the passage of a house."

Diana Royle gathered up her embroidery and her book.

"If you are going to talk that sort of nonsense, Cynthia, I shall go to bed," she remarked sternly, and left Cynthia still gazing into the fire.

Cynthia had not been speaking with affectation. The terror with which her father had for so long inspired her had left its mark deep, as Robert Daventry upon his death-bed had understood. He was dead--yes, but she could not rid her thoughts of the dreadful destiny which he had proposed for her. By so little she had escaped it. She would look round the room with its books and its dainty appointments, and feel the arms of her chair to make sure that all was real.

"If he had carried me away!" she would cry. "If he had come back with the law at his side and had carried me away!" And the streets of Buenos Ayres would pass before her eyes in a procession of blazing thoroughfares and dimly lighted lanes. And because she had escaped by so little, she looked out upon all unknown things with apprehension. Moreover, Daventry's disclosure to her upon his death-bed had, in a strange way, added to her apprehension. There were three people--thus her thoughts ran; two of them seeking to hide from her knowledge which they thought would cause her pain; and she the third, seeking to hide from them, just for the same reason, that the knowledge was hers already. The years of terror had been needless, yet they had been endured, and it was love itself which had inflicted them. Kindness then could do just the same harm as the deliberate will to hurt. She took that thought into her heart of hearts, and because of it dreaded what might come through when the door opened upon the world.

With the coming of the spring, however, there came a stir in her blood. It was a spring of sunlit days and warm, soft nights. The great garden bursting into leaf and blossom, the annual miracle of tender green, the return of the birds, and the renewal of melody quickened the girl's pulses, gave to her a lightness of spirit, and made her dreamily expectant of wonders. She walked of an evening under her great cedar trees, with the flowers and the paths glimmering pale in the warm dusk, and the earth whispered to her of things as yet beyond her knowledge; throbbing moments of life, dreams minted in events. She woke eagerly to the clear, early mornings and the blackbirds calling on the lawn; she lingered on that lawn when the windows in the house were alight and the nightingales sang in the copses, and from some distant wood the clear, double note of a cuckoo was borne to her across the darkness. There came an evening in the middle of May when she burst her sheath like any bud on the bole of one of her chestnut trees. She stood a creature of emotion. The soft wind brought to her ears the chimes of the clock in the great church tower at Ludsey. Desire for the adventure overswept her fears. Her feet danced, and her youth had its way with her.

She could see through the long open window Diana Royle in the drawing-room. She ran across the grass.

"Di!"

Some new sound in her voice, a leap, a thrill, made Diana look up. She saw a look in the girl's face, a light in her eyes, a soft color in her cheeks which quite transfigured her.

"I have been rather a brute, Di," cried Cynthia. "We will go to London."

"When?"

"As soon as we can pack."

A telegram was sent off to Mr. Benoliel, who was now in Grosvenor Square. He was bidden to work his quickest and his best. The furnished house in Curzon Street was still unlet. It was secured, and by the beginning of June Cynthia had come to town. There she was of course unknown. But she had made many friends in Warwickshire. Mr. Benoliel set his shoulder to the wheel; and she had a handsome balance at the bank. Add to these advantages her looks, and it will be seen that it was fairly smooth sailing for Cynthia during her first season. She danced, she dined, she lunched at Hurlingham, she went to plays and to the opera, she rode under the trees of the Row in the morning, she went up in a balloon; she came with both hands outstretched for new experiences. Yet she grasped them with a certain wariness. Eager she was, but her eagerness was guarded. For dim in the shadows at the back of her mind there was still the image of the mirror and the door. She had been in London less than a month when Harry Rames was brought to her side by Mr. Benoliel.

They talked for a moment upon immaterial topics, and then Mr. Benoliel turned to Harry Rames:

"So it is all settled, I hear."

"Practically," replied Rames. "I have still to be formally adopted as prospective candidate by the Three Hundred, but that will be done at a meeting on Monday night."

"Then there is no longer any reason why we should keep the matter secret, especially from Miss Daventry, who lives not five miles from your constituency. Cynthia," and both men turned toward her, "Captain Rames is going to stand for Ludsey at the next election."

Captain Rames smiled modestly, expecting congratulations. He liked congratulations, especially from pretty girls, but he was disappointed. He saw only a wrinkle of perplexity upon Cynthia's forehead and a shadow in her eyes.

"Why?" she asked.

"You disapprove?" said Rames.

Cynthia drew back.

"I have no right to disapprove," she said coldly, and Harry Rames planted himself sturdily on both his feet in front of her.

"Nevertheless you do," he insisted.

In spite of herself, a faint smile of amusement played about Cynthia's lips as she watched him. She felt constrained to accept his challenge.

"I should have thought--" she said with a trifle of hesitation; "it's not my business, of course--you may think it an impertinence--but since you challenge me, I should have thought that you would have done better to have gone back to the Antarctic again."

"That's just what Smale said," remarked Mr. Benoliel, and he moved away.

"That's just what Smale said, what every one will say. But it's all wrong," Rames exclaimed emphatically. "I was very glad to go South. I am very glad now that I went; but once is enough."

A little wrinkle of disdain showed about Cynthia's mouth.

"No doubt there were many hardships."

Captain Rames was nettled.

"Yes, there were, Miss Daventry, a great many, and singularly unpleasant ones. I have been twenty-four hours in a sleeping-bag with two other men. The sleeping-bag was sewn up on the inside, it was within a tent, we were so close together that we could only turn round one at a time, and we smoked in the bag, and still we were deadly cold. And I hate being cold. Yes, there were hardships, and though it's easy enough to remember them lightly here in the Admiralty, they were not delightful when they happened. But I should face them once more if I wanted to go back. Only I don't. I never want to see an ice-pack again as long as I live."

The bluff confidence with which he spoke convinced Cynthia that it was not a fear of the hardships which had affected him. There she had been wrong, and she made amends.

"I have no doubt the hardships wouldn't deter you if you wanted to go," she admitted. "But what I don't understand is why you don't want to." And a greater emphasis crept into her voice than she had meant to use, and gave to her words the wistfulness of an appeal. "I should have thought," she cried, "that you could never have rested until you had finished what you had begun."

"That's true to the letter," he replied. "That's why I am standing for Ludsey."

Cynthia looked up at him in surprise.

"I don't think that I understand," she said quietly, and she made room upon the couch at her side. Harry Rames took the place. The appeal in her voice was a flattery which he quite failed to understand. Though Cynthia was young, and though she walked no longer in her enchanted garden, something of that spirit of romance, which had guided her there, had revived in her of late. Captain Rames was one of the chosen men for whom the turnstile had revolved; now that she met him in the flesh she could not forget it. He was of her dreams, he had marched in the procession of heroes, and though disillusionment had come to her he still wore a look of the heroic in her thoughts. All the more because disillusionment had come to her she wished him to retain the look. Her appeal was a prayer that he should stamp it upon his image for good and all.

"May I explain it all to you?" he asked. He sat down beside her, and in answer to that gentle appeal of hers to make the best of himself, he drew for her clearly and succinctly and proudly the picture of a man on the make. "I went South, first and last, to get on in the world," he began. "As I say, I was very glad to go. The journey was a great experience. Yes, three years of my life were very well spent upon it; but they were very well spent, not because the journey was a great experience, but because it is now the great help to me in getting on, which I always thought it was going to be."

He took no notice of the disappointment gathering upon Cynthia's face. He was not aware of it. Here was a girl of remarkable loveliness, wistfully appealing to him to explain the inner workings of his mind, and he was delighted to gratify her wish.

"I can hardly remember the time when I was not diligently looking for a chance to get on. I was poor, you see. I am so still, indeed. I had none of those opportunities which money commands. I had somehow to create or find them. There's a motto in gold letters above the clock in the great hall at Osborne, the first of all mottoes in its superb confidence:

"'There is nothing the navy cannot do.'"

Cynthia turned to him with eagerness.

"Yes," she said with a smile. "For a boy to have that plain and simple statement before his eyes each day, that's splendid. I suppose a boy would never speak of it, but it would be to him a perpetual inspiration."

"Yes," said Rames, "if all he thought of was the navy; if his ambitions were bound up with the navy. But mine weren't, you see, and I used to worry over that sentence even then. 'There is nothing the navy cannot do.' Very well. But that didn't mean that this little particular, insignificant cog-wheel in the navy machine was going to do anything special, or, indeed, anything at all. And I wanted to do things--I myself, not the navy."

"To do things?" Cynthia asked quietly, and her lips drooped a little at the corners, "Or to become a personage?"

Captain Rames laughed good-humoredly.

"I can meet you there, Miss Daventry. There's no contradiction in the phrases. To become a personage is to secure the opportunity of doing things, and when you are a personage you soon find things which want doing. After all, how many of the great statesmen started out to be big men first. They had ideas, I grant you, but they had to make themselves big men by hook or by crook before they could carry them out. Look at Disraeli. I have been reading up these fellows. He did a lot of things. He got the Suez Canal shares. He is the author and begetter of the Imperial Idea. That's what you remember and admire him for. Yes; but don't forget his velvet trousers, and his habit of reciting his epic poems in the drawing-room after dinner. He set out first of all to be a personage. So do I in my small way. He chose velvet trousers and epic poems. I went down toward the South Pole. We each chose the path of least resistance."

Cynthia was silenced, but not convinced. There must be hundreds of instances to confute him, only for the moment she could not remember any of them. And one quality in Captain Rames impressed her.

"You speak as if you had thought all these things out," she said.

"I have had to," he replied.

"I wonder that you went into the navy at all."

"My father put me there," he answered.

Cynthia looked him over again, noting the strong, square face, the direct, the practical, common-sense, uninspired look of him. He would get on without a doubt. There was a great deal of force to push him on, and no great delicacy of character to hold him back. Scruples would not trouble him, and he would not fail of friends. He was of the type which makes friends easily. Even she herself was attracted. He would get on probably by trampling upon others, but he would do it good-humoredly, and with no desire to cause unnecessary pain. There are men, after all, who put nails in their boots to do the trampling.

"I wonder, with your views," she said, upon an impulse, "that you didn't leave the navy long ago and go into the city."

Harry Rames looked at her quickly.

"It's rather curious that you should have said that; for, a few years ago, I was actually thinking of the city, and wondering whether I could make a fortune quickly there."

Cynthia laughed suddenly. Her suggestion had been uttered in sarcasm. Youth is disinclined to rate the making of money high in its standard of careers. Captain Ramos would never have passed the turnstile had she spoken with him when the turnstile was.

"What held me back," he continued, quite unconscious that he was toppling off a hero's perch,--and indeed he would have been totally indifferent had he known,--"what held me back was the knowledge that I should be beginning too old. One has so very little time," he exclaimed with a touch of passion in his voice. "I would like to go on living and living and living for a century. As it is, one begins at twenty at the earliest, and then with luck one may have fifty-five years--that's all," and the prospect of the disintegration of his powers at the early age of seventy-five affected him with so much melancholy that Cynthia laughed again, but this time with a clear and joyous ring of amusement.

"Never mind, Captain Rames, I am sure you will live every day of your fifty-five years, and that is more than all can say."

"They are only thirty-five now," he grumbled. "However,"--he was not to be diverted from the pleasant business of unfolding his character,--"I might still have gone into the city, when one morning in June, as I was walking round the corner of Buckingham Palace to Constitution Hill, I saw on the other side of the road the president of the Geographical Society. I knew him slightly. I had read of the expedition; I was aware that he was organizing it. It came upon me in a flash, 'By George, here's my chance at last,' and I ran across the road and applied for the command."

Cynthia nodded her head.

"So that's how you became connected with the expedition--a pure piece of chance," she said slowly. "If you hadn't turned round that corner to Constitution Hill----"

"Oh, I should have dropped across something else, no doubt," said Rames.

"And now you are going into Parliament."

Cynthia was endeavoring to readjust her forecasts with the facts.

"If I get elected," said Rames.

"Oh, you will get elected," replied Cynthia confidently, but there was no admiration in her confidence. It was almost disdainful. "They will call you 'Breezy Harry Rames,' and they will elect you by an immense majority."

"I am very glad you think that," Rames returned imperturbably; and he leaned forward with his elbow on his knees and spoke to her upon an altogether different note; so that the disdain died out of her face. He told her how in answer to Henry Smale's invitation he had gone down to Westminster in the afternoon, had sent in his card, had waited by the rails in the great round of St. George's Hall. Smale had come out from the House, and had fetched him down the stone passage into the lobby. A great man was speaking, and the lobby was nearly empty. But he finished his speech in a few moments, and the doors burst open and there was an eruption of members from the Chamber. Some stood in groups talking eagerly, others hurried to the libraries and the smoking-room, and barristers walked up and down in pairs, talking over their cases for the morrow. There was not a thing in that lobby, from the round clock above the doors of the House to the post-office and the whip's rooms which had not impressed itself vividly upon Rames's mind. Every now and then the doors would swing open as a member passed into the Chamber, and just for a moment Rames had a glimpse of the green benches, saw the great mace gleam upon the table, the books and the three clerks gowned and wigged behind it, and behind the clerks the dim figure of the Speaker under the canopy of his chair.

Of what he saw on that afternoon Rames spoke with an enthusiasm and a modesty which quite took Cynthia by surprise. He saw dignity in every detail, was prepared to magnify with great meanings the simplest ceremony and form. He could not but impress her with his picture, so greatly impressed was he himself, so keenly had he longed to walk unchallenged down that forbidden way between the rails and to pass through the swing doors over the matting to his place on the green benches. People in the streets might sneer, or go about their business unconcerned. The cynics might talk of the Ins and Outs, and speak of Parliament as the most expensive game in which a race of players of games indulges, but there in that small room, with the soft light pouring down from the roof, and very often the morning light streaming in through the clerestory windows, the great decisions were ratified which might hamper or advance the future of forty millions.

Henry Smale had paced the lobby for half an hour with Rames, setting before him clearly the risks which he would run.

"I don't want to advise you one way or the other," said Smale, "but it is not as if you had no career, and you should come to your decision with your eyes open. I speak to you as to one of the ambitious. If you go in, I take it, you go in with an eye on the Treasury bench. Well, I can tell you this: the House of Commons makes a few, but it breaks a few, and if it advances some, it mars a good many. Poverty is a serious hindrance, for it means that you cannot give the time to the House of Commons which it now claims."

"There are the barristers," objected Rames.

"The House of Commons is in their line of business," returned Henry Smale. "The highest offices of the law are reached through the House of Commons. Moreover, the questions which arise for debate here have often been the subject already of suits in the law courts. They have acquired, too, the knack of extracting rapidly the essential things out of a paper or a bill. Thus, the barristers come especially equipped. Yet, even so, very often they do not make their mark. And here is a point for you, Captain Rames." Henry Smale turned with a warning finger upraised and stopped in his walk. "The most distinguished men enter this House and never get the ear of it. The House of Commons is not ungenerous, but for eight hours a day through a long portion of the year people are talking in that Chamber there, and it will not provide an audience unless, first, the speaker has something of his own to contribute, and, secondly, can express his contribution. It does not, on the one hand, ask for oratory; it is not, on the other, content even with exhaustive knowledge; it demands character, personality, the power of coining out of your knowledge some judgments of your own, the power of explaining your judgment in clear and intelligible phrases sufficiently vivid to arrest its attention. I admit at once that if you succeed, success here is sweeter than anywhere else; its recognition is so immediate. But, on the other hand, here disappointment is more bitter. To come in with ambition, and to be left behind in the race--there is no destiny more galling."

"Yes," said Rames quietly, "I have thought over these things. There is that risk. I am prepared to take it."

"Very well," returned Smale, and once more he turned on the stone pavement, and with Rames at his side retraced his steps. "Let us suppose that you have got the ear of the House, that the benches fill up when you rise, and men stand at the bar to listen to you. Well, even so, you may lose your seat, and you may not yet have established yourself firmly enough to make your party find you another. There you are--out, your dreams dissolved, your ambitions stopped, yourself miserable, and your presence in this lobby an insignificance. Where you walked by right, you come as a guest; you have been, and you are not; you must turn to something else, while your thoughts are here, and very likely you are already too old to turn to something else."

"You put the worst side of it all in front of me, Mr. Smale."

"No," replied Mr. Smale. "Visit the political clubs a couple of months after a general election, talk to the defeated candidates who two months back were members, you will know I am talking the truth. The place enmeshes you. And mind, not because of the sensations. The sensations happily are rare. It is a humdrum assembly. I remember once taking a foreigner into the strangers' gallery at the time of a European crisis. An indiscreet letter had been sent. The foreigner was elated. He said to me, 'This will be very interesting. The Commons will discuss the letter which has so convulsed Europe.' But it was doing nothing of the kind. It was discussing whether the Tyne, Durham, and Hartlepool Railway paid its employees sufficiently well to justify Parliament in allowing it to build a bridge across a stream of which you have never heard."

Captain Rames smiled.

"I see a good many men in this lobby," he rejoined. "I do not notice that any of them are bored. Indeed, for the most part, they seem very busy."

"That is one of the tragedies of the House of Commons," Smale replied. "There are so many men in who during the whole of each session are extremely busy doing nothing; they haven't a moment to spare, they do nothing with so much energy and persistence. One moment they are in the library writing to a constituent who wants to know why the medal which his father earned in the Crimea has not yet arrived; the next moment they rush into the House because the famous Irishman with the witty tongue is up; they are off again to the outer lobby to tell a visitor that he can't see the Prime-Minister--'Industry without work, idleness without rest,' that is how this House was once described, and, believe me, the description is not inapt."

Thus said Henry Smale, but Harry Rames was not to be turned aside.

"I will take all these risks very willingly, Mr. Smale," he cried, "I want to be in here."

Henry Smale smiled, ceased from his arguments, and clapped Rames in a kindly fashion on the shoulder. "I have done my duty," he said. "Come!"

He led Rames through a little doorway at the side of which sat three or four messengers, and at the end of a narrow passage tapped upon a door.

"Come in," said a voice, and as Smale ushered in Harry Rames a man of pleasant address and an exquisite suit of clothes arose and welcomed them.

"Hamlin," said Henry Smale, "this is Captain Rames."

Mr. Hamlin shook hands cordially with Rames and invited him to a chair.

"We shall be very glad to have you in the House," he said. He beamed. He seemed to have been waiting for Captain Rames to complete his happiness. "I think Ludsey was suggested."

"Benoliel suggested it," said Smale. "He's a good judge too."

"There is no candidate arranged yet. I will write to Ludsey at once."

Smale and Rames left the room together.

"I should think you might consider that settled," said Smale.

Rames thanked him and referred to Hamlin's charm of manner. Smale's small eyes twinkled.

"That's why he sits in that room. He's the chief Whip." And shaking hands with Rames Mr. Smale abruptly returned to the House.

The gist of the conversation with Smale Rames told to Cynthia in the reception-room at the Admiralty, and she listened with a growing interest. Then once more his note changed. He spoke with a boyish enthusiasm of his aims. To force an entrance into that arena; the entrance gained, to fight himself into the station of a great man; ultimately to govern and exercise authority--the note of personal ambition rose to a pitch of exultation in his voice. Of principles he obviously had no care, theories of politics were to him of no account. He was the political adventurer pure and simple. Cynthia sat with her eyes of dark blue clouded, and a real disappointment at her heart. She raised her face to his, and a little smile trembled upon her lips, and even her voice shook ever so slightly.

"You have been very honest to me about it all," she said. "I thank you for that."

Captain Rames was a trifle bewildered. He could not see that he had anything to conceal.

"Good-night," she said as she rose, "I see my friend Mrs. Royle waiting for me."

She gave him her hand and moved away for a few steps and then stopped. Harry Rames was at her side before she had stopped. She turned to him timidly with the blood mounting very prettily into her cheeks.

"I suppose," she said, "that your journey to the South really counts now for very little in your thoughts. Yet you must have had a great many wishes for your success sent to you from all parts of the world before you started. I wonder you can forget them all, and leave that work unfinished."

It seemed to Captain Rames that she had hit upon a rather far-fetched argument to persuade him to a second journey to the South.

"Well, I am getting a good many wishes for my success now, and I hear them spoken," he said with a smile. "It is true that I got all sorts of messages and telegrams before I sailed to the South. But to tell you the truth I was rather too busy to read them. I have got them all tied up somewhere in a brown-paper parcel."

Cynthia seemed actually to flinch. She turned away abruptly.

"I wanted to ask of you a favor," said Rames. "Mr. Benoliel said that you lived near Ludsey. You could do a great deal if you would help me. Will you?"

Cynthia turned back to him, her eyes shone angrily, the blood came into her cheeks in a rush.

"No," she said decisively, and without another word she walked away.

"I might have struck her," thought Captain Rames. He knew nothing of a telegram from the Daventry estancia which lay forgotten in that brown-paper parcel.

None the less he walked home across the Mall treading upon air. Great people had moved out of their way to make his acquaintance; Cabinet ministers had promised to speak for him; important ladies had smiled their friendliest. He looked back upon the days of his insignificance, and his heart was buoyant within him. Certainly one girl with dark-blue eyes and a face like a rose-leaf had presumed to disapprove of him. But there! Girls! You never knew what odd notions nested in their pretty heads. If a man on the make steered his course by a girl's favor, he would soon shipwreck on a snag. However, this girl must be soothed down. Harry Rames could not afford to have an enemy at Ludsey. But he had no doubt that he could soothe her down. He walked home, softly whistling under his breath.

Cynthia for her part went home in a different mood. She had lost another illusion to-night.

CHAPTER XII

LUNGATINE

The threatened dissolution was, after all, postponed, and through the autumn months Captain Rames went busily up and down between London and Ludsey. He made his head-quarters at an hotel on a climbing street in the thick of the town, and spent his days in the public view and his nights at meetings and at local festivities.

Cynthia Daventry, five miles away, heard stories of his indefatigable energy and once or twice she met him in the streets; and once or twice he snatched an afternoon and swept over in a motor-car to see her. She welcomed him with a pleasure which she rather resented, and not for worlds would she have asked him how his campaign was faring. She did not, however, have to ask. For either Diana Royle was present and eagerly questioned him, or if Cynthia were alone he plunged into the subject himself. Captain Rames was at some pains to amuse her and he succeeded. Little incidents of the campaign, whether they told against himself or not; sketches of queer characters whom he came across; an anecdote now and then, drawn from the ancient history of the City--he poured them out to her, making it quite clear with an apparently ingenuous frankness that he had deliberately stored them in his memory purely for her amusement. He was engaged in the work of soothing her down. Diana Royle would rhapsodize after he had whirled away in a cloud of dust.

"What a wonderful man! How energetic! How clever!"

"And how complacent!" said Cynthia.

"What high principle!" Diana gushed lyrically. "What character!"

"And what cunning!" added Cynthia, with a droop of her lips.

Diana tapped the floor with an irritable foot.

"Very well, darling. Look for an angel, by all means. You will be very glad of a man later on." Then she laughed pleasantly. "But I am not deceived. You talk lightly of him when he is gone, but when he is here you fix your big eyes on him, and, though you say nothing, every movement of you asks for more."

Cynthia was startled.

"Well, perhaps I do," she admitted. "I suppose that I have a kind of hope that I will hear, not more, but something different from what I am hearing."

"That's so like you, my dear," Diana rejoined; she was all sugar and vinegar. "If Julius Cæsar came back to earth, you would want him different. But that's the way with romantic people. They look for heroes all day and never see them when they knock at the front door."

Cynthia laughed good-humoredly. There was this much of truth in Diana Royle's attack. She had been searching through the words of Harry Rames all the while when he was uttering them for a glimpse of some other being beside the man on the make. Certain qualities she recognized. Enthusiasm, for instance. But it was enthusiasm for the arena, not for any cause to be won there. A shrewd foresight again was evident. But it was foresight to pluck the personal advantage. Here, it seemed to her, was the conscience of the country stirring on all sides to the recognition of great and unnecessary evils in its midst, and Harry Rames was alone unaffected. Yet in a measure she was impressed. He had so closely laid his plans. He gave her yet more evidence when he came again.

"I have got a rule or two," he said. "All demands for pledges from leagues and associations go into the waste-paper basket. I'll answer questions if they are asked me by a man in my constituency. I won't put my name to a general proposition and post it to London. Many a good man has been let down that way. Then I won't canvass. I won't solicit a vote. I don't believe in it. There's one only point of view for a candidate: that the electors are doing themselves a service by electing him, and not doing him one. You have got to persuade them of that."

"Don't you find it difficult?" asked Cynthia, innocently.

Rames laughed.

"Yes, I do," he said. "The electors have their point of view, too. But I won't canvass, I am there at my hotel if any one wants to see me. I am at public meetings, and I go to social functions. That's a good move," and Captain Rames nodded his head. "You meet the fellows on the other side and if you can get them friendly, you stop them coming out hot against you. Makes a lot of difference, that. Then there's wisdom in taking a firm stand upon a point or so. Your own people, treat them properly, will always give you a bit of latitude, and a reputation for courage is a fine asset in politics as in anything else."

"But you mustn't overdo it, I suppose," said Cynthia ironically.

"Oh, no, you must be careful about that," replied Rames seriously. "What you want to produce is an impression that you are not pliable, that industries will be safe under your watch--that's for the business men--and that social advancement will not be neglected--that's for the artisans. You know the election is coming now," he suddenly exclaimed. "Do come to one of my meetings!"

Cynthia looked doubtful.

"I don't think," she said, "that I believe very much in any work which--I don't express what I mean very well--which hasn't a great dream at the heart of it."

Rames looked up into her face quickly and grew suddenly serious. He made no comment upon her words, however.

"After all that's no reason why you shouldn't come to one of my meetings."

Cynthia smiled.

"I will come to the last one on the night before the poll," she replied reluctantly.

"I shall hold you to it," said Harry Rames, and he went away well pleased with his visit. Cynthia was popular in Ludsey. So Cynthia should sit on that momentous evening in the front row upon the platform. Also he would make for her benefit an unusually effective speech. Cynthia from the window watched his motor-car spin away in a whirl of dust. He was going to preside that evening at a meeting of the Salvation Army.

The dissolution took place on the fifteenth of January. But the real contest had begun a fortnight before in Ludsey. Harry Rames rushed into it as if it had been a foot-ball rally. He spoke all day, in factories and outside factories, in halls and schoolrooms and from club-room windows. He ransacked the morning papers for new pegs on which to hang his arguments; he kicked off at foot-ball matches and the aim of the kick was entirely political; and at the end of three weeks even he was very tired and inclined to recognize an element of humiliation in the conduct of a successful campaign.

It was eleven o'clock at night. There was to be but one more day of it, but one more meeting to-morrow night, the big, final rally on the eve of the poll. Harry Rames lay outstretched upon his sofa with his pipe between his lips cradled pleasantly upon that reflection, when the door of his room opened and a waiter brought in a card. Rames waved it aside.

"I can see no one."

"The gentleman said that his business was important."

Rames grumbled and took the card from the salver.

"M. Poizat," he read. "A Frenchman. Certainly not. I won't see him."

The waiter, an old English servant, a rare being nowadays, even in a country hotel, stood his ground.

"He's lived in Ludsey a long time, sir."

"Oh, has he!" said Rames. "Tell him I am out."

The waiter shook his head.

"He has already told me that you are in, sir. Come, you had better see him, sir. Perhaps he's the ha'porth of tar."

"Oh, very well," said Rames. "But I tell you, William, that I am in the mood to assert my rights as a man."

"Mustn't do that, sir, until the day after to-morrow. You are only a candidate till then."

William retired. Rames fell back upon his sofa. He meant to lie there prone upon his back, even if his visitor held all the votes of Ludsey in the hollow of his hand. Then the door opened and was shut again. A little, puckish old man stood in the room, danced lightly on his feet, skipped in the air, twirled before Captain Rames's astonished eyes and finally struck an inviting attitude, both arms extended and one foot advanced, like the pictures of the quack doctors in the newspaper advertisements.

"Oh, he's out of a lunatic asylum," Captain Rames almost groaned aloud. "He won't even have a vote."

The little man skimmed forward with agility, fixing a bright and twinkling pair of eyes upon the prostrate candidate.

"How old do you think I am?" he asked, and he whirled his arms.

"You are the youngest thing I have ever seen," replied Rames with conviction. "I didn't know that people were even born as young as you are."

"I am seventy-three," exclaimed the little man with a chuckle. He squared up at an imaginary antagonist and delivered a deadly blow in the air.

"Do you mind not doing that!" said Rames mildly. "My nerves are not what they should be, and if you do it again I shall probably cry. I suppose that you are M. Poizat----"

"I am, sir," said the little man. He changed his tactics. He no longer whirled his arms in the air. He advanced to the sofa and suddenly put up his foot on the edge.

"Feel my calf!" he said abruptly.

Captain Rames meekly obeyed.

"You ought to have a medal," he said languidly. "You really ought. At seventy-three, too! For myself I am like butter, and rather inferior butter, on a very hot day."

M. Poizat nodded his head.

"I know. That's why I am here!" He looked about the room and with the importance of a conspirator he drew out of his pocket a medicine bottle filled with a brown liquid. "Why am I so young?" he asked. "Why is my leg of iron? Listen to my voice. Why is it so clear?--It's all 'Lungatine,'" and with immense pride he reverently placed the bottle on the mantel-shelf. He turned again to Captain Rames.

"I heard you to-night. I suffered with you. What a voice! How harsh! How terrible! And yet what good words if only one could have heard them! I said to myself: 'That poor man. I can cure him. He does not know of Lungatine. He makes us all uncomfortable because he does not know of Lungatine.' So I ran home and brought a bottle."

"It's very good of you, I am sure," said Rames, "But look!" He pointed to a table. Throat sprays, tonics, lozenges, encumbered it. "The paraphernalia of a candidate," he said.

M. Poizat smiled contemptuously. He drew from his breast pocket a sheaf of letters.

"See how many in Ludsey owe their health to me!" he cried, and he gave the letters to Rames, who read them over with an 'oh' and an 'ah' of intense admiration when any particularly startling cure was gratefully recorded.

"You are a chemist here I suppose--naturalized, of course?" asked Captain Rames.

"I have a restaurant," M. Poizat corrected him. "Lungatine is merely one of my discoveries."

He sat down complacently. Captain Rames started up in dismay upon his elbow.

"I have a great deal to do to-morrow," he said piteously. The plea was of no avail. Captain Rames was in the grip of that most terrible of all constituents, the amateur inventor. M. Poizat drew his chair to the side of the sofa and went through the tale of his inventions. It was the usual inevitable list--an automatic lift which would work with absolute safety in any mine, a torpedo which would destroy any navy, a steel process which would resist any torpedo, and a railway-coupling.

"I'll bring you the models," he cried.

"No, no," cried Rames, springing from his sofa in dismay. Then he laid his hand on the inventor's shoulder and smiled wisely:

"Royal commissions for you," he said. "They're the fellows for models. I'll see about some. Royal commissions for you. Thank you for your Lungatine. Good-night, my friend, good-night."

Gently, but firmly, he raised the inventor from his chair, while he shook hands with him, and conducted him toward the door.

"You have your hat? Yes."

"A tablespoonful six times a day in a wineglass of water."

"Yes. The instructions, I see, are on the bottle."

Captain Rames opened the door with his pleasantest smile.

"To-morrow at your great meeting," said M. Poizat, "I shall be there. I shall hear what you say. Your voice will ring like a trumpet. And perhaps at the end of your speech, you will say that it is all due to Lungatine."

A frosty silence followed upon the words. Captain Rames said indifferently:

"You have been in England a long time. You are naturalized, of course?"

M. Poizat did not reply to the question.

"Perhaps you will say that it is all due to Lungatine," he repeated softly. "Perhaps you will say that. Who knows?"

Captain Rames looked up at the ceiling.

"Ah, who knows?" he said enigmatically.

M. Poizat shook hands for a second time and went down the stairs. Captain Rames closed the door, took the cork from the bottle, wetted the tips of his finger, and tasted the brown liquid. It was a simple solution of paregoric.

"I don't believe the fellow's naturalized," cried Rames, and he raised the bottle in the air above the coal-scuttle. But he did not let it drop.

"Perhaps he is though," he thought. He poured away a portion of the liquid amongst the coal, replaced the cork, and set the bottle prominently upon the mantel-shelf so that if M. Poizat took it into his head to call again he would see it there. Then he betook himself to bed; and M. Poizat figured in his dreams, a grotesque, little, capering creature, a figure of fun, as indeed he was, to the eyes of wakefulness. There are people upon whose faces nature writes plainly hints of tragic destinies, and M. Poizat had certainly no relationship with these. But then nature is apt to be freakish.

CHAPTER XIII

THE NIGHT BEFORE THE POLL

The walls of the great Corn Exchange were draped with banners and hung with gigantic mottoes. Cynthia sat in the front row of chairs upon the platform with Isaac Benoliel upon one side of her, and beyond him Diana Royle. It was the first public meeting at which she had ever been present, and now that the shy uneasiness at the prominence of her position which had troubled her when she took her seat was passing away, she gazed about her, eagerness in her eyes and a throb of excitement at her heart. In front of her a rostrum had been built out from the edge of the platform so that the speakers might stand upon the exact spot whence the voice carried with the greatest sonority. The rostrum was railed and hung with red cloth; the chairman's table, with the inevitable water-bottle, occupied it; and the small, square space was the only empty space in all that cavern of a hall. A few rows of chairs for members of the association were ranged at the front upon the floor; behind the chairs the people stood packed and massed to the doors, most of them men. The one gallery was crowded to its furthest nook; behind Cynthia the platform was thronged. Wherever her eyes turned she saw faces, faces, faces, all set in one direction, all white under the glare of light, all inclined toward the empty rostrum. It was the eve of the poll. There was a tingle of excitement in the air, a hushed expectancy. Only when Cynthia raised her eyes did she lose the vague feeling of suspense. Overhead a skylight in the roof was covered with a horizontal blind. One tattered corner hung down and as she looked up from the indistinguishable throng of faces, it arrested her attention as something especially individual and definite and single.

Suddenly came a buzz and a stir. The chairman was seen to rise from a flight of steps at the side of the platform. He was followed by a tall, gaunt, loose-limbed man with a bony face, a white moustache, and a high, bald head. He had the look of a soldier. Cynthia took no heed of him. He stalked before her and sank unnoticed in his place. Behind him came Harry Rames, and as he passed along the narrow gangway between the crowded chairs, those who had seats sprang to their feet; and three thousand people broke like a wave into a flutter of handkerchiefs and a shattering thunder of applause. Above the applause a chant gradually swelled, two lines of a tune rather like a chime. Cynthia could not hear the words, but the sound, with its rise and fall, surged backward and forward against the walls of the Exchange for a full minute.

Mr. Benoliel leaned toward Cynthia.

"They have given him their foot-ball song. In a city of artisans, keen on foot-ball, that's a good sign."

Cynthia nodded. But she hardly heard, she could not have answered. Here was something quite new to her, and overwhelmingly new. The thunderous outburst had taken her by the throat; for a second she felt choked; she had no part in politics, yet emotion woke in her and the tears sprang into her eyes.

"What's the matter, Cynthia?" asked Diana Royle.

Cynthia replied with a break in her voice between a laugh and a sob.

"I don't know. It's just the crowd, I think."

"And the enthusiasm of the crowd," added Mr. Benoliel. "You make me feel very old, Cynthia. I can listen to it quite unmoved now. But there was a time when I couldn't without a choking in my throat. It's the splendid faith of the crowd."

Cynthia, arrested by the phrase, looked quickly at Benoliel. Greatly as she liked him she was never quite sure of him. Kind as he had been to her she always suspected some touch of the charlatan. He had the look of a man quite in earnest.

"I wonder," she said, "whether mere magnetism is enough to arouse it."

Mr. Benoliel did not answer; for the chairman rose at his table; and while he spoke the harmless necessary words, Cynthia took stock of Harry Rames, who was seated in the rostrum at the side of the table in front of her and a little to her left. The last weeks of exertion had left their marks; the flesh had worn thin upon his face; there were dark hollows beneath his eyes; he had gained a look of spirituality which did not belong to him. He was nervous; his hands, with the long fingers which never seemed to accord with the rest of him, moved uneasily and restlessly from the buttons of his coat to the slip of notes which he had placed upon the table. Cynthia was deceived by the look of him as she had been deceived by the fervor of the gathering. The outburst was not entirely, was not even chiefly, a tribute to the candidate. Ludsey was a political city, and by three weeks of speeches and agitation political feeling had been whipped to a climax of excitement. It sought and found its outlet to-night at this final rally before the poll.

The cheers broke out again when Harry Rames rose and leaned his hand upon the rail of the rostrum. When they died down he began to speak--first a faltering word or two of thanks. Then his voice suddenly strengthened and rang firm. His fingers ceased to twitch, and he turned over in his mind the consecutions of his thoughts as though he were turning over the pages of a book. All that he had planned to say came clearly to him in its due order, and brought the comforting assurance that the rest would follow. He was master of himself, and being master of himself set his audience at ease to listen, Cynthia among the rest. Anxious as he himself, she knew now that the speech would go right on to its considered end. She leaned forward, all ears to catch the words, and all eagerness to read into them, if she could, the something more which was not there.

But she could not; yet it was a night of triumph for Harry Rames, "Breezy Harry Rames." She recalled her own phrase with a disappointed droop of the lips more than once during the next hour. He was going to win. She had no doubt of it. Confidence swept from his audience to him and back again in waves. And he savored the joys of the orator as he never had before. He had the arts of the platform, and more than the arts, a power to bend his audience to sympathy. He knew that night the supreme reward, the hush of a mass of people constraining themselves to silence and even to immobility while a voice, low as a whisper, sounded audibly in every nook. He played with the suspense, prolonging it to the last moment of endurance, and then, by a sudden swoop to a sharp, clever phrase, drawing the audience to its feet and coining the silence in a stormy tumult of applause.

He had the gift of speech; Cynthia gladly conceded it. An aptness of homely words, an absence of all extravagance, and a voice resonant and pleasant as a clear-toned, bell impressed her more than she had expected to be impressed. A day's rest had restored his voice for the time, even though M. Poizat's Lungatine had not contributed to the restoration.

She was surprised, too, by a certain shrewdness in the matter of the speech. It was not so much of the platform as his manner. There was very little reference to the navy. "I don't mean to be considered a 'service member,'" he had said to her once. "No one pays attention to the service member in the House of Commons." But here and there came views which struck her as new and worth consideration.

"If you could teach the wives of the artisans to cook and to take an interest in cooking, you would have done a great deal more to solve the question of intemperance in this country than if you closed half the public-houses," he cried once and developed his theme with humor and some courage. He drew a picture of a wife putting her husband's supper on the fire, ready against the time when he should come home from his factory, and then running out into the street to talk to a neighbor and leaving the meat to grill to the toughness and dryness of leather.

"The man comes home, sits down to it, and rises from it unsatisfied. What does he do? He goes out and strolls round to the public-house. Put a good meal, well-cooked, inside of him, and he'll not be so disposed to move. He'll be inclined to smoke his pipe by the fire in his kitchen."

He passed on to other topics. The whole speech was clever and was uttered on a lift of enthusiasm. But again Cynthia argued, it was the enthusiasm for the arena, not for a cause. It was ambition without ideals, power without high motive.

Diana Royle inclined toward her.

"Aren't you satisfied now?" she asked.

"Oh, he will get on," said Cynthia; and then she suddenly sat upright in her chair, with her lips parted and the blood bright in her cheeks.

"But, after all," Rames was saying; his voice was beginning to grow hoarse and he raised his hand in an appeal for silence, "here are we discussing the work to be done, and leaving out in our discussion the great necessity. I don't know what you think, but to my notion there is no greatness in any work unless it has a dream at the heart of it. The world's work is done by the great dreamers. Well, here is my last word before the poll, perhaps the last word I shall speak in this constituency."

He was interrupted as he had meant to be by loud repudiations of such a possibility.

"No, no!"

"You're a member already."

"We'll put you in."

Such phrases broke in upon the words and then a cheery voice, louder than the rest, shouted from the back of the hall:

"Never fear! You're well patronized in Ludsey, Captain."

A burst of laughter followed upon the words, and a flush of annoyance darkened Rames's face.

"I will remind my friend that I am not a public entertainer," he said. "And it's really against the spirit represented in that sentence that I wish to direct my first words. I have my dream too--a dream. I speak openly to you--at my very heart. Let me tell it you. It involves a confession. When I first came to Ludsey six months ago, when for the first time I saw from the windows of my railway carriage across the summer fields the tall chimneys and high, long roofs of its factories, the delicate steeples of its churches, it was to me just a town like another. I will be frank, it was just a polling-booth. But as I got to know your city that error passed out of my thoughts."

Cynthia leaned forward. He had used her own words. She could not but be flattered by his use of them. They had been acclaimed, too, by this great gathering, and she was proud of that. Not for anything would she have had their authorship revealed, but she was proud to hear them used, proud, too, because they seemed to have led, if she dared believe her ears, Harry Rames out of his detested breeziness into a contemplation of something other than the personal gain. She could hardly doubt him now; he spoke with so simple a sincerity. She had a sudden glimpse once more of her enchanted garden wherein she had walked with and helped the great ones of the earth. To help, herself unknown except by those she helped!--that had been the dream when she had encouraged dreams; and it sprang once more into life now as she listened.

"It is a city," Rames continued, "where a few steps will take you out of the thronged streets into some old garden, quiet with the peace of ancient memories; some old close of plaster and black beams; some old room with windows deep-set in four-foot walls and wide hearths of centuries ago. And round about these old places stands a ring of factories where in good times the lights blaze until the morning and the whir of its machines never ceases from your ears. It is a city whose continuous life is written for all to see upon its buildings. Here kings and queens have tarried on their journeys; there chambers of commerce hold their meetings. From small and ancient beginnings it has been made by the activity of generations of men into a modern industrial city. Well, I have my dream. It is to be one little link in the continuity of its life and to do my share of service in the forwarding of its prosperity."

A shout answered his words. He had his audience in hand. He stilled it with a swift gesture and his voice rang out with a laugh which had all the exultation of battle.

"Well, we shall know to-morrow night. We are in the ice-pack now, but we are coming to the outer rim of it. We can see the blue water already. We shall be sailing smoothly upon it this time to-morrow night."

He had been chary of references to the voyage which had made his reputation; all the more, therefore, this one struck home. He sat down tempestuously acclaimed, and turning in his chair held out his hand to Cynthia Daventry.

"I am glad that you came," he said. "I have achieved two triumphs to-night. I have brought you and Mr. Benoliel to your first political meeting and both of you are on my platform."

He shook hands with Isaac Benoliel and with Diana Royle. Cynthia leaned a little forward.

"I, too, am glad that I came," she returned with a smile. Because of those last words of his, friendship was warm in her toward Harry Rames. She added, "You knew then that I was here--just behind you?"

Rames nodded.

"Yes, but I was too nervous to turn to you before I had made my speech. The flesh wears a little thin after three weeks of this. One gets jumpy. Even the tattered corner of blind hanging down there from the skylight seemed to-night charged with some important message." He spoke, ridiculing the fancy, and Cynthia, with a smile and a quick lift of her eyebrows, cried:

"I noticed that too."

"Then for the first time," said Rames, "we have something in common. You and I are probably the only people in the hall who noticed it. We have a bond of union."

"A strip of tattered blind!" said Cynthia.

"Well, there was nothing at all before," said Captain Rames, and he suddenly turned back to his seat. For the tall, gaunt man was on his legs.

Cynthia neither heard his name nor followed his speech with any particular attention. It was indeed difficult to follow. He was an old hack of the platform with all the sounding phrases at the tip of his tongue. Rolling sentences, of the copybook, flowed out of him; declamations too vague to be understood were delivered with the vigor of a prophet. But he interspersed them with the familiar clichés of the day and each one received its salvo of applause. To Cynthia he was a man not so much stupid as out of place. She could imagine him at the head of a cavalry squadron. Here he seemed simply grotesque.

On the other hand, Captain Rames did not; and the contrast between the two men bent her to consider whether, after all, she had not been wrong in her condemnation of his new career. She was in the mood to admit it; and when the meeting broke up and the crowd was pouring through the doors into the street, and those upon the platform were descending its steps, she found herself alone for a second on the rostrum with Harry Rames.

"Perhaps I was wrong," she said. "I remember what you told me of Mr. Smale. A vivid gift of phrase--he thought that necessary. You have it."

"On the platform--yes. But the platform's not the House," said Rames. "Smale told me that too. I have yet to see whether I shall carry the House."

"Yet those last words," said Cynthia--"about the city and the continuity of its life and your pride to have a little share in it. Oh, that was finely done."

And upon Rames's face there came a grin.

"Yes, I thought that would fetch 'em," he said.

Cynthia stepped back. Once again it occurred to Rames, as it had done on the night of their first meeting at the Admiralty, that just so would she look if he struck her a blow.

"Then--then--the city is still a polling-booth," she stammered.

"Yes," said Rames.

The hero newly perched upon his pediment tumbled off again.

"You used what I said to you because you just thought it would go down."

Rames did not deny it. He remained silent.

"I remember," she continued, "it was no doubt a foolish thing I said. But even when I said it, you were thinking this is the sort of thing that will take."

That she was humiliated, her voice and her face clearly proved. Yet again Rames did not contradict her. Again he was silent. For there was nothing to be said.

"You do not allow me many illusions about you," Cynthia said gently, and she began to turn away.

But now he arrested her.

"I don't mean to," he said quickly; and by the reply he undid some portion of the harm he had done himself in her eyes.

CHAPTER XIV

COLONEL CHALLONER'S MEMORY

It had been arranged that Mr. Benoliel's small party should take supper with Harry Rames at his hotel. As they stood waiting at the foot of the platform the agent came to them from the outer doors.

"The way's clear now," he said. "I think you can go."

They passed through the empty hall, Cynthia first at Harry Rames's side, and in that order they came out upon the steps. A fine rain was falling, but the crowd had not dispersed. The great light over the door showed the climbing street thronged. Coat collars were turned up, hats were pressed down; and so as Rames and Cynthia came out they saw in the glare beneath the rain just a mass of swaying, jostling black things, round black things moving indecisively this way and that like some close-packed herd of blind animals. Just for a moment the illusion lasted. Then Rames was seen and of a sudden the heads were thrown back, the hats shaken high, and all those black round things became the white faces of living men, their eyes shining in the light, their voices shouting in acclamation.

Captain Rames took a step back.

"Did you see?" he cried to Cynthia.

"Yes. They are not animals to draw your chariot," she replied. "They are men."

"Yes, men--men to govern," he answered. His was the spirit of the old Whig families. Though he was not of them, he meant to force his way among them. To govern the people, not to admit it to government, to go far in appeasing it, but not to give it the reins, that was his instinct. He wished to retain the old governing class, but he meant to be one of it. His ambitions soared to-night, and reached out beyond this hilly, narrow street. He led these men now who stood acclaiming him in the rain. His thoughts shot forward to other days when every town in England might at his coming pour out its masses to endorse his words.

He waved his hand toward his companions and the crowd made a lane for them across the street to the hotel. Rames himself was carried shoulder-high, and set down within the doors. He led the way up the stairs to a big room upon the first floor overlooking the street, where supper was laid. A great shout went up from the street as they entered the room.

"They want you," said Mrs. Royle.

"No," replied Rames. He opened a door into a smaller room in which no lights were lit and pulled up the blinds. Across the street under a great clock was a newspaper office and in the windows the election returns of the night were being, displayed. All along the line victories were gained for Rames's party. Arthur Pynes, a young manufacturer, and the chairman of the association, to whose energy the organization was due; an ex-Mayor, a Mr. Charlesworth, and one or two hard fighters of the old school joined the group in the dark room. One of them, a rosy-faced contractor with a high laugh, who had presided over the association in its darker days, leaned against the window by Cynthia Daventry.

"He'll have to appear on this balcony to-morrow night, as soon as he can after the result's declared," he said. "You see, the windows are all boarded up on the ground floors opposite."

"He'll speak from here?" asked Cynthia.

"He'll speak, but they won't listen," replied Mr. Arnall. "I remember Sir William Harris, the last time he was elected before he was made a judge--" and he ran off into stories of the old days until the windows of the newspaper office were darkened and the crowd at last dispersed.

"Let us go in to supper," said Rames, and they all passed into the next room. "Will you sit here, Mrs. Royle, and you here, Miss Daventry?" He placed Diana Royle upon his right hand and Cynthia upon his left. "Pynes, will you take the chair next to Mrs. Royle, and Colonel," he addressed the tall, gaunt man whose flowing platitudes had left nothing in Cynthia's mind but a recollection of sonority, a booming as of waves in a hollow cave, "will you sit next to Miss Daventry?"

The colonel bowed and prepared to take his seat. But he was a punctilious old gentleman and stood upon the ceremonies.

"You have not introduced me, Rames," he said.

"I beg your pardon. Miss Daventry, this is Colonel Challoner. He has made his own seat a safe one--a county division which polls a week later than we do, and he lives in it. So when I applied at head-quarters for help at our last meeting Colonel Challoner was kind enough to volunteer."

Cynthia shot a startled glance at her neighbor. Her own name was Challoner too; and all that was terrible in her recollections was linked with it. Of course, it did not follow that this Challoner was any relation of hers. There must be many families of that name. Nevertheless, the sudden sound of it caused her a shock. The blood rushed into her face. She made a movement. Almost she shrank away. Challoner, however, was taking his seat. He noticed the quick movement; he did not appreciate the instinct of fear which had caused it.

"Ah, it is true then, Miss Daventry," he said. "We have already met. You remember it, too."

Cynthia was startled.

"No, Colonel Challoner," she replied quickly. "I don't think that we have. Indeed, I am sure we have not. I should surely have remembered if we had."

"That is a pretty thing for a young lady to say to an old man," the colonel answered with a smile. "But my memory is a good one. I never forget a face."

He had the particular pride of all men with good memories, and ambition had intensified it into an obstinacy. For he had his ambition, and successive disappointments had only strengthened its hold upon his heart. He aimed to be Under Secretary of State for Foreign Affairs. He had been military attaché at so many Embassies, the post, to his thinking, was marked out for him. At each new promotion to the Cabinet, at each general election, he was sure that he could no longer be overlooked. He ran from platform to platform to increase his claim upon the office should his party be returned. A telegram from the chief whip had brought him to Ludsey, would send him to-morrow into Yorkshire. Now, surely, his turn must come! He had one persistent fear, lest he should be thought too old. And he clung with an almost piteous reiteration to the accuracy of his recollections as a vindication of the alertness of his powers.

"When I saw you upon the platform I was quite sure that it was not for the first time, Miss Daventry," he insisted.

"During the season, perhaps," Cynthia replied. "At some reception or ball. Did you hear that, Colonel Challoner?" and she turned quickly toward Mr. Arnall, who was telling an old story of the days and the hustings when broken heads were common about the doors of the polling-booths.

Cynthia laughed eagerly with the rest in her anxiety to keep Colonel Challoner from plying her with questions. She was ready with her answers, but greatly she feared, lest by probing into his memories he should understand of a sudden where he had seen her before. And for a time she was successful. The confidence which had run from man to man in the great Corn Exchange an hour before was present at this supper-table and kindled them all to cheeriness. The ex-Mayor said with a pleasant drawl, which was his habit:

"Do you remember Taylor the Democrat, Arnall? He fought two elections here within three months and then went bankrupt. He was an adventurer and the most eloquent man I ever heard. But he was a caution."

"Yes," cried Mr. Arnall, with a clicking laugh at the back of his throat. "Do you remember his meeting down by the club? 'Gag that calf,'" and Mr. Arnall spluttered with delight.

"That's it," said the ex-Mayor. "You must know that Taylor stood as a Democrat, Captain Rames. That's where the fun comes in. He wore a blue swallow-tail-coat with brass buttons and his hair down to his shoulders. 'Your father was a miller,' one fellow shouted from the crowd. 'Gag that calf,' cried Taylor and he held up his arms in the air. 'Look at these fair hands. No work has ever sullied them.' That did him all right."

A quiet, elderly man leaned over the table.

"Did you notice the flag upon the chairman's table, Captain Rames?" he asked. "It was woven out of Ludsey silk fifty years ago. It's the true Ludsey blue. My father wove it for Sir William Harris's first election, and the other fellows swore they would have it on the polling-day. But we carried it about the streets from morning to evening, with twelve big fellows to protect it. It was nearly down once, I remember. I was a lad at the time--at the corner of Stapley's Lane. But we saved it and it was your table-cloth to-night, Captain Rames. It brought us victory then. It will again to-morrow."

The stories were continued. They were often not very pointed; often enough the humor was far to seek; but they were alive. They were told with infinite enjoyment, and the smallest details were remembered over decades. Cynthia began now to listen to them for their own sake; she was learning with surprise the value of politics to the lives of men in a busy city of the provinces. But the colonel at her elbow was not longer to be diverted.

"I think it must have been in Dorsetshire that we met," he said. "I live near to Wareham."

Cynthia looked at him quite steadily.

"I have never been in Dorsetshire in my life, Colonel Challoner."

"Yet I associate you with that county," he persisted. "Now, why should I do that, Miss Daventry? You have not been to my house, I know. For since my wife died and my son went away, I have not had so many young people to stay with me as I should have liked."

From the moment when Colonel Challoner had claimed her recognition, Cynthia had not doubted that she was sitting next to a relation. And Colonel Challoner's location of his home in Dorsetshire, near to Wareham, had confirmed her belief. She knew quite well how it came about that he had seemed to recognize her, that he associated her with his own parish. She knew because upon one unforgettable night she had crouched in a great chair in a dark room and through the panels of a door had heard her father claim her as his daughter. He, too, had recognized her as Colonel Challoner now did, and just by the same means. For there was a Romney hanging upon the dining-room wall in that house near Wareham which might have been a portrait of herself. But until this moment she had not guessed what degree of relationship bound her to the old man at her side.

Now, however, she knew that too. The hesitation, the gentle wistfulness with which he had spoken of his son struck home at her. She was this man's granddaughter. She was moved by what he had said. A big house empty of young people must be a place of melancholy and hollow as a shell. Yet she would not reveal herself. She had it fixed now as an instinct of her nature that she would never wear the name of Challoner, nor admit a link with any of that name.... But she turned toward her grandfather with a greater sympathy.

"You have given up your whole life to politics now?" she asked, and a wave of pity swept through her. It could not be possible that he should win any success in that sphere, and she was young and could hardly conceive of life at all without success.

"Yes. I left the army twenty-five years ago. Sometimes I think that I may have made a mistake," he answered. "But it is too late for me to go back upon a mistake, even were I sure that I had made one. Politics is all I have now. I have no longer any family. And I have politics in my bones. I do not know what I should do if I lost my seat. I should probably die." He spoke with absolute simplicity, absolute sincerity: Cynthia was greatly moved. An old futile man without wife or family in a big, empty house, feeding himself from day to day with the disappointments of a hopeless ambition--it made for her a dismal picture. She contrasted it with the other one before her eyes--Harry Rames at the head of the table, confident, comfortable, young as politicians go, with the world a smooth sea for his conquering sails; and once again an unaccountable resentment against Harry Rames flared up within her. Almost she wished that for once he might fail. Almost she revealed herself then to Colonel Challoner. But she did not. She had painfully learned a great gift-- silence.

She knew very well with what relief she would wake on the morrow to the recollection that she was still Cynthia Daventry and not Cynthia Challoner.

"I expect that what I say will sound extravagant to you, Miss Daventry," Colonel Challoner continued. "You at your age could hardly understand it."

The spell which was upon Cynthia was broken. She looked thoughtfully about the table.

"I should not have understood it an hour ago. I was inclined to think it really didn't matter very much in the long run who was in and who was out, that the things which wanted doing and which legislation could do, would get themselves done sooner or later by one side or the other and perhaps by both; and that for the rest the nation went on its way, leaving the talk and the honors to the politicians because it had no time for either and doing the work itself."

Colonel Challoner laughed.

"That's a definite point of view, at all events."

"I expect that I was drawing my ideas from another--" she was about to say "country," but checked herself lest she should be asked what country and so put Colonel Challoner on the track of her relationship to him. She went on hastily: "But since I have been sitting here, I have learned how much of color politics can bring into the lives of men."

And Colonel Challoner looked at her and cried:

"That's it, Miss Daventry. Color! That's the great need. That's why the quack religions flourish in the back streets. We all need it--all except the man there at the head of the table," and Colonel Challoner looked a trifle enviously at Harry Rames. "He has it and to spare."

The door opened by a few inches at this moment and a wrinkled pippin of a head was pushed in. A pair of little bright eyes surveyed the company and then the door was thrust wide open and M. Poizat stepped lightly in.

Harry Rames rose and shook hands with the little Frenchman. Colonel Challoner stroked his white moustache.

"You were present to-night?" said Rames. "What a difference, eh?"

"Yes, I was proud," M. Poizat returned. "But always I waited for some little word--some little word which did not come."

"One always forgets an important point and generally the most important. It is the experience of all speakers," said Rames. He turned to the table. "I must introduce to you M. Poizat, and if ever your voices are hoarse in Ludsey, please ask for Lungatine."

Rames drew a chair to the table, pressed M. Poizat into it, and filled for him a glass of champagne. The little man was delighted. He drank Captain Rames's health, he bowed to the company; and his hand was arrested in mid-air, holding the wine-glass by its stem. Colonel Challoner was gazing fixedly across the table at him. A look of trouble took all the merriment out of M. Poizat's face.

"I have seen you before, M. Poizat," said Colonel Challoner.

Cynthia began to think that the colonel had a mania for recognizing people.

"I am *Mr.* Poizat, an Englishman," the little confectioner answered hurriedly.

"Naturalized," said the colonel.

"It is true," said M. Poizat reluctantly.

"If you had only said that last night," thought Harry Rames. "You would have got your advertisement, my friend."

But he said not a word aloud, and M. Poizat continued:

"But it was a long time ago. And all the years since I have spent in Ludsey."

Colonel Challoner shook his head.

"It was not in Ludsey that I saw you. For I was never here in my life before."

M. Poizat shrugged his shoulders.

"We have sat opposite to one another in a train perhaps. We have run against one another in the traffic of a London street."

"No, it was on some occasion more important. I do not forget a face."

"Nor I," said M. Poizat. "And I have never seen yours, sir, until this moment;" and though he spoke with spirit his uneasiness was apparent to every one at that table.

Colonel Challoner sat back in his chair and let the subject drop. But he was not satisfied. He was even annoyed at his failure to identify the Frenchman, and he sat relentlessly revolving in his mind the changing scenes of his life. Meanwhile the talk drifted back to by-gone elections and this or that great night when some famous statesman was brought into the town and never allowed to speak one audible word. Mr. Arnall mentioned one whose name resounded through England.

"Next night in Warrington he said that he had been struggling with the beasts at Ephesus," said Mr. Arnall with a chirrup of delight. The old Adam was strong in him at this moment and his own solemn exhortations to hear all sides clean forgotten. Suddenly Colonel Challoner broke in upon him. He leaned across the table and with a smile of triumph stared between the candles at M. Poizat.

"It was in a corridor," he said, "a vast bare corridor--somewhere--a long time ago. You were coming out of a room--wait!--wait!--No, I cannot name the place," and he sank back again disappointed.

But M. Poizat's face wore now a sickly pallor.

"In no corridor--nowhere," he stammered and his eyes, urgent with appeal, turned toward Harry Rames.

Harry Rames did his first service for an elector of Ludsey. He glanced toward Mr. Benoliel, who rose.

"It is getting late," said Benoliel, "and Rames has a busy day in front of him."

"I will order your motor-car round to the door," said Rames. He rang the bell and the rest of the company left the table. Diana Royle and Cynthia sought their cloaks in the adjoining sitting-room. Harry Rames took M. Poizat by the arm and led him to the door.

"I am very grateful to you," he said. "Good-night." And even as M. Poizat's foot was over the threshold the voice of Colonel Challoner brought him to a halt:

"One moment. I remember now. You come from Alsace, M. Poizat."

"I come from Provence," cried the little man, facing about swiftly with a passionate, white face.

Harry Rames had begun to think Colonel Challoner rather a bore with his incomplete reminiscences. That thought passed from him altogether. He had but to look at the two men to know that some queer and unexpected moment of drama had sprung from their chance meeting at this hotel at Ludsey. They stood facing one another, the little Frenchman in the doorway with fear and rage contending in his face, his mouth twisted into a snarl, his lips drawn back from his gums like an animal, his teeth gleaming; the colonel erect above the table with the candle-light shining upward upon a triumphant and menacing face.

"You were in Metz in '71," cried Challoner. "So was I. I was a lad at the time. I was aide to our attaché. That's where I saw you, M. Poizat--in the long corridor of the Arsenal. Yes, you were in Metz in '71."

And behind M. Poizat appeared the waiter announcing that Mr. Benoliel's motor-car was at the door.

CHAPTER XV

THE MAYOR AND THE MAN

St. Anne's Hall stands tucked away in a narrow street of Ludsey by the spacious square; and from its ancient windows you look out between the lozenges of stained glass upon the great church of St. Anne with its soaring spire and its wide graveyard. Into this hall the ballot-boxes were brought from the polling-booths on the next evening, and at long tables in the Council Chamber the voting papers were sorted and counted. Harry Rames walked from table to table. He seemed to see nothing but crosses against his opponent's name. He did not dare to put a question to any of the scrutineers standing behind the sorters. The very swiftness with which the votes were counted impressed him with a sense of disaster. For the first time he began to ask himself how he was to shape his life if to-night he were defeated. Thus an hour passed and then the chief constable drew him aside to a bench under the musician's gallery at one end of the room.

"I've been watching the tables, Captain Rames," he said, "and I think you are going to be elected."

"You do?" said Rames eagerly. "Yes, and I shall be very glad if you are."

"Thank you," exclaimed Rames. He could have wrung off the chief constable's hand in the fervor of his gratitude.

"Oh, I am not speaking as a politician," the chief constable returned with a smile. "I have the order of my city to look after. That's all I am thinking about. If you weren't by any chance to get in, I am afraid there would be trouble to-night in Ludsey. And I want you if you are returned to get back to your hotel at once. It's important from my point of view that you should show up on your balcony as soon as possible after the result is declared."

"I see," said Rames.

"I will take you out the back way through the police station," the chief constable continued, "and there's a lane opposite which will lead you straight to your back door. You had better run, I think. For your own friends would tear you to pieces to-night without noticing they were doing you any harm."

The chief constable suddenly changed his tone. One of the scrutineers on the side of Rames's opponent had drawn close to them. The chief constable had no intention to allow a suspicion that he favored one side more than the other. He raised his voice.

"You have noticed our tapestry, perhaps. It is quite invaluable, I believe. We lent it two years ago to the South Kensington Museum. There was an American millionaire here the other day who wished to buy it."

Raines looked across the room.

"Isn't there some portion of it missing?" he asked.

"Yes. That disappeared in the Commonwealth times. Let us go and look at it."

Rames walked at the chief constable's side up the floor of the room toward the dais where Mr. Redling the Mayor, with his chain of office about his shoulders, sat in his big chair in the centre of the long council table. His mace lay upon the table in front of him, and he surveyed the busy scene over which he presided with an imperturbable gravity. But Mr. Redling was a genial soul with a twinkling eye and a red, round face like a crumpled cherub's; and as Harry Rames advanced toward the dais, Mr. Redling beckoned to him with a discreet twist of the finger of a hand lying idle upon the table.

Harry Rames took a seat beside the Mayor at the long table and again words of comfort were poured into his ears in a gentle undertone.

"I think you are going to do it," said Mr. Redling, repeating almost word for word the utterance of his chief constable. "Of course, I couldn't take any part. But you know what I should have been doing if I hadn't been Mayor, don't you? But I have asked quietly here and there about your chance and I fancy it's all right."

He winked, and his face broke into triumphant smiles. He was a man. Then he remembered again that he was a Mayor, and he sat a pillar of municipal propriety.

"It's good of you to say that," cried Harry Rames in a low voice. "I needed to hear it, I can tell you."

Mr. Redling looked at his face. The three weeks had taken a heavy toll of him. He had thinned and sharpened; his eyes were heavy and very tired; for the moment his buoyancy had gone.

"Yes," said Mr. Redling. "An election takes a good deal out of one. And these two hours are the worst of it when the fight's all over and there's nothing to do but wait. Gives you a kind of glimpse into what women have to put up with all their lives, eh?"

Harry Rames glanced at the Mayor with interest.

"Why, I suppose that's true."

Mr. Redling nodded his head.

"Yes. It teaches you that sitting with your hands in your lap isn't the same as sitting soft, after all."

Harry Rames felt comfort steal in upon him from the neighborhood of the little Mayor. Mr. Redling was that rare bird, a strong politician without a fad, and, therefore, a veritable haven of refuge to a candidate in the cudgelling of an election. On the few afternoons when Harry Rames had been able to snatch a half hour of leisure he had been wont to run round to the Mayor's house and spend a restful interval with one of the Mayor's cigars. Mr. Redling laid his Mayoralty aside with the silk hat he invariably wore, and when he took off his chain of office he usually took off his coat too. He had had his ups and downs, and as he discoursed upon his city in his shirt-sleeves, Harry Rames never failed to draw comfort from his talk, so strong a spirit of human friendship breathed from him.

"They like you here," continued Mr. Redling; "both sides. Take us for all in all we are not violent people. Give us the right sort of man, and we'll be sure he won't do us harm, whatever his politics," and then as Mr. Benoliel, who was acting as one of Rames's scrutineers, came to him with a doubtful voting paper, he switched off to another topic; and it happened quite naturally that he chose the very same subject as the chief constable had done.

"Have you noticed our tapestry?" he asked. "We are proud of it. An American gentleman, a Mr. Cronin, came over here last week with Mr. Benoliel to see it. And after he had seen it, he wanted to buy it."

"Oh, did he?" said Benoliel as he handed the voting paper to the Mayor. "But I might have guessed that he would. I brought him over from Culver, and we met Mrs. Royle just outside here. She came in with us. Mrs. Royle seemed as interested in the tapestry as Cronin himself."

While Mr. Redling examined the voting paper, Harry Rames cast an eye over the tapestry. The æsthetic qualities formed a quite insignificant element in his nature. Of art he thought nothing at all. It noted in his mind long hair and an absence of baths--such was his ignorance. The only picture-gallery into which he had ever entered was the Royal Academy; and the only occasion upon which he had ventured over that threshold was the Academy dinner to which he had been invited after his return from his Antarctic expedition. He had a primitive appreciation of scarlet as a color and he recognized that women upon canvas could look beautiful. There for him art ended. So he gazed at the tapestry with a lack-lustre eye. There was no vividness of color, and the human forms worked upon it had an angularity and a thickness of joint which pleased him not at all.

"I suppose it's very beautiful," he said.

"It's unique," replied Mr. Benoliel; "that's why Cronin wanted it. Let a thing be unique, he'll not trouble his head so much about its beauty, and I am told he will ask no questions how it comes to be offered to him."

"Well, he offered us a hundred thousand pounds," Mr. Redling remarked with half a sigh. Ludsey was growing at a pace which made it difficult for the borough council to keep up with it. Mr. Redling thought of baths and schools and houses. "A hundred thousand pounds--a good deal of money for a municipality to refuse. But of course, we did. We couldn't let that tapestry go." He returned to the voting paper and gave his decision upon it. Harry Rames drifted down again into the body of the hall. He troubled no more about the priceless tapestry swinging under the high carved roof in this ancient place. He was a man of his own day, absorbed in its doings, and wondering always in a great labor of thought how he might make his name familiar in all men's mouths before nightfall swept him into the darkness. His anxieties were now diminished, his heart beat high. For here were two men, both experienced in elections and both convinced that he would surely win. So the first small victory, it seemed, was won. He crossed to the row of windows and looked down through a lozenge of white in the painted pattern into the street below. And having once looked he could not again withdraw his eyes.

It was a night of January, dreary and loud with a roar of falling rain. A light wind carried the rain at a slant so that it shot down past the street lamps like slender javelins of steel. And exposed to that pitiless assault a silent crowd of men stood packed together in the narrow street between St. Anne's Hall and the railings of the church. A few, a very few, carried umbrellas over their heads, the rest stood with their coat collars turned up about their throats and their hands deep in their pockets. No one moved, for there was no room to move; and all the faces were uplifted under the brims of their soaking hats to the great window beyond the hall whence the result should be declared. The patience of the throng, its acquiescence in discomfort, as though discomfort were the ordinary condition of its life, suddenly caught hold of Harry Rames. He took a step, nay, a stride forward. Last night when he had come out of the Exchange and the herd of animals had been transfigured into the uplifted faces of men, his thought had been:

"This is for me."

But now his thoughts changed. The men of Ludsey did not wait in vain that night. For Harry Rames the glamour faded off the arena. At the very moment when the bars were being withdrawn for him to enter it the exultation of battle died out of his heart. He woke to something new--the claim of the constituency. The longer he looked, the stronger the claim grew, the more loudly the silence of that throng proclaimed and shouted it. They stood under the javelins of the rain, the men who had voted for him. They emphasized their claim by their extraordinary quietude. Almost they menaced.

"A queer sight," said a voice at his elbow.

Harry Rames turned. It was Mr. Arnall who had interrupted him.

"I shall not easily forget it," said Rames, drawing a breath, and then with an irritable outburst he said: "They look to Parliament for more than parliaments can do, to candidates for more than members can achieve. Each election is to open paradise for them."

"And whose fault is that?" asked Mr. Arnall dryly.

Rames nodded.

"Ours, I suppose," he said; and behind him in the room there was a bustle and a grating of chairs upon the floor. The votes had been sorted. The candidates and their friends gathered about the long table on the raised dais.

"They are taking yours first," said Mr. Arnall to Harry. "That's a good sign."

The papers cast for Harry Rames were brought to the table in sets of fifty. They were placed crosswise, one set on the top of the first, and the third on the second, until five hundred had been counted. Against that pile of five hundred votes a second rose. Gradually the orderly heaps of paper extended along the table's edge in front of the Mayor. There were half a dozen now. Rames's agent stood by them like a bull-dog on the chain. The half-dozen became ten, eleven, twelve. And as the twelfth heap was completed a quick movement ran among all of Rames's friends. He had polled now half the electorate of the city. One more set of papers and he was in.

It was laid next to the others at that moment, and Rames's hands were silently grasped and shaken. But the heaping up of the votes went on. There were three more piles to be added before the end was reached. Eighty-four per cent of the electorate had recorded their votes. Harry Rames had won by a majority well on to two thousand. He stood there in a buzz of congratulations, with a sudden vacancy of mind and thought. He remembered the extraordinary agility with which Mr. Redling whipped out of the room, trying to say unconcernedly:

"I'll just announce the result at once."

He heard the storm of cheers in the street below. That patient silence was broken now in a hurricane of enthusiasm and even through it he could distinguish the words of the exultant cry:

"Rames is our man!"

He saw the Mayor return, much out of breath. He proposed the vote of thanks to the returning officers, with the usual eulogy of his opponents and depreciation of himself. But even at that moment the claim of the constituency would importunately obtrude and find acknowledgment in his words.

"You look to me very likely for more than I can do," he said simply. "At all events you shall have what I can."

But the most memorable achievement that night was the reply of Mr. Redling.

As he rose to his feet to acknowledge the vote of thanks, the man ran forward and got a fair start of the Mayor. He cried out, all one bubble of delight:

"I need hardly say, gentlemen, how utterly I rejoice at--" and then the Mayor put on a spurt and caught up the man--"at the admirable manner in which this contest has been conducted by both sides."

But the correction deceived no one. Mr. Redling's politics were known, and so, in a general splutter of good-humored laughter, the Ludsey election came to an end.

The Mayor turned from the table wiping his forehead.

"I nearly made a bad break there," he said in a whisper. "They won't come at you again, I think. I reckon you have got Ludsey, Captain Rames," and then Rames felt the hand of the chief constable laid upon his arm. He was rushed across the Mayor's parlor, down the stairs through the police station, where the police at their supper rose and gave him a loud cheer.

"Silence!" cried the chief constable savagely. He opened the street door and peeped out.

"All's clear. Run--down that alley opposite. Say something from your balcony, never mind what--they won't hear more than two words."

"That's just all that I want them to hear," cried Rames.

He had foreseen that moment. He ran with one or two of his friends to the back door of his hotel. A path was made for them through the crowded hall. He came out upon the balcony, and up and down the hill as far as his eyes could see the street was thronged. He stretched out his hand. He had a second of absolute silence, and in that second his voice rang out:

"My constituents----"

The roar which answered him showed him that once more his foresight had served him well. No other word of his was heard. But any other words would have spoiled the two which he had uttered.

CHAPTER XVI

WORDS OVER THE TELEPHONE

The next two hours were for Rames of the tissue whence nightmares are woven. Rames was conscious that he made speeches and still more speeches and yet others on the top of those, until speech-making became a pain in the head for which there was no anodyne. He made them from windows--one at that very window where Taylor, the lily fingered democrat, had by a single sentence won immortality and certain defeat--he made them from tables in club-rooms which he no longer recognized; where men, packed tight as herrings, screamed incoherencies in a blaze of light and the atmosphere of a Turkish bath, or standing upon chairs beat him, as he passed beneath them, on the top of the head with their hats in the frenzy of their delight. For two hours Ludsey went stark mad and Harry Rames had reached exhaustion before a gigantic captain of the fire brigade lifted him panting and dishevelled out of the throng, and drawing him into a small committee-room locked the door against his votaries.

"Better wait for a little while here, sir," he said; and it was one o'clock in the morning before he ventured to return to his hotel.

By that time the madness was already past. There was still noise in the blazing rooms of the clubs. But the streets were empty and up the climbing hill the city was quiet as a house of mutes. A placard in the window of the newspaper office recorded the figures of the election, and the boarding which protected the shops opposite to his hotel shone white in the light of the lamps. But for those two signs, even Rames might have found it difficult of belief that so lately this very hill had rung with cheers and seethed with a tumultuous populace. To-morrow, however, the sirens of the factories would shrill across the house-tops at six and the work of a strenuous industrial town begin. Ludsey had no time to dally with victories won and triumphs which had passed.

Nor indeed had Harry Rames. He rang the bell at the door and entered the hall quickly. There was something which he should have done before now, though only now he remembered it. With a word to the porter, he went into the office and switched on the electric light. He crossed to the corner where the telephone was fixed and called up the White House. A woman's voice, very small and clear, came back to him over the lines. He recognized it with a thrill of satisfaction. It was Cynthia Daventry's.

"Oh, it's you yourself," he cried eagerly, and he heard Cynthia, at the other end of the telephone, laugh with pleasure at his eagerness.

"Yes," she answered. "I thought perhaps you might ring me up."

So she had waited--just that they might talk together for a few moments. Harry Rames, however, did not answer her. It seemed to him from the intonation of her voice that she had more to say if she would only make up her mind to say it. He stood and waited with the receiver at his ear, and after a little while Cynthia spoke again upon a lower note.

"I am glad that you did. I should have been disappointed if you hadn't."

"Thank you," said Rames.

He spoke very gently. There was no smile of triumph upon his face. It had become of vast importance to him within the last two hours to know how her thoughts dealt with him; and he was not sure. There was friendship between them--yes. But how far on her side did it reach? He had no answer to that question.

"You have heard the result?" he asked.

"Yes. Mr. Benoliel telephoned to me at once from the Mayor's parlor."

"I ought to have done that," said Harry Rames.

"Oh, no. You were making speeches," replied Cynthia with a laugh. She was at all events not offended by his omission.

"And you are glad that I have won?" he asked. And again she waited a while before she answered; and when she did speak it was with that little spirit of resentment which Rames had heard before in her voice.

"Well,--since your heart was so much set on winning,--yes, there you have your triumph--I am glad that you won."

Cynthia meant what she said, but she was reluctant to mean it. She spoke, too, under a constraint to speak. She had a picture before her eyes of the man at the other end of the line quietly waiting upon her, certain perhaps of what she would say. And the picture and the sense of compulsion were both an offence to her.

"Good-night," she added curtly and with a sharp, quick movement she hung up the receiver. The little clang of metal travelled along the line to Harry Rames and emphasized her resentment.

But he was not disturbed by that. On the whole he looked upon it as a favorable sign. So definite a resentment implied that she was interested and set a value on their friendship. Rames went upstairs to bed, but he was too tired to sleep and his thoughts raced ahead and scouted in the future. He had leaped the first obstacle in the race, but that once leaped and looked back upon became a tiny thing compared with those which lay ahead.

"Will she? Will she not?" he asked. All hung upon the answers to those questions. He was poor. He must marry. He must marry money and even money was not enough. Other qualities were needed to help him to the great career. But they were all there, a few miles away, possessed by the young mistress of the White House. She had looks and manners and a distinction of her own. You could not be in a room with her, however crowded, and be long unaware that she was present too. Only--would she?

He had very little to offer her--beyond this earnest of future success which he had won to-night. And six hundred and seventy others would have won just the same opportunity before the year was a fortnight older. Moreover, Cynthia was romantic and he was not. For all her friendliness he was a bitter disappointment to her. He recognized it all and began to regret that he had not donned the glittering cloak of romance which so often she had held out to him. But his foresight came to console him.

"I could never have lived up to it," he reflected. "She would have found me out. I have been honest with her and she likes honesty."

Certainly there were points in his favor. Rames took heart. She had run the gauntlet of the drawing-rooms through a London season. Men had gone down before her satin slippers, men ancient and modern. Mothers of daughters had frowned upon her, mothers of sons had smiled. Young Lord Helmsdale, adored of the ladies, had pursued her, and it was his habit to be pursued. Yet she had come out of the throng to Warwickshire heart-free. Of that he was sure.

Besides, she had waited up to speak to him. That was something,--not very much, perhaps,--but surely something. Also, since he had wished to win, she was glad that he had won. Rames's memories took him back to the night when they first met at the Admiralty. Not thus had she spoken then. She had moved toward him since that night--reluctantly, slowly. Yet she had moved.

He was still casting up this ledger of his chances when a lonely booming sound broke upon the stillness of the night and penetrated through the open window like some melancholy siren of the sea. It was repeated and repeated, growing louder with each repetition yet hardly more articulate, and without any change of intonation. And every now and then it was interrupted for a few seconds by a dull crash. Rames tried to thrust it from his notice.

"Will she? Will she not?" he asked himself. But the booming sound would not be denied. It was as the wail of some utterly friendless man who cared not whether his fellows slept or waked. It was thoroughly pitiless. Nearer it came to the hotel, and now wavering, heavy feet could be heard to beat an irregular accompaniment. The occasional thud was explained. A very drunken man was staggering up the hill and from time to time he fell upon the pavement, unconscious that he fell, barely aware only that his long-drawn cry had ceased. Rames thought of him as a malignant creature determined to inflict torture--until the sound at last sifted itself into definite words. "Vote for Harry Rames!" the nightfarer cried aloud to a city which had already done so; and at times he dropped the Harry and inserted an epithet of color common no doubt in his vocabulary. He passed beneath the windows and with many a tumble faded into distance, invoking the unresponsive gas lamps.

Rames turned over on his side with relief.

"My dear," he whispered, "take his advice and vote for Harry Rames! I shall owe you much, but I'll make it up to you. I'll not ask you till I am sure I can. I must risk Helmsdale carrying you off."

He fell asleep and even the tune the clock chimes in Ludsey church played at four o'clock in the morning did not make him stir. But at the White House just at that hour Cynthia waked. It was not the clock which waked her. It seemed to her that she had heard a step in the corridor. She sat up in her bed and in a few seconds was sure of it. Some one was moving very stealthily about the house. For a moment her old horror gripped her. Here was her father come at last with authority to claim her. She sat staring wide-eyed into the darkness, flung back to the days when she was a child. Then her reason reasserted itself. Her father was dead. The blood flowed again to her heart. But the stealthy sound continued. She heard a door gently latched. She sprang out of bed, opened her own door, and switched on the light. The corridor was empty to the edge of the shadows. She peered into them. She saw nothing, and no sound reached her now.

"Who is it?" she asked in a loud voice, and no answer came to her. She waited in her doorway with a hand to her breast. The plank of a stair cracked loudly, close to her; but no footsteps made it crack. She went back into her room.

Yet she had not been mistaken. Any one in the road that night might have seen a light ascending past the windows of the staircase and then moving through the upper rooms, until at last in one it remained for a long time. The light was carried by Diana Royle. She passed up the staircase to an unfurnished room used for the storage of old boxes and discarded things. From the corner of this room she rolled out a great bale, dusty with years, and tied up like a carpet with an old piece of rope. She cut the rope and spread it out upon the floor, cautiously and silently. Then lowering her candle she examined it. With a smile upon her lips she stood up again. She fastened the bale and dragged it back into its corner. The smile did not leave her lips. Chance had led her up here some weeks ago. She had discovered the bale and had wondered what it was. An old carpet? A disused curtain? Now she knew. In an attic of this old house she had discovered the lost strip of the Ludsey tapestry.

CHAPTER XVII

A REFUSAL

"So you have refused young Helmsdale."

Three months had passed since the Ludsey election. The air was warm and golden and already the world whispered of summer, yet not too loud lest it should seem to boast and so be balked of its desire. Parliament had met, London was full, and in the country the foxes and the pheasants had leisure to attend to their own affairs. And with the rest Cynthia had come to town. She rode on this morning out of the park, where the buds were running along the branches of the trees like delicate green flames, about eleven o'clock, and turning out of South Audley Street into Curzon Street, she saw Mr. Benoliel waiting upon the pavement in front of her new house. As she stopped her horse before the door he reprimanded her:

"Cynthia, you have refused him."

Cynthia blushed. Then she exclaimed:

"But how in the world could you know! It isn't half an hour since I refused him." Then she bent down over her saddle and gazed at him in the fulness of admiration. "But you know everything. It wouldn't be of much use trying to keep things from you, would it?"

Mr. Benoliel smiled grimly.

"Yes, that's the way, Cynthia, and no doubt a neater style of doing it will come in time."

Cynthia sat upright, swift as a spring, and remained so, with her nose in the air, haughty for five complete seconds. Then curiosity restored her to her sex and she swooped again over her saddle.

"How did you know?"

"He borrowed a horse from me this morning," said Mr. Benoliel--"a good horse. He was very particular that it should be a valuable horse. So I gathered that he wanted to make on this morning of all mornings a specially favorable impression."

Cynthia's lips twitched.

"You lent him a very good horse," she said. "But the horse didn't tell you."

"That's where you are wrong, Cynthia. The horse did," said Mr. Benoliel. "Ten minutes ago, as I was turning out of Grosvenor Square, I met my very valuable horse being led by a ragged beggarman whom I had never seen in my life before. I asked him what the dickens he was doing with it and he explained that as he was standing by the rails in Hyde Park a young man rode up to him in a violent rage, dismounted, tossed him the reins and a shilling and told him to lead the rotten beast back to Grosvenor Square. Just fancy that! My horse! I might have lost him altogether."

Cynthia tried her best to look indignant at so treacherous a return to Mr. Benoliel's generosity, but she could not and she rippled suddenly into laughter.

"He was horribly angry," she said.

Mr. Benoliel turned his wrath again upon Cynthia.

"And no wonder!" he said. "Helmsdale's not used to being refused. He is young. He is good-looking. He has a social position----"

"And he has a profile," added Cynthia. "Please don't forget that. But you can't if you know him, or even if you don't, can you? Have you ever fixed your eyes steadily upon him, Mr. Benoliel? Do the next time you see him, and within twenty seconds he will show you his profile. He will turn his head quite slowly and show it you, just like a man at the music-halls disclosing the newest sensation. I couldn't marry a profile, even though it was mounted on your horse." Then she bent down to him again coaxing him: "You didn't really want me to marry him, did you? You see, I don't love him."

Mr. Benoliel seemed to think this answer insufficient.

"Love would come," he answered.

"That's what he said," exclaimed Cynthia.

"And you?" asked Benoliel.

Cynthia bent her eyes steadily upon him.

"I answered, 'Lovers would come.'"

Mr. Benoliel looked up at her with a wry face.

"You know too much, my dear," he said, and Cynthia threw back her head, with her face suddenly clouded and sullen.

"Oh, yes," she cried bitterly. "I have eaten of the tree--and lately--very lately."

And at the sight of her distress all Mr. Benoliel's indignation vanished.

"I know," he said gently. "That's why I wanted you to marry, Cynthia."

"Is that the remedy?" she asked. And she shook her head slowly. "I am frightened of it."

She called to her groom, dismounted from her horse and taking Mr. Benoliel by the arm cried:

"Come in. You haven't seen my house since I bought it. You shall tell me what you think of it, now that it's finished."

She ran up the steps and turned to him at the top with a look of compunction in her face:

"I talk to you of my troubles," she said. "I have no right to--no, neither to you nor to any one. I am ashamed of myself. I have food to eat, clothes to wear, money to spend, and friends. Yes, I am very fortunate," and her mind winged back to a dark night on the estancia when she had crouched in a big chair, listening to horrors set ready for her. "I ought to be grateful," she cried with a shudder at her memories. "Come in!"

She led him through the rooms and claimed his enthusiasm for this or that rare piece of satin-wood or mahogany. It had been a great joy to her in the early days of the year to ransack the dealers' shops and grow learned of Hepplewhite and Chippendale. She told Mr. Benoliel stories of her researches, seeking to recapture some savor of that past pleasure. But her sprightliness became an effort and in her own sitting-room she turned abruptly to him:

"But I have a distaste for it all now," she said and sat down in a chair. "I have no longer any pride in the house at all."

Mr. Benoliel stood over her and nodded his head in sympathy. She was distressed. She had a look of discomfort.

"Yes, I understand that, Cynthia," he said.

She took off her hard hat. It pressed upon her temples and made her head throb.

"How much do you know?" she asked.

"That Mrs. Royle is leaving you."

"Yes," said Cynthia moodily. "We have agreed to separate. Do you know anything more?"

"Yes. The missing panel of tapestry hangs again in Ludsey Town Hall."

"Yes. It was lying in a lumber-room under the roof of my house in Warwickshire. How long it had been lying there, or how it came there, I can't discover. Diana ran across it by accident. It was tied up in a bale like an old carpet. She didn't think it of any value--until she went one morning to the Town Hall with an American millionaire who was anxious to see the tapestry and buy it if he could."

"Yes. I took Cronin there myself. He was staying with me and I drove him into Ludsey and met Mrs. Royle in the street. That was the day before the election. We all three went into the Town Hall together. I remember Mrs. Royle saying that she had never been in the building before. I pointed out the tapestry and explained that a wide strip of it was missing. I think I suggested that it would one day be turned out of some old cupboard."

Cynthia nodded.

"That no doubt helped her to the truth. Anyway, she tried to persuade me to sell it. She merely told me that it was valuable and that I could get two thousand pounds for it. I didn't connect it with the Ludsey tapestry. I thought that it might be worth while to bring it up to this house; and I refused to sell. Diana urged me again, however, and but that I don't like selling things, I would have let her sell it, just because she was getting tiresome about it. Then Hartmann, the Bond Street dealer, called on me a month ago and told me what the strip was."

"Why did he call?" asked Benoliel.

"He was in the deal with another man. Both apparently were selling to Mr. Cronin, and they quarreled over the division of the profits. So Hartmann came to me in revenge. He told me that Diana was to get eight thousand pounds if she could persuade me to sell and that they meant to sell the tapestry afterward to Mr. Cronin for twenty-five thousand pounds. It's not a pretty story, is it?"

"No," said Benoliel. "So you gave it back to Ludsey?"

"Yes."

"Does Mrs. Royle know that you are aware of her share in the transaction?"

"Yes. We haven't ever talked of it, but she knows and proposed of her own accord that we should separate. We couldn't go on living together, could we? It would be too uncomfortable. I couldn't trust her."

"When does she go?"

"In a week or two, now," said Cynthia. "She has taken a little house on the north side of the park. Of course, for my father's sake"--thus she always spoke of Mr. Daventry--"I am looking after her;" and she suddenly struck her hands together. "Oh, but it's all rather sordid, isn't it?"

"Yes," said Mr. Benoliel. He was troubled and perplexed. "And what are you going to do?" he asked.

Cynthia shrugged her shoulders.

"I must engage a companion."

"That doesn't sound very satisfactory."

"What else can I do?"

"Marry!" said Mr. Benoliel.

Cynthia rose petulantly to her feet.

"No," she cried. "That I won't do." She turned away and looked out into the street, a storm of rebellion at her heart. Why should every one want to marry her off? Even her friend, her adviser, who should have stood by her, had turned, it seemed, against her. She came back to Mr. Benoliel, but he stood with so distressful a countenance that her indignation died away, and with a pretty compunction she made her apology:

"I know that you are thinking of me. I am sorry if I seemed to forget it. Forgive me! But you can't really want me to marry just so that I may not be alone."

"My dear," said Mr. Benoliel gently, "It's a very good reason."

Cynthia shook her head.

"For a girl?--I am little more. No. I may come to that belief in the end when I am older. But not yet. I must have a better reason now. There are too many years ahead of me."

Mr. Benoliel smiled, with a little wistfulness in the smile.

"Dreams, Cynthia, dreams," he said.

"I am losing them," she returned, and with a smile too, the smile of humor, not of amusement. "I am making haste to lose them against my will. But this one I'll keep for still a little while. I'll still dream that while I am young I must have a better reason for marriage than the fear of being alone."

"Very well, Cynthia," said Mr. Benoliel disconsolately. "I'll hope you are right."

He left the house and Cynthia sat down for a long time in her room. She had run to the extreme of melancholy with the determination of youth to make the very worst or best of life's daily provision. She had never felt so keenly the vanity of her illusions. She had seldom felt so lonely, she was sure. Even Harry Rames nowadays left her severely to herself. Why didn't he come to see her? She asked the question with indignation. She had never seen him since the supper-party at his hotel in Ludsey on the night before the poll. She had never heard his voice since he had spoken to her over the telephone just after his election. Very likely he had grown tired of her appeals to him to be different from what he was. No doubt she was a bore. Sadly Cynthia admitted it. Yes, she was a bore, and Diana Royle was treacherous, and Harry Rames never came to see her, and, take it all in all, it was a gray and dismal world.

CHAPTER XVIII

A MAIDEN SPEECH

Yet to her astonishment Harry Rames came that very week on the Friday afternoon. Cynthia received him with an elaborate dignity. There was no acidity in her welcome, neither was there any joy. She seemed intensely unaware that she had not seen him for three months. Her nose was perhaps a trifle too high in the air, but she was not conscious of it. On the whole she was greatly pleased with her demeanor. She was behaving as a woman of the world to whom one acquaintance, more or less, is a matter of complete indifference. She offered him tea, and seating herself upon a sofa in front of the table poured it out. Harry Rames took his cup with humility. Cynthia was quick to notice it, no less quick to be gratified by his exhibition of a quality which hitherto he had lacked. He was abashed. He was ashamed. He was uneasy. No doubt he had come expecting the flattery of questions. Her unconsciousness of the length of his absence put him at a loss. When he spoke, it was with difficulty. And then, suddenly, Cynthia saw his lips twitching at the corners. He was not abashed at all. He was simply trying not to laugh. Cynthia grew hot. Alas! her great dignity had barely sustained her in contentment for five minutes! The old indignation shone in her eyes. The indifferent great lady vanished. Almost before she was aware of it she was talking in broken, resentful sentences--as any other ordinary girl might have done who had been wounded and whose wound had betrayed her into speech.

"People who insist on making friends with other people who didn't at the beginning want to be friends at all, haven't the right afterward to drop being friends calmly, without a word of explanation. Of course, if people are bored--but even then they should have guessed they were going to be bored before they perhaps made other people count a little--oh, not so much, of course, but just a little--on their friendship. No, I object to that. It's hateful--and then you saunter in as if--No." Cynthia, oppressed with a sense of utter isolation in a most neglectful world, which probably hated her when it stopped to think of her at all, was perilously near to tears. She took refuge in sarcasm of a crude kind:

"You probably wouldn't understand that suddenly to stay away after you have been friendly is rather humiliating to a girl. But you will take it from me, won't you, that it is so?"

She spoke as one giving a kindly lesson in tact to a boorish person. But her lips shook. Harry Rames rose from his chair and crossing the room took up the *Times* which lay still neatly folded in its original square upon a table.

"You have not opened your paper to-day," he said; and once more he saw Cynthia flinch as though he had struck her a blow--flinch and sit dumb, with her great eyes full of pain.

"Oh, please don't make any mistake," he said quickly, and with the newspaper in his hand he came back to her side. "I wasn't taking what you said carelessly. But if you had read your *Times* to-day you would have understood, I think, why I have stayed away till now. You might, perhaps, have guessed why I have come this afternoon."

Cynthia took the newspaper from him and unfolded it, with her eyes resting in doubt upon his. Then comprehension came to her. She turned the pages quickly and stopped at one particular sheet of closely printed columns. "Oh," she cried, "you have made your maiden speech."

"Yes, last night."

In a second her resentment was forgotten. She was all smiles. She reached out an eager hand to him. "It was successful? But why do I ask? I have watched the newspapers ever since the House met. I thought you were never going to speak."

"I always meant to hold back at the beginning," said the wise Harry Rames. "There were new men tumbling over one another to speak on the address; I let them get that start of me without any fear. I wanted to learn the way of speaking which carries you home in the House of Commons."

Cynthia laughed and made room for him on the sofa at her side.

"Yes, there I recognize you."

"Besides," Rames continued, "the address fights the election over again, sums it up, and parades its consequences--consequences already known to all. It's very difficult to make any real mark in the debate on the address. So while the other men talked I sat quiet. Night after night through the address, through the two months which followed it, I sat in the House, listening and watching. And I learned my lesson."

"Yes?" said Cynthia.

"I learned that the House scoffs at oratory and has no use for perorations; that it won't listen to leading articles; that it won't tolerate conceit, except in the biggest men, and hates it in them; that it is conscious of dignity and requires the same consciousness in the members who address it. It requires too that the man who intervenes in a debate should contribute something out of himself."

"Does it always get that?" asked Cynthia in bewilderment.

"No, indeed. But, on the other hand, it goes out into the lobby, or it talks. Smale's a wise man. He told me once that hardly ever did a Parliament produce more than three new men. Just think of it! For five or six years, for six or eight or ten months in each of those years, there's one perpetual flow of talk during eight hours of the day in that Chamber; and yet out of all that sludge of talk only three men emerge of any account. I want to be one of the three men in this Parliament. Otherwise you are right and I am wrong. I have mischosen my career. So I sat quiet and learned my lesson."

"Until last night," said Cynthia.

"Yes, my opportunity came."

"With a subject on which you could contribute?"

"Well, on which I thought I could," said Rames; and once again Cynthia wondered at the patience with which he had sat night after night awaiting his moment, and yet counting calmly as among the possibilities of failure his own incompetence. "It was Asiatic immigration."

Cynthia made a grimace.

"Sounds dull?" asked Rames. "Very likely. But it's an important question for us and one that's going to be still more important in the future. You see, as a power, we are in a queer position. We are at once the white people resisting the Asiatic immigrant, and the Asiatic immigrant wanting the outlet of immigration--but I won't make my speech over again to you. I raised the question myself on the colonial vote, and here is what I said,"--he took the newspaper from her hands, folded it, and gave it back to her. Then he sat quietly by her side while she read the speech through. She appreciated the labor and thought which had gone to its making; the half column which the *Times* gave to reporting it enabled her to realize that it had been delivered with a vivid economy of phrase which gave his meaning aptly and never frittered it away. If only the trouble had been taken and the speech delivered for the sake of the question! The question was a big one. Cynthia understood that through the spectacles of Harry Rames's speech.

"You made a great success?" she asked turning toward him. She noticed that he was sitting very still beside her, as though he set great store upon her judgment. And in a voice of greater warmth she said:

"But of course you did."

Again Rames took the newspaper and again he folded it. He pointed to the first leader, from which his name stood out in bigger type than the rest of the text.

"It doesn't so very often happen that the *Times* takes the subject of its chief leading article from a man's first speech in the House of Commons."

Then he folded the paper again at the parliamentary report and pointed to a paragraph here and there. "That's what the leader of the opposition said. Here's the reference the colonial minister made when he wound up the debate. You see, both dealt with my speech."

There was a note of quiet elation in Harry Rames's voice. He had taken another step along the chosen path. He had passed through another of the ordeals.

Cynthia did not answer. She sat with the newspaper on her knees, gazing forward with perplexed eyes. She looked almost disheartened.

Rames noticed the look and smiled.

"I know what's troubling you, Miss Daventry. You are wondering whether it isn't, after all, the horrible truth that a desire to get on and excel can achieve quite as much, and be quite as useful to the world, as enthusiasm for a cause, the pure, genuine enthusiasm to make the world better."

Cynthia turned to him with a start.

"Yes, I was wondering just in that way."

"Well, I'll answer you," said Rames firmly. "The desire to get on achieves more and better things than enthusiasm for an idea."

"I can't believe it," cried Cynthia in revolt.

"Think it over," continued Rames. "Enthusiasm for cause blinds you to the harm, the injustice which you may do in furthering your cause. The desire to get on makes you appreciate the cause, and weigh it, yes, but it makes you weigh also the methods of advance."

"No, no," cried Cynthia. "You push a garden roller over all my frail illusions. Some day, I think, you'll pay;" and she turned suddenly toward him. "Yes, I'm afraid you'll pay."

She glanced down at the paper and suddenly swept it off her knees. His were ignoble views; she was sure of it. But none the less he was her friend, and she took refuge from his views, as was her wont, in her friendship. After all, he had come hot from his little triumph to tell her of it. She recognized that she was making him an ungenerous return.

"Tell me what you felt when you got up to speak! Were you nervous?" she asked, and Rames relaxed from his attitude of vigilance and leaned back with a laugh.

"I should have run away if I could," he said. "But I couldn't. I had taken the trouble to make flight impossible. The House goes into Committee over the estimates. I had asked Smale to speak to the Chairman of Committees. He had done so. An opportunity had been made for me. I had to make the best of it I could."

"Tell me," Cynthia insisted; and as more than once he had done before, having lost ground in her thoughts, he marched forward and unconsciously regained it. For he drew her with humor and a vivid truth the picture of a man in one of the ordeals of his life. He neither posed as the triumphant hero for whom there are no difficulties, nor did he exaggerate his terrors or apprehensions so that his ultimate success might glow the brighter. He was true to himself, as he had always striven to be with Cynthia. The labor of forethought, the stress of fear, the strain upon the nerves, and the tiny victory won as the consequence were set before her in their due proportions. He ceased to be a thing of cold calculations and inevitable triumphs. He became a man, stiffening his knees against tremors and alarms.

He had walked down to the House early on that Thursday. For his speech had been thought out, and there was nothing more for him to do, and now he must keep moving. He went down onto the broad terrace over the Thames, and there, during the hour of questions which precedes debate, in a cold wind he wandered miserable. One tall and burly policeman was the calm guardian of that deserted place. Harry Rames walked from the Speaker's house to the House of Lords and back again, trying to repeat over to himself the argument of his speech. But the policeman loomed too large between him and it. Rames detected something supercilious in his imperturbability. No doubt he knew that Rames that day was going to make his maiden speech. He must have seen so many pace this terrace during the hour of questions with the same apprehensions. The signs would be visible.

Rames turned his back upon the policeman and leaned on the parapet. But the speech would not come. He had left the opening sentences to the moment when he should be upon his legs. For he must link what he had to say onto what already had been said, lest he should lose altogether the effect of spontaneity. The rest he had prepared and rehearsed, and rehearsed again, with the intention to know it so well that he should be free to twist into its scheme the speeches made immediately before. But now that he tried to say it over on the terrace it lost altogether its continuity. The argument halted; the chosen words failed him; he stumbled from unconnected epigram to inappropriate metaphor; he clung to half-remembered phrases, and with a sinking heart repeated them, and repeated them--and repeated them. He shut his eyes. The great effort was going to be just a failure of fine talk--the mere scrap-heap of a speech.

He looked down at the brown water, followed it eastward below the bridge; and then his eyes were caught by a small torpedo-boat lying opposite at a mooring in front of St. Thomas's Hospital. And the aspect of this familiar thing smote him down to the depths of abasement. But for presumption he might now be in command of a great battle-ship doing the things he had been trained to do, and doing them with confidence. And his thoughts swept him away to Spithead; and the vision of a great, dark battle-ship, sitting steadily in a tumbled sea between Southsea and the Isle of Wight, clear of the Solent fairway, and west of the checkered forts, rose up and drew him for a moment as with chains. He hated his ambitions; he thought of this dreadful hour to which they had lured him. He saw the day pass and the evening come up out of the sea and the lights begin to glow upon the foreshore, a cluster at Southsea pier, a little chain running up the hill of Union Street, at Ryde, and close down by the water's edge tiny lights in cottages and houses like glow-worms in a forest.

Then another step sounded on the pavement and he turned away from his vision. After all he might be laughing at all these fears in an hour's time, he took the courage to reflect; and he went up the stairs and across the lobby into the Chamber itself. He looked for a seat on the second bench below the gangway, but the House was full.

Colonel Challoner, again passed over in the choice of under-secretaries, looked up at him from the corner seat, and noticed the blue-book and a volume of Hansard under his arm.

"Are you going to speak?" he asked.

"If I can get called," said Rames.

Challoner made room for him at his side.

"I mean to say a word or two myself," he said, "but we shall probably neither of us get a chance. Those front-bench men think it beneath their dignity to take less than an hour."

Certainly, so far as the first speech was concerned, Colonel Challoner was right. It was delivered from the opposition bench by an ex-minister, William Kenway, a man of a kindly and generous disposition who yet managed by some perversity of tact to rasp the temper of the House from wall to wall. For a full hour he stood there now, saying the wrong thing with determination, giving little lessons with the air of a school-master, irritating by a certain priggishness his friends behind him as well as his opponents in front.

Rames sat and listened. He realized that the very opportunity which he wanted was being given to him. Kenway, with a white paper in his hand, came to the problem of Asiatic immigration. Rames was no longer trying to remember the consecution of his speech. He sat waiting for the long speech to end, making a note or two, grasping at a beginning for his speech, and clinging firmly to it.

When Kenway sat down, he found himself standing upon his legs. He was aware at once that some one was standing beside him, Colonel Challoner. Both men had risen. Almost he resumed his seat, and then he heard his name called by the chairman, and from a very long way off an encouraging cheer reached his ears.

He was conscious of the lack of a table in front of him or the barrier of a platform--something on which he could rest a hand. He felt strangely defenceless without it. He faltered through his opening sentences in a voice which sounded to his ears weak and thin as a ghost's. He saw a member take off his hat on the opposite benches, rise, and make his way out; and at once he was certain that he was making a dismal failure. Suddenly he remembered one member who had risen to speak, had been called upon and had sunk back in his seat without uttering more than a few unintelligible words. Was his to be the same fate, he asked himself? And asking himself he lost the thread of what he was saying and with a gasp retrieved it.

"It seemed to me," he said in describing the scene to Cynthia, "that I stood there dumb and helpless for twenty seconds. As a matter of fact, the interval was so short that not even my neighbors noticed it. I suppose that I only paused for the fraction of a second, really."

"Yes," said Cynthia, and the trifle remained in her mind.

He was speaking, too, with a haze before his eyes and his hands clutching at the edges of his coat. But he went on, and then quite suddenly the haze thinned so that he saw the House and he heard his voice ringing out clear and firm, not loud nor arrogant, filling the Chamber and with just that note of deference which he had planned to strike and had struck because the deference was sincere. He turned in his place. He was no longer conscious of the need of a table in front of him; he looked down the House toward the clock above the entrance door, and he saw that the bar was thronged with members. Curiosity, no doubt, had brought them in from the library and the smoking-room and the lobby when his name went up on the tape--he had, after all, a reputation. He, the least romantic of men, had some aura of romance about him in that assembly; enough at all events to invite a momentary interest. But they stayed, and as he spoke in a voice that went steadily forward with the rhythm of marching men, he saw now one, now another come out from the throng at the bar and slip into a seat. With a throb of joy he realized that he was not failing, that now he was not going to fail. The House had filled since he had risen and on all the benches there was a great quiet. He turned toward the Speaker's chair. The space at the sides of it was crowded too. He saw more than one cabinet-minister standing. Above, behind the grille, he saw the big hats and shadowy forms of the ladies in the gallery, and here and there the gleam of an ermine stole against the light behind them. That happened to him again which had happened in the Corn Exchange at Ludsey. He turned over the consecutions of his argument like the pages of a printed book. He was master of himself. He worked in his predecessor's points and replied to them with force and without offence because they were just the points he had foreseen. He provoked interruptions from his opponents; he had foreseen them and was ready, and the cheers broke out from the benches about him and behind him. He spoke for just twenty minutes. The applause, generous and friendly, came from both sides of the House when he resumed his seat. The Prime-Minister leaned across the gangway and shook him by the hand. And as for the great battle-ship at Spithead, anybody could have it as a gift.

Rames leaned back in his chair and closed his eyes. So the third step of the great career had been taken. He had been chosen candidate, he had been elected member, he had made something of a small triumph out of his maiden speech. Now he would wait without any hurry. He would make one speech more later on in the session, perhaps two--not more than two, certainly. And next session he would plunge boldly and take up his part in the impromptu debating on the Committee stages of Bills. In that work lay the real test of parliamentary capacity.

Thus he planned, and content with his plan he opened his eyes again. At once he was made uneasy. He met the eyes of a small, white-haired man with a deeply lined, brown face who was watching him fixedly from the benches opposite. This was Albert Coulter, a man of many expeditions in untravelled countries, when there were countries still untravelled, whose name had become a signal for dark whispers. A callous selfishness, when selfishness might mean the life or health of his companions, and a relentless severity with his natives, was rightly or wrongly imputed. The survivors of his expeditions came back with queer stories. But he had never failed until the moment, when at the age of fifty and with the looks of seventy, he had entered the House of Commons. There, an interesting yet ineffective figure, he sat day after day, solitary, disliked, with brooding eyes under a bristle of gray eyebrows which seemed to be haunted with sinister memories of deep tropical forests and days long past. His eyes rested upon Harry Rames now, not enviously, not encouragingly, but without expression, almost indeed like the eyes of a dead man. Their fixed gaze chilled the blood of Harry Rames and all his satisfaction was marred. He had to move from his place and beyond the reach of those brooding eyes before he shook the impression off. And even now so distinct was it in his memories that he omitted it altogether and deliberately from the story he told that afternoon to Cynthia Daventry. He related in its place another incident which had happened later in the evening.

"We had a division," he said. "I was walking through the lobby and just at the turnstiles where the clerks tick off our names, I found Henry Smale in front of me. The R's and the S's go through the same turnstile. He turned round as I passed through behind him, and said to me in a low voice, 'You have the ear of the House now. Keep your eye on the treasury bench.' That from Smale, who was dissuading me to enter Parliament, means a good deal."

Harry Rames turned and looked at Cynthia.

"Yes," said Cynthia.

There was a smile upon her face rather wistful, rather ironic.

"So you have turnstiles in your House of Commons," she said slowly.

"No. Did I say turnstiles?" he asked. "There's no actual barrier which revolves. But there's only room for one at a time to pass between the desks. The clerks stand at the desks and register your votes for publication. Otherwise where would party government be?"

"You mean if the votes weren't published men would vote according to their convictions?"

Rames nodded.

"But it's a superficial view," he said. "You have got to take the sum of your policy. As a whole, is it better than the other fellow's? That's what you have to ask yourself when you are going to register a vote upon some particular point which may help to turn your government out and let the other fellows in."

"Yes, I see that," said Cynthia; and once more her eyes fell upon the *Times* and she was suddenly conscious of a queer pride. Others to-day were aware of the success which Harry Rames had made; probably she alone was aware of the thought, and the apprehension and the tribulation of soul which had gone to the making of the success. To the others he would just be one of the inevitably successful--what indeed she had herself been wont to think him. To-day, however, he was to her human as he had never been. He had shown himself to her, bleating with fear like an ordinary man at the approach of the fateful moment which was to put him to the test. He had drawn the picture with a sense of humor, but he had not blurred it. Would he have drawn it for any one else, she asked herself? She turned impulsively toward him:

"I wanted you to come to me this week," she said impulsively. "And I thank you very much for telling me not merely that you succeeded, but how near you were to breaking down. But," and she hesitated for a few moments, "I should have been still more grateful if you had come to me the day before you made your speech."

"I almost did," said Harry Rames.

CHAPTER XIX

AND A PROPOSAL

Cynthia smiled, but she did not believe.

"I think," she said, "that this is the very first time you have gone beyond the truth to say a pleasant thing to me."

"It is the truth," he insisted. "I almost did more than come to you. I almost asked you to let me inflict my speech on you before I made it in the House."

"Oh, I wish you had!" cried Cynthia. "It would have made a difference to me this last week--a great difference." Then she turned swiftly toward Harry Rames with a glance of distrust. "Why didn't you come then?" she asked coldly. "There was nothing to hinder you. You knew that you would be very welcome. I should like to have known beforehand what you were going to say;" and once more a gentle wistfulness crept into her voice. "I should have liked also to have heard you in the House. I should have liked, in a word-- not to have been shut out."

"You weren't shut out," Harry Rames exclaimed. "You mustn't fancy that! It's not true. If I did not come, it was really because I had you in my thoughts. Yes. I stayed away deliberately because of a saying of Smale's which I know to be true, which I quoted to you at Ludsey."

The distrust grew stronger in Cynthia's mind. What had Smale to do with the matter? Her face hardened. Harry Rames had, till this moment, at all events, been honest, had always stood apart in her eyes by reason of his honesty. Must she strip him now of that quality even as she had to do of the other, the imagined ones?

"What saying?" she asked.

"That many a man may cut a great figure upon the platforms who will never get the ear of the House of Commons. I wanted to be sure that I was not one of those--before I came to you."

A particular significance in the intonation of the words warned her--and then troubled her. She looked at him swiftly, and as swiftly looked away. The blood mounted into her face and flushed her throat.

"I wanted to be sure that I should come not quite empty-handed," he continued.

Cynthia made no pretence to misunderstand him, and no answer. All was explained to her now: why he had stayed away, why he now returned--all those particulars which he had told her she might have guessed, and not one of which had to this moment entered her head. She had never stepped beyond the border-line of friendship in her thoughts of Harry Rames--never once. She was startled now that she was asked to. She needed time to adjust herself to the new point of view. He had been honest with her, after all. That was her first instinctive recollection.

"So I am here now to ask you to marry me," he continued. He spoke very quietly and simply. He did not simulate any passion, and again in her heart comparing him with that other wooer in the Row, she thanked him for his honesty.

Still she made no answer, but calmness had returned to her. She sat looking out of the window, straight ahead of her, with her chin propped in the palm of her hand. She was quite still, and the stillness of her attitude was no greater than the stillness of her mind. There was no throb of joy at her heart. But Harry Rames had been honest with her, and she had been taught not to expect so very much.

"I think you know whom you will be marrying," he resumed. "I have tried to make what I know about myself clear to you as well as to me. You once agreed that I left you no illusions about me."

"Yes. On the platform at the Corn Exchange in Ludsey," Cynthia replied. "I remember quite well. I remember your answer too: That you did not mean to."

"Yes," said Harry Rames. "That was my answer."

Cynthia paused for a few seconds. Then in her turn she began to question him.

"So even then you were thinking that if you succeeded in Parliament--this afternoon would come?"

"Yes."

"Perhaps even before then?"

"Yes, even before then."

Cynthia nodded her head. With a smile in which there was irony and a little of her old resentment, she remarked:

"Yes, you have always looked ahead."

Harry replied simply and gravely:

"Always."

"Thank you," said Cynthia.

She thanked him because he was so perfectly honest with her. He admitted--for his words were no less than such an admission--that he had deliberately thought of her because she had money. On the other hand, it was true that he had stood by and left the opportunity open for any one to snatch until he could himself bring something into the partnership. That weighed with her in his favor.

"Will you tell me when you first began to think of me in this way?" she asked with an earnestness which to Harry Rames appeared quite singular. To his direct mind the one question which needed answering was whether she meant to marry him or no.

"Does the exact date matter?"

"Very much."

Rebellion again broke out in Cynthia. "I believe it is quite a usual question for maidens to ask on these occasions. But no doubt I ought to have asked it with a deeper bashfulness."

Harry reflected. Here was one of the nice subtleties of the feminine mind which somehow he must satisfy.

"It was after I had driven out once or twice from Ludsey to see you. That is as near as I can put it. It was after I had got to know you a little."

"As soon, in a word, as you concluded that I would suit the place." Though the sentence was phrased still in the ironical form, the irony had suddenly gone from her voice. She was so relieved that a smile trembled about her lips. Her next words gave the reason of her relief.

"So really and truly you want me personally--as well."

The question would have sounded vague to a stranger, but these two understood that it was her fortune which she omitted to name. Cynthia knew, as she could not but know, that her wealth had first set his thoughts running toward her. But it was some personal quality which in the end had decided him to ask for her. He must have money--yes, but other help than money as well. It was a satisfaction to her pride that he found it in her.

"Yes," he returned. "A wife can do so much for a man in politics if she is the right wife. I should be very glad if you would marry me," Rames resumed. "I think that we should get along together very well, and together we might do important things."

"Be important things," Cynthia corrected.

Harry Rames smiled.

"That's an old quarrel of ours, Cynthia. I mean 'do' this time."

Cynthia looked at him quickly. She was in the mood to find in that hope the strongest of appeals.

"You really think so?"

"I do. I should owe so very much to you. I should be conscious of my debt. I should try with all my strength to pay it back."

Cynthia gave him her face frankly now. A smile of confidence quite lit it up.

"I have no doubt of that," she said; and then the smile faded, and there came a look of longing.

"But I would rather, of course, that it were work for love of me, than work to repay me. There's a difference, isn't there? But I suppose one can't have everything, and--perhaps--I might be content to help you on."

She fell again to a wistful silence, pursuing the vision of a happiness which might have been down an avenue of bright imagined years. The happiness did exist. She had seen the evidences of it often enough. All men were not *tant soit peu cochons*, as she had once heard an unhappy French lady describe them, nor were all women neurotic. She had heard of lovers who felt that they had been waiting for one another since the beginning of the world. But it seemed that such happiness was for others, not for her.

"Tell me!" she said. "When you were making your speech, after the agitation had passed and when you were master of yourself, you looked up to the ladies' gallery, you said, and noticed the women behind the grille?"

"Yes."

"Well--it is a little difficult to ask the question--But"--she stopped for a moment or two, and then went on with an appealing timidity, while the color once more mounted into her face--"but I suppose that then--when you knew you were making a success--it never came into your mind that you would have liked to have got me up there in the gallery while you were speaking?"

The temptation to lie was strong upon Harry Rames now. The very timidity of her appeal moved him. It taught him that the truth would hurt her much more than he had ever dreamed. He hesitated. For the first time in her company he was at a loss.

"The truth, please," she pleaded earnestly. "You said that your mind was free, that you could stand outside yourself and look on at what you were doing, as artists do. It never once occurred to you that you wanted me up there in the ladies' gallery, too, at the moment of your success, to witness it--to--yes, to share it with you?"

The word was out at last--the word which she had been striving with her modesty to reach.

"Be frank, please," she prayed.

Harry Rames was at a loss how to wrap the brutal truth up so that it should not hurt overmuch. He had no other intention at this moment. He was for once not considering what effect his answer would have upon his own prospects and future.

"You were in my thoughts," he said. "That's true. For I was thinking that now I could come to you. But, yes, I wanted to be sure of myself first."

"Yes," said Cynthia slowly, and with humility she analyzed the meaning of his words. "You never thought of me as a kind of inspiration to an even greater success in the future if you succeeded now, or as a kind of consolation if you failed. It may be vanity to say so, but I think that is what a woman in whom you were interested, and who was interested in you, would have liked you to have thought. I was, after all, shut out, wasn't I? I was to hear of the achievement after it was done and over, and I was neither to share the preliminary fears, nor feel the revulsion when the triumph came."

"Yes, but look at it from my point of view. There are many who want to marry you--men with something to offer. It wouldn't have been fair if I didn't bring something in my basket too."

"Fair!" cried Cynthia scornfully. "Oh, I know, that's the point of view of the man--at least," and as she realized that she had been unjust, her face dimpled to smiles, "of the men one rather likes." For it occurred to her that Lord Helmsdale would have been troubled by no such scruples.

"No," she said. "You wouldn't have borrowed another man's thoroughbred so that you might cut a dashing figure while you proposed."

Rames had no idea of what she meant, and he behaved as he usually did when unintelligible things were said to him by women. He asked for no explanations and just took no notice of Cynthia's words. He sat quietly at her side and waited.

The clock struck the hour. He put his hand into his pocket, and at the movement Cynthia started.

"There is no hurry," said Harry Rames. "I was only getting out my cigarette case. May I smoke?"

"Of course," replied Cynthia; she was relieved that she need not answer upon the moment. She was still in a great perplexity; and while Harry Rames smoked his cigarette she sought this way and that for a light to guide her. Here was not the marriage of which she had dreamed. No. But he was honest. It was possible, too, that she might be able to help him on, as he had said. And it might be well worth doing. It might be true that the ambitious men are the world's best servants, and not the men possessed with ideas. Ideas, she remembered, with a bitter little smile at her folly, had once given the right of entrance to her enchanted garden. But she had travelled far from its gateway, and the flowers were all dead in it, and its pathways overgrown. It might be that the fixed idea meant the narrow vision. Harry Rames might be right; and if he were, by helping him on, she would make her money of real and great value. It was a gray world anyway--and Harry Rames was honest. She could trust him--though he wounded her.

She turned suddenly toward him.

"Do you remember the supper party at Ludsey?" she asked.

"Of course," he replied: "And the little Frenchman, Monsieur Poizat."

"I was not thinking of him," said Cynthia. A sentence or two spoken at that table by Colonel Challoner had leaped into her memory. Politics meant color in the lives of men. It was the craving for color which fired enthusiasm in the towns of the provinces. Well, she herself craved for bright colors in her life too. Might she not get them out of the paint-pot of politics just as men did?

"If I were to say yes," she remarked, "I would not be content to be merely the witness of your success. I must share the fears which go to make it. I could not sit quiet and twirl my thumbs, shut out from the hopes and apprehensions and endeavors, and just smile admiringly at the result. I must share everything."

"Of course," said Harry Rames. "From the moment you say 'yes,' you share everything. I meant that too when I said that I needed your help."

He spoke gravely and sincerely, and again Cynthia said, "Thank you."

She sat for a little while longer, hesitating upon the brink. To say "yes" would solve the question of a companion. Oh, certainly, there were practical advantages in the acceptance of Harry Rames's proposal. She would have to abandon the hope of beauty in her life. Color, excitement, interest, she might get. But the beautiful life would not be for her. Still, under no circumstances, perhaps, might it have been for her. No one, she reflected, and with some sadness--no one by his approach had ever set her heart beating to a quicker tune. Perhaps there was some defect in her, some want of human passion, she reflected, which placed her in the second rank of women. When Cynthia was humble there was no girl so humble as Cynthia. And, after all, Harry Rames was honest. To that one stable point all her questions brought her back.

She moved at last, and Harry Rames rose and stood before her.

"Well?" he asked.

Cynthia dropped her hands loose at her sides and answered with a smile:

"Why not?"

It was in those words that she accepted him. There was no spirit in them, and very little of expectation. But she had come to expect not very much; and she had travelled a long way from the garden of her dreams.

"After all, there's a turnstile in this affair, too," she said, with a note of bitterness. "A very important one too. For it leads not into a garden, but straight to the treasury bench."

Harry Rames was bewildered. But he made no comment. Women were queer, and it was good to disregard their moments of excitement. Cynthia sprang up the next moment and laid her hand upon his arm.

"Oh, yes, we'll follow Mr. Smale's advice, Harry," she cried, "and we'll keep our eyes on the treasury bench. Why not? Now go, and come back to-morrow."

She was laughing a little wildly, and Harry Rames had the sense to take her at her word. He went out of the room, and Cynthia flung herself down upon the cushions and cried for an hour by the clock.

"Well," she said to herself at the end, as she rose and dried her eyes, "Mr. Benoliel will be satisfied. That's one thing." Almost she seemed to blame Mr. Benoliel for the fact of her engagement.

CHAPTER XX

AT CULVER

The odd thing in the affair, however, was that Mr. Benoliel did not seem satisfied. Cynthia asked him over the telephone the next day to come to her, and when he came she told him of her engagement.

"But no one knows of it as yet except yourself," she added; "and no one is to know, for the present. I want it kept a secret."

"Oh!" said Mr. Benoliel, looking at her curiously. "And why?"

"There will be a certain amount of ill-natured talk," Cynthia returned in a confusion. "And I want the time for it to be as short as possible. It will cease after we are married."

"People will say that Rames is an adventurer, who is marrying you for your money," said Mr. Benoliel bluntly, and Cynthia turned on him with spirit.

"Lord Helmsdale's mother will, and other mothers would have said the same of Lord Helmsdale if I had married him."

"So it's to spare the feelings of Harry Rames that you are keeping your engagement secret," said Mr. Benoliel with an ironical wonder. "I should never have suspected him of such delicate susceptibilities."

"Well, I should be uncomfortable too!" cried Cynthia, bending puzzled and indignant brows at him. "I think you are quite horrid."

Benoliel sustained her indignation unabashed.

"Is that the only reason, Cynthia?" he asked.

"You wanted me married," Cynthia continued. "You ought to be very, very pleased."

Mr. Benoliel, however, was not to be lured from his question into a discussion upon the propriety of his feelings. He repeated it.

"Is fear of gossip the only reason, Cynthia, which makes you keep your engagement secret?"

Cynthia again showed signs of confusion. Mr. Benoliel wore his air of omniscience. She sat down upon a chair.

"What do you mean, Mr. Benoliel?"

"This," said he. "I have noticed that the young ladies who keep their engagements secret are not, as a rule, very much in love with the men they are engaged to. They leave themselves a loop-hole of escape."

Cynthia's cheeks flamed. Certainly she had intended to spare Harry Rames and herself some uncomfortable weeks. But would she have minded those weeks had she cared for him? The question came swiftly, and as swiftly was answered. Had she cared for him she would have wanted to wear him like a ribbon on her breast for all the world to see. She realized it with a pang. She would have run quickly forward to meet the gossip and do battle. But she had not run forward. It was true that she had left herself a pathway of retreat, and rather by instinct than from any deliberate plan. Her wariness had prompted her. Once more she had wanted to be safe. But nothing of this was she going to acknowledge to Mr. Benoliel.

"I think you are extraordinarily horrid," she said again with a cold dignity, and hoped that her stateliness would crush her inquisitor.

"When do you propose to marry, then?" he asked.

"Just before Whitsuntide. The House will rise for ten days, I hear, at the least. We shall announce the marriage just before the House rises;" and that indeed was the plan upon which she had agreed only that morning with Harry Rames.

"Then there is no hurry," said Mr. Benoliel. "Perhaps you and Captain Rames will pay me a visit in the country before Whitsuntide comes."

He spoke as though he accepted the situation, and turned to other subjects, fearing to confirm Cynthia in obstinacy by any show of opposition.

"Certainly," she said; "we shall be pleased to come;" and a month later she and Harry Rames came one Friday afternoon to Culver.

The house stood within hearing of the bells of Ludsey, but on that side of the city opposite to the White House. Benoliel had built it himself, and to those who knew the man but slightly it was an astonishing production. Captain Rames, for instance, whose taste was not very meticulous, never ceased to marvel at it. Even this Friday afternoon, as the car swung round a turn of the country road and the thing stood before him, he contemplated it with amazement. It was nothing but a monstrous new villa of red and yellow brick, a pretentious ghastliness of towers and flashing glass rising from the middle of a small bare field within twenty yards of the roadway. An avenue of fir-trees not yet shoulder-high wound to the front door, and there was no need for it to wind. Circular beds of glaring flowers disfigured the new lawns, and little bushes of evergreens, which would one distant day make an effort to be shrubberies, gave to the house a most desolate and suburban look. It seemed wonderful to Harry Rames that so nice and delicate a person as Mr. Benoliel could bear to live in it at all; and still more wonderful that with a dozen of the most beautiful houses in England bosomed in deep meadows and whispered to by immemorial elms, within an easy motor-ride to choose from as his models, he should have devised this unconscionable edifice.

Sir James Burrell, the surgeon, however, who was sitting opposite to Harry Rames in the car, and next to Cynthia, took a different view. He gazed at the house with satisfaction. For it would add yet another subtle paragraph to his character sketch of Mr. Benoliel.

"How extraordinary," he cried, "and yet how like the man! That's just the house which Benoliel would have built. Only one had not the insight to guess it. I love it!" and he leaned his head out of the window and chuckled at the building's grotesqueness. "Yes, I love it. The fitness of things appeals to me." And he turned to the astonished Captain Rames. "You don't see the exquisite appropriateness of that--let us not call it a house--that detached residence to Isaac Benoliel?"

"Well, I don't," said Harry Rames. "He always seemed to me to set up as a lover of beautiful things."

"And the love is genuine," said Sir James, fairly off at a gallop upon his hobby. "He doesn't set up. The love is almost a quality of his race. Yes, but his race doesn't always know what things are beautiful. There's the explanation of that building--race, which confounds logic and is quite untroubled by inconsistencies. There's Benoliel's race in every line of it. He's of the Orient. He loves flamboyancy and gaudiness. He may conceal it carefully from us. But every now and then it must break out, and it has run riot here. Does the East repair and mend? No, it lets its old buildings decay and builds afresh. That's why Mr. Benoliel passes by your stately houses all up for sale in their parks and builds this villa. Remember, Captain Rames, though Mr. Benoliel talks with you and walks with you, he doesn't think with you. Behind those old tired eyes of his, he thinks as the East thinks."

Thus Sir James Burrell, and the car stopped at the front door before he could utter another word. He was not sorry, nor indeed were the other occupants of the carriage. He was merely trying his new paragraph on the dog, so to speak. He needed time to eliminate the unnecessary, and make it vivid with the single word, and fix it up with a nice juxtaposition of paradoxes and altogether to furbish it for presentation.

"He does talk!" said Harry Rames to Cynthia.

"Yes, doesn't he," she replied with a laugh, and then grew serious. "But I wonder whether he's right. I wonder whether Mr. Benoliel thinks and judges from principles which are true to him, but not true to us." Her eyes rested with a strange and thoughtful scrutiny on Harry's face.

"Why should you trouble?" said Harry Rames.

"It makes a little difference to me," said Cynthia. "Perhaps more than a little."

For old Daventry's last words weighed upon her. He had bidden her in troubles and difficulties to seek advice from Isaac Benoliel. He had thought much of his wisdom. She had herself accepted it as a thing beyond question, and a timely help. Now, she began to ask herself, was his wisdom, if it was born of the East and tempered by the instincts of his race, fit for service in her generation and for her people? She pondered the question during the next two days, and leaned more and more to Sir James Burrell's way of thinking from a trivial reason; the inside of Culver agreed so completely with its exterior. Its flamboyancy set the eyes aching. Its wall papers were indigestibly rich with colored flowers, and never was there a blue so vividly blue as the blue of his velvet curtains and triple-pile carpets. It is true that there were treasures of art in Culver, glowing pictures of the early Flemish school, with their crowds of figures, each one a finished miniature, and behind the crowds the clear sky and translucent air; there were marvels of jade, and glorious little statues of silver and marble, but their delicate beauty was spoilt and lost in the riot of gorgeousness which framed them.

One homely place alone there was in that building. The great hall, all colonnades and galleries, occupied the centre of the house. But on each side of the wide chimney, where of an evening, even in the summer, a fire usually burned, a great screen was drawn; and these screens enclosed a space before the fire set about with comfortable chairs, a sofa or two, and little mahogany tables, and made of it a place of comfort. In this space on the Sunday night Cynthia came to grips with Isaac Benoliel, and understood at last his life, and something of his philosophy.

It was eleven o'clock, or a little later. The ladies were retiring for the night. Cynthia herself had her foot upon the lowest step of the stair, and was thinking that after all she was to be spared an argument, when Mr. Benoliel came from the corridor of the smoking-room where he had left the men.

"Will you give me a few minutes, Cynthia?" he asked, and she turned at once and walked to the fire. She stood with a foot upon the rail of the hearth and a hand upon the mantel-shelf, quiet but mutinous. Mr. Benoliel followed her and sat down in a straight-backed arm-chair, facing the fire, and a little way behind her.

"You have not yet announced your engagement, Cynthia?" he began.

"No."

"Yet Whitsuntide is very close. Perhaps you have thought better of it?"

"No."

Mr. Benoliel looked at her as she stood, aggressively showing him her back, and smiled at her, with some amusement, a great deal of affection, and a little pity.

"Of course," he said, "I have not much right to interfere, and yet I should like you to hear, Cynthia, what I have to say. Otherwise I shall fail your father."

Cynthia turned about at once, and her manner toward him changed with her movement. The appeal of his voice and words had its effect upon her, and not that alone. Mr. Benoliel was so neat and supple, he sat with so upright a figure in his chair, his hair was so black and sleek and thick that she was seldom really conscious of his age. But at times, as now, when by chance she looked straight into his eyes and noticed their fatigue and their patience, and how the light had quite gone out of them, it came upon her almost as a shock that this was an old, old man; and because she was surprised she exaggerated his age, and gave to him in return for his pity the cruel pity of youth. She was in the mood almost to admit his right to interfere. But her gift of silence and the weariness which had become instinctive checked her. She moved forward to him with a gracious deference--that was all--and said, standing in front of him:

"I am glad of course to hear anything you have to say, Mr. Benoliel. You disapprove of my marriage."

"Yes."

"Yet you wanted me married."

"To the right person."

"Lord Helmsdale," said Cynthia, with a little pout of disdain.

"Youth should marry youth," returned Mr. Benoliel.

He looked the girl over from head to foot. She stood in front of him in her delicate frock of soft white satin and lace, long-limbed and slender, with the gloss of youth upon the heavy curls of her fair hair, and the rose of youth on her cheeks, and the sheen of youth upon her white and pretty shoulders. She was the color of a flower, and had the freshness of a flower upon a morning of dew. From the tip of her slim satin slipper to the ribbon in her hair, she was dressed with a daintiness which set her beauty proudly off. To Mr. Benoliel she was radiant and wonderful with youth.

"Yes," he repeated, "youth should marry youth, Cynthia, especially when it is such rare youth as yours."

Cynthia was pleased. She knew a compliment when she heard it.

"You have shifted your ground, Mr. Benoliel," she said, smiling down at him.

"No," he answered.

"It was social position, which you wanted me to marry in Lord Helmsdale."

"That, too. Yes. I don't make light of it. I am old enough not to blow a trumpet round the walls of Jericho in these days," he said. "But I did not tell you all my thought. I am an old man, and there are certain things I am shy of talking about. I am like you in that, Cynthia, eh? We neither of us wear our hearts upon our sleeves or are fond of talking sentiment. But I am compelled to to-night. I think the most beautiful thing in the world is a couple of young lovers facing all the unknown future, hand in hand, high of hope and courage, and serious with the uplifting seriousness of love. Now you are not in love, Cynthia, and he's not young. So, from my point of view, on both sides this marriage falls short of the marriage which should be."

"Captain Rames is not old," replied Cynthia. She omitted all reference to the point in which she herself failed according to Benoliel's standard. Isaac Benoliel noticed her admission, and, though he made no comment, he became still more determined to prevent the marriage if by any means he could. He had drawn his bow at a venture. With that touch of charlatanism which made him delight in posing as omniscient, he had stated as a fact what he only suspected. But she would have denied the suggestion, and indignantly, had it been false. He was sure now that she did not care for Harry Rames as a young woman should care for the man she is to marry. Moreover there had been a note of involuntary regret in Cynthia's voice as she had answered him. It seemed that she too agreed with him as to what should have been, and grieved that it was not to be.

"No," he conceded, "Captain Rames is not old. But neither is he young. He is forty, or thereabouts. He has lived by eighteen years longer than you have. And so--I will tell you the truth, Cynthia"--and he leaned forward with his hands upon his knees and his eyes shrewdly watching her face--"and so I am afraid. Yes, I look forward into your future, and I am afraid."

He saw Cynthia wince. So often had she spoken just such words to herself. Ever since she had crouched by the door in the dark room at the estancia, fear had walked at her heels with its shadow thrown upon the road beyond her feet. Was it to lie in front of her all her life? Here was her chosen adviser thinking her thoughts. She was not to be comforted by Sir James Burrell's reasonings. Mr. Benoliel might be altogether compact of the Orient. None the less his words knocked shrewdly at her heart. She sank down at the end of a sofa close at Mr. Benoliel's side, her face all troubled and discouraged.

"But I accepted Harry so that I might be safe," she cried tremulously, "so that I might no longer be afraid," and then sat with her cheeks afire, conscious that she had betrayed herself.

"I mean--" she corrected herself hastily.

"Just what you said, Cynthia," rejoined Mr. Benoliel. Once more he had shot his arrow at a venture and reached the mark. He had now for the first time the key to her. Much was explained to him. But he spoke as though the explanation had long been known to him.

"Yes, ever since I have known you, you have lived in fear, Cynthia," he said.

Cynthia did not again deny the truth. She found a better argument in the recollection of old Mr. Daventry's death-bed.

"But there was no reason for the fear," she cried. "It was groundless. I tortured myself for nothing. It was all due to a foolish mistake." She hesitated, choosing her words so that they might carry some sort of conviction and yet reveal nothing. "The mistake arose because--people--were silent--and they were silent because they wished to spare, and thought that knowledge would hurt. It was the silence which hurt."

"This time," said Mr. Benoliel, "silence shall not do harm. Nor shall a thought to spare. I will be frank with you as to why I am afraid, if you will listen to me. I shall have to tell you a little about myself. I shall not spare myself."

He spoke with reluctance. For he was reticent about himself. Cynthia realized suddenly how very little she knew of him, though she probably knew him more intimately than any one else, except the separated wife in Eaton Square. He had kept his secrets better than she had kept hers. Now he was going to reveal himself, and certainly to open old wounds for her sake.

"Thank you," she said gently. "I shall know of what you are afraid, of something perhaps which I may now be able to avert. But I ought to tell you at once, that nothing which you say can change me."

CHAPTER XXI

MR. BENOLIEL'S WARNING

Mr. Benoliel, however, persisted.

"I daren't be silent, Cynthia. There are just three great crises--some would say three great catastrophes--birth, marriage, and death. The first and the last happen. They are outside our control. But about the middle one we do ourselves have a word to say; we can direct it. And it's the most important of them all. For it means the beginning of life for others, and the making or undoing of our own. Therefore you can't afford to trust to luck, Cynthia."

"I am not trusting to luck at all," said Cynthia confidently.

"Aren't you?" asked Mr. Benoliel. "You are proposing to marry a man, nineteen years of whose life--whose man's life--if you understand me, you have had no share in, no influence upon, and have now no real knowledge of. I am not suggesting that the conventional other woman is somewhere in the background, waiting to appear at the marriage ceremony with a baby in her arms," he continued with a smile. "But during those nineteen years how many things must have happened to him, trials and miseries and elations, to modify and mould his character? And since you are ignorant of the things which happened to him, how can you know the man?"

"Yet I think I do know him," said Cynthia, and her confidence increased. She could meet Mr. Benoliel on this battle-ground. "And without laying claim of any particular insight. For he has always been careful that I should know him. From the very first day of our acquaintanceship he has spoken and acted quite deliberately in order that I might have no illusions about him. He has wanted me to know him just as clearly as he knows himself."

Mr. Benoliel shrugged his shoulders.

"Does he know himself?" he asked.

"Better than most men," said Cynthia. "He has set out to use himself as a machine and he has studied the machine unceasingly, its limits and its capacities, so that he might use it to its fullest power." She recalled Harry Rames's foresight, the careful laying of his plans, the queer modesty which underlay his ambition to excel. She turned triumphantly to Mr. Benoliel. "Oh, yes, he knows himself a good deal better than youth can know itself."

"Ah!" said Mr. Benoliel, raising a warning finger. "I was waiting for that. I admit that youth doesn't know itself. But then it's not so important that it should. There's not, after all, as yet, so very much to know. But take it this way. Suppose that you and Captain Rames were both young and of an age! Suppose that he had the nineteen years which separate you in front of him instead of behind him!"

"Well?" said Cynthia.

"Why, then, when he reached forty, you, the wife, would know him better than he would know himself. A wife always does, if she lives in sympathy with her husband. I am presuming that. You would know him a good deal better than he knows himself now. The solitary nineteen years, of which now I dread the consequences, you would have shared. That's the point. And you wouldn't be running the danger you are running now."

"What danger?" asked Cynthia impatiently. "Of what are you afraid?"

"I am afraid of the latent things," Mr. Benoliel answered. "I am afraid of the seeds which may have been sown in him during these nineteen years, and of which the plant has not yet shown. I am afraid of latent desires, fancies, ambitions, latent cravings of which he is not yet aware, and which may some day come to life with overwhelming strength. Haven't you seen men suddenly change for no apparent reason to the ordinary observer, drop from all their established habits, begin again upon another plane? I have, and that's the change I am afraid of now. For it's one you would be powerless to avert, since you would not even suspect it until it had actually begun."

He turned toward Cynthia, and with a smile upon his face summed up his argument.

"Make no mistake, Cynthia. I am not making light of Captain Rames. In a way my fears are an actual tribute to the man. But I am afraid that out of a life so busy, and so keen as his has been, so fraught with incidents, so varied, something may suddenly seize him and catch him back and hold him; some craving, some ambition in which you will have no share, and which will separate you forever."

He spoke with so much earnestness that Cynthia was impressed against her will. She was sure that he was speaking with knowledge of a kindred case. Certain words he had dropped made her certain that the kindred case was his own.

"But supposing that such a change came," she said with hesitation, "must it separate?"

"No," said Mr. Benoliel gently, "not if both bring to the marriage love. Then I don't think it need." He glanced at her swiftly, and said with a sudden sharp note in his voice: "But what if the marriage be only a bargain, Cynthia? What then?" and the blood rushed into the girl's face as he looked at her.

"I'll tell you," he cried. His voice rose and a kind of sombre passion rang in it. "One party doesn't keep the bargain, or keeps it half-heartedly, as an irksome thing, and day by day the separation grows more complete, until you are living with your enemy or living quite alone."

His voice dropped again to a whisper on the last words. He finished and sat lost wistfully in his own recollections, and forgetful of Cynthia at his side. After a little while his lips moved, and, as an old man will, he spoke a word or two to himself. Cynthia's ears caught the words.

"It was my fault, and it couldn't be helped," he said, and so again fell into a long silence, with his eyes upon the coals of the fire. At length Cynthia touched him gently upon the sleeve.

"I should like--the instance," she said timidly.

Isaac Benoliel roused himself with a start.

"Yes. I mean to give it you."

"But I have no right to it," Cynthia insisted. "You must remember that."

Benoliel shook his head and smiled.

"You are a young girl starting out on life. You have every right to it, Cynthia."

"I mean that it cannot change me," she said. "I would like to hear it--yes. But it is only that I may understand and be ready. And if you think that reason insufficient, don't tell me. I shall thank you, all the same, for offering to tell me."

"You mustn't take the warning literally," he said. "I am of the East, you know. So is my story"; and a sudden relief swept over Cynthia. He was not of her people, his stand-point would not be hers, his warning might not apply to her. She thought of Sir James Burrell's words. Discouragement sat more lightly upon her than it had done during the last hour. There were certain curious phases in Mr. Benoliel's life which were not understood--sudden disappearances, for instance, during which no one met him to bring back to London the place of his abode. He was recognized as a man apart. Yes, he was of the Orient, and he might have no message for her ears.

"It was my race which caught me back," Benoliel began, and Cynthia's courage increased. But his story was only just begun.

CHAPTER XXII

AND AN INSTANCE TO ENFORCE IT

"You knew, I suppose, that I was married?"

"Yes," said Cynthia.

"And that my wife lives?"

"Yes."

Mr. Benoliel nodded and shifted in his chair.

"You have also very possibly heard a good many speculations about my origin?"

"A good many," said Cynthia.

"Well, here's the truth. I am a Barbary Jew. I come out of Morocco, the one country where you'll find the East to-day. Already in Tangier, the city given over to the foreigner, you will come across some traces of it. But ride for a few hours out of Tangier, straight to the south, pay your dues and cross the Red Hill, and you'll have both feet planted in the East, and may breathe in some of its enchantment. Go forward for another day or so, and you may pass perhaps some tall Arab, striding through the crowd outside El Ksar, carrying a stick stretched across his shoulder-blades. He'll speak to no one, stop for nothing, and all will make way for him. That's the Imperial Courier, on his way to the coast from Fez. He'll not sleep upon the way, and he'll take no food lest he should sleep. He'll be in Tangier three days after he has left Fez. He's the penny post. Ride on still further, cross the Sebou, travel over a vast plain by a track beaten by the feet of men and animals, yet strangely enough a track which never runs straight, though the plain is bare, but winds and turns, and winds again over the face of the country." Mr. Benoliel's eyes were fixed upon the fire; he spoke, lingering upon his words. He had grown forgetful of the purpose which drove him to reveal himself. Another and a strange aspect of him was presented suddenly to Cynthia. The dilettante and the exquisite had vanished. He spoke with a kind of yearning in his voice. His thoughts had drifted out through the doorway of his abominable villa. He was walking in the starshine over the wide empty plain of the Sebou, steeped in the enchantment of which he had spoken. Dimly she foresaw whither he was leading her.

"Yet a day and you come to a wall of hills. Right ahead of you a cleft opens--that's the pass to Fez--a troublesome place, by the way, for Barbary Jews, since the Z'mur tribe has a way of taking toll in that narrow pass," Benoliel explained with a smile, and seemed to become once more aware of Cynthia's presence.

"But a little further to the right from a break in the sky-line of the wall, a regular broad staircase seems to descend. It becomes a track, it zigzags across the face of the cliff, like a piece of string, to the plain. That's the road to my home," and he suddenly threw back his head and sat alert--"the city of Mequinez--the most eastern of the cities of the East, where the great gateway of mosaic, built by Christian captives, crumbles slowly to ruin, and the Jew must not wear shoes in the street, must walk barefoot with a black gaberdine upon his body, and a black cap upon his head. I ought to resent that, eh, Cynthia?"

He looked at her, and answered the question himself. "But I was born there," and to him the answer was sufficient.

"In Mequinez!" said Cynthia, striving to bridge the distance between this actual house in the green of Warwickshire and that distant city with the great mosaic gate in Barbary. Mr. Benoliel helped her a little to see it.

"Yes, in the Mellah of Mequinez, Cynthia. That's where the Jews are crowded; an evil-smelling place you would call it, close and airless, with narrow alleys and houses huddling together, and a reek of rancid cookery. Yet it's a town of spaces; there's a good square before the gate. There are great silent palaces, with gardens and lakes. There's room in Mequinez--but not for us. We were shut up in the Mellah at six o'clock at night like children. And we were not all poor. The Mellah was gaudy with the bright handkerchiefs and dresses of the women, and their satin and silk scarves. There was a great deal of money in the Mellah of Mequinez, and a great deal more owed to it by its Moorish lords and masters in the city. But that didn't make any difference. Remember you are in the East in Mequinez, and a Moor who owed me a thousand pounds would make me strip off my shoes in the street, if he met me wearing them. A pretty picture of dignity, eh, Cynthia?"

Cynthia did not answer. She was puzzled by Benoliel now, and she did not wish to interrupt him. He sat beside her, neat and trim and scrupulously clothed, with no jewellery but a pearl stud in his shirt-front, and pearl links at his cuffs, a person utterly modern and used to good manners. Yet he spoke of the Mellah in Mequinez not with the air of one recollecting unclean days, now, thank God, altogether done with, but rather with a kind of relish and contentment that such places should be. She had to cast an eye about that flamboyant hall before she could in any way reconcile Mr. Benoliel with his words.

"I was not one of the rich, however," he continued. "I was a poor boy. I lived with an aunt, for both my parents were dead, and picked up a few copper flouss from time to time as I could. My aunt wasn't very kind. I was terrified of the Moors and their dark, contemptuous faces. There's a wall outside Mequinez, one of many which run out into the country and stop--but this one runs further than the rest. It was built or rather begun--for, like all things in Morocco, it was never finished--by some old king, so that a blind man might be able to find his way from Mequinez to Morocco City without a guide. I was always fascinated by that wall, and wanted to follow it--and never to come back. I hated Mequinez. Finally I ran away one morning with a pedlar of my race who wanted a boy to help him. He and I and a donkey, which carried his stock in trade, slipped out early from the town, and climbed northward onto a great rolling plateau of grass and asphodel, which reached away past the white sacred city of Mulai Idris, on the hill of Jebel Zarhon, past the Roman ruins of Volubilis, to that gap in the sky-line of the cliff where the road leads down to the plain of the Sebou. It was spring-time, there were irises up to our knees, the asphodel bushes were in flower and the air on this wide upland, with Jebel Zarhon on our right hand, was sweet and clean. We walked, brushing through the bushes, our shadows shifting as the sun rose--I had a sense of freedom. We stopped and ate at a little stream, and went on again. I can remember all the details of that day, even to a great glowing field of mustard, which shone like yellow silk----"

Mr. Benoliel pulled himself up with a laugh.

"But I needn't tell you about all that," he cried. "Here's the point. At the top of a roll in the turf, just by a miserable little tent village, I sat down upon the ground, while the pedlar bargained over his wares, and I took what I meant to be my last look at Mequinez. I could see the city below me far away, and very small in the sunshine, with its buildings all confused. I made up my mind then that I would be a rich man, and that never--never would I pass between the ruined walls up to the gateway of Mequinez again, that never--never would I look on it even from a spot so far away as this. We went over the brow of the hill, and I saw Mequinez no more. In a fortnight we came to Rabat upon the sea. There I learnt the great lesson."

He sat still for a few moments, with his chin sunk upon his chest. He seemed to be wondering whether, after all, the lesson was so great a lesson, and worth the learning.

"Yes?" asked Cynthia. "What lesson?"

"We crossed the river from Sallee to Rabat, where the great plants and cactuses hang down the walls," he explained. "It was evening. I said to the pedlar: 'We must hurry to the Mellah.' And he answered: 'In Rabat there is no Mellah.'"

"No Jews, then," said Cynthia.

Mr. Benoliel shook his head and laughed.

"That's what I thought, Cynthia. But I was wrong. There were Jews in Rabat, but they wore European clothes, they lived in houses, in the best positions-- for of course they had all the money, that goes without saying, in Morocco as in most other places--they were people of importance, consuls and vice-consuls; they were allowed to walk in the governor's orange garden. I was astounded. I asked how this could be. And I got my answer between cuffs from my pedlar. It was the influence of the Europeans. Rabat is a sea-port with European trade. That was the great lesson: the Europeans do not have Mellahs."

"So you decided to come to Europe," said Cynthia.

"Not quite at once," said Mr. Benoliel shrewdly. "I was a boy and very ignorant. I had to find out first whether a Jew could make as much money in Europe as he could in Morocco."

Cynthia laughed in spite of herself; and Mr. Benoliel quite misunderstood the reason of her laughter.

"Well, I didn't know anything about Europe at all," he said seriously. "But I made inquiries. Oh, I heard stories. The Jews of Rabat talked of London, and of hotels in London. There was one who said--and it was repeated to the pedlar, who told it to me, but I would not believe it--'We kept it up all June, every night, till four o'clock in the morning, in the American Bar.' They were gay dogs in London, the Jews of Rabat, and they made money enough to keep it up all night till four o'clock in the morning, in the American Bar. So I decided to come to London."

All Mr. Benoliel's humor had deserted him. He was speaking with intense seriousness. He was a little Barbary boy again, learning with amazement the extraordinary latitude which Europe allowed to its Jews.

"So I ran away from the pedlar," he resumed; and now at last he smiled. "You will never guess, Cynthia, in what capacity I came to England. I came with a troupe of Moorish acrobats who were going to appear at one of the music halls in London."

"You!" Cynthia exclaimed.

"Yes. I found them on the beach at Rabat, with their baggage, waiting for the surf to go down. The Elder Dempster steamboat was lying outside the bar, a mile from the shore. They wanted a boy who was light. They took me."

"And you appeared at the music halls?" Cynthia asked.

"Oh, yes," said Mr. Benoliel, "I appeared. I learnt some simple somersaults and balancings, and I looked after the baggage. That lasted for a year. By that time I had learnt some English and I left them. I am not going to bother you with the next twenty years of my life. I got on as others have done--office-boy to confidential clerk--the usual process. I meant to make money, you see--all the time, hour by hour, I meant to make money. I was with a great firm of financiers who had got themselves into a tangle over some Eastern business. I had mastered the subject; I was by my origin fitted to cope with it; and I saw a way out of the trouble. The firm came to me, and with the firm my opportunity. I asked for a salary of seventeen thousand pounds a year. The firm refused. I went on at my old two hundred and fifty for another month. By that time the trouble had grown more grave. It was a real crisis, meaning perhaps dishonor. The firm came to me again and accepted my terms. It took me a year to put matters right, and at the end of the year I was, of course, dismissed. But I had seventeen thousand pounds, and I knew what to do with it."

"You made it into a great fortune," said Cynthia.

"By the time I was forty," replied Mr. Benoliel. "And then I began to think about marrying."

Cynthia stirred and leaned forward. Benoliel turned swiftly toward her.

"Ah," he said, "you are beginning to appreciate the similarity between my case and Rames's. But it doesn't date from the age of forty at which we both began to think about marrying. No! Strip our careers of the accidents of race and country and occupation, and you will find the similarity right there in our boyhood and our youth. We were both adventurers, both determined to get on, he to his ends, I to mine. Well, at forty-one I married."

Mr. Benoliel hesitated. His wife was living. He was a man of some sensibility, and a delicate reticence of mind made it repugnant to him to lay before another the manner of his marriage and its troubles. But he looked again at Cynthia, and the freshness and the youth of her, and the trouble in her big dark-blue eyes, which were fixed so intently upon his face, persuaded him. He might be exaggerating. His fears might be quite vain. But suppose that they were not? Every line of grief graven in the girl's young face would be a whole epistle of condemnation.

"Our marriage was a bargain, too," he said frankly. "My wife brought social position, I money. But there was less risk in our bargain than there will be in yours."

"Why less risk?" asked Cynthia.

"Because we who are Jews make good husbands," said Mr. Benoliel; and Cynthia cried out indignantly:

"I am not afraid that Harry will make a bad one."

"I don't say either that he will," Mr. Benoliel returned calmly. "I only say that as a rule the Jew makes a good husband. He believes in the family. Can you say as much of the Christian? No. Therefore there was less risk in our bargain. And still it did not turn out well."

"Why?"

"Because I was forty-one and my wife twenty-three. Yes, that's the truth at the end of it all. There were eighteen years of experiences and struggles in my life which my wife had not shared; and out of those eighteen years there sprang a passion in me which I, least of all, expected, and which I could not combat. I became homesick for my country, and for that city on which I had turned my back with joy."

"You?" cried Cynthia. For a moment she thought herself listening to a fairy tale. "You wanted to go back to the humiliations, to the Mellah?"

She recalled the feminine nicety of his house in Grosvenor Square, the bright silver--not too much of it--the elegance of its mahogany furniture, which was never allowed to crowd the rooms. She recollected those dinner-parties at which the great men of the earth were entertained with so much pride. It could not be that he wished to return to the crowded Jewish quarter, noisome with the reek of rancid cookery, where the gates were locked on its inhabitants at six o'clock of the night! But Mr. Benoliel replied with an energy and a fire which she had never known him manifest before.

"Yes. I wanted to go back. How and when the longing first came to me, I can't tell you. But it did come, and, having come, it grew. I felt day by day more and more of a stranger amongst a strange people. That road winding up the cliffs to the break in the sky-line above the plain of the Sebou--I began to dream of it! Then I used to lie awake at night and travel along it, past the pillars and arches of Volubilis, and the little white city of Mulai Idris, on the shoulder of Jebel Zarhon--right over the upland, and down through the asphodel to Mequinez. Finally, I had to go. I told my wife. We had got on together up till then, no better, no worse than other people. She stared at me with amazement, with suspicion, as at a stranger, and from that moment our relations changed. She knew quite well to what I was going back, to what I wanted to go back--the Mellah, the gaberdine, and the rest of it. And--it was natural, I think--she despised me. I was quite aware of her contempt, and--was indifferent to it. I wanted to go back. And I did."

"You did?" said Cynthia. And then, "I see. I see."

She understood now these mysterious disappearances of Mr. Benoliel when he vanished from his clubs and his haunts, and no man brought news of him.

"Yes, I went, and as I went London and the years in London dropped away from me. I was happy. I went down with my mules into Mequinez, and put my European clothes away in a cupboard in the Mellah. I stayed in Mequinez three months."

"But how?" asked Cynthia. "What did you do?"

Mr. Benoliel smiled.

"Business," he said. "I traded. I lent money. Then I came back to England--refreshed as a man comes from his bath. But my wife hated the whole business. At first she would not hear a word of what I had been doing. Then she became curious--morbidly curious. There was no end to her questions. What humiliations, what indignities had fallen to me amongst the Moors--she was never tired of hearing. And as she questioned and I answered, she would sit looking at me, with eyes in which contempt grew ever more bitter, looking at me as one looks upon a stranger. Quarrels followed. I went back to Mequinez, after a year or two, and again after another period. And every time the pull of the place became stronger. It was after my third visit that our marriage came to an end. We gave a great dinner-party, and when our guests had gone, she told me that our life had become intolerable to her."

Mr. Benoliel did not spare himself. It was rather a grim scene which he had to describe--the last one of many quarrels which had sprung from their estrangement. "You leave me for those squalors. You return to me fresh from them;" that was the burden of her accusation. She was not of his race or of his people. She had no sympathy with, or comprehension of, the intense craving which from time to time assailed him to go back to his own place, or of the utter weariness which overtook him of the life of London, in which he played an actor's part. The squalor and humiliation of his days in Mequinez got upon her nerves, filled her with disgust, and made his companionship repugnant.

"You can understand that, Cynthia?" he asked, and Cynthia, since frankness was demanded of her, agreed.

"Yes, I can understand that," she answered gently. His story was to her fantastic and fabulous. It belonged to the East--as he did. Only by keeping in mind that he, underneath the veneer of his manners, was of the East could she accept it as truth. She did so accept it. But she looked at Mr. Benoliel with curious eyes, and was conscious of a feeling very like aversion. Within the half-hour he had grown a stranger to her even as he had done to his wife. That he should leave the order and the cleanliness of his home, depart from the company of cultured people--he the dilettante--don the gaberdine, go joyfully back to the dirt and squalor of his Mellah, humbly take off his slippers and walk bare-foot at the bidding of any Moor who passed him by-

-that Cynthia could not understand. But that his wife should find life with him intolerable when he came back from his degradation, refreshed as by a bath, to resume existence at her side--that she did thoroughly understand.

"So we separated," said Mr. Benoliel.

"Yes," said Cynthia. "But there's no parallel between your case and ours. What happened to you cannot happen to us."

She was not sure. There was appeal in her voice. She pleaded to him to agree with her. She clung desperately to her one small piece of knowledge. Mr. Benoliel was of the East. Harry Rames was not.

"There is a parallel, and a close one," Mr. Benoliel insisted. "What happened to us may happen to you. Out of the experiences of eighteen years in Captain Rames's life, experiences in which you have no share, some unsuspected craving may even now be fermenting which may turn the course of his thoughts, and snatch him back from you."

"He would fight against it," said Cynthia.

"Even so, it would stand between you, and it would grow."

Cynthia was silent for a moment. Then she said timidly:

"Even then there is one condition according to you which would avert the risk."

"Yes, one. Love."

And again Cynthia was silent. Then she burst out, striking her hands together in a violence of revolt:

"But I know him! I know him!" and with the words still in her ears, she doubted them. Mr. Benoliel's warning had alarmed her. But it had alarmed her chiefly because it had brought home to her how very little she might really know of those whom she met daily, and with whom she was most intimate. Here was Mr. Benoliel. She had thought she knew him, and so well that she could play with him, and twist him to her wishes. He had spoken for half an hour, and, lo! she had never known him.

"Do all men hide themselves?" she cried. "Do you all build up barriers about you, and lie hidden within? Oh, but Harry's honest--honest;" and again she caught at her old argument and consolation.

She rose from her seat abruptly.

"Thank you very much for all you have said. I am grateful. I shall not forget it. Good-night;" and she moved away to the foot of the stairs. She stopped then and turned back, as though in half a mind to say more. But as Mr.

Benoliel rose, and she looked at him, a shadow darkened her eyes and she seemed to shrink from him with that slight sense of repulsion.

"Good-night," she said again, and hurriedly went up the stairs. His story was too new in her thoughts. What she had it in her mind to say, she left untold.

But Mr. Benoliel was none the less to be informed of it that night. He sat late in the hall after the lights had been turned out, with only the firelight flickering on the hearth. He had read the aversion in Cynthia's face which his story had provoked. He had made a sacrifice of her affection. But he had made it for her sake, and he did not regret that he had spoken. None the less he was disturbed. He might have done no good, and he had reopened an old wound of his own. He sat there knowing that if he went to bed he would not sleep; and in a little while he heard a noise in the corridor leading to the billiard-room. The door into the hall was softly opened, and the wavering light of a candle dimly lit up that cavernous place. The screen stood between Benoliel and the intruder. He could see nothing but the light of the candle shaking upon the walls above the screen. He did not move, he heard some one moving across the floor of the hall; he kept his eyes fixed upon the opening between the screens; and he saw Captain Rames pass across the opening. He sprang up with a low cry. Rames was coming from the corridor where his bedroom was to the foot of the stairs up which Cynthia had gone. At the cry Rames stopped, and, holding the candle above his head, peered into the shadows. Mr. Benoliel came quickly toward him.

"Where are you going, Captain Rames?" he asked.

"To my wife," said Harry.

Mr. Benoliel stared at Harry Rames.

"You and Cynthia are married?"

"Yes."

"When are you going to make your marriage public?"

"On the day the Whitsunday holidays begin. We shall have it announced in the evening papers. We shall already have left for Fontainebleau."

So after all Mr. Benoliel had spoken in vain. He might have spared his breath, and retained in a fuller degree Cynthia's liking and respect. He knew now what she had turned back from the stairs to tell him.

"Give her this message," he said. "Tell her to forget what I said to her;" and he moved away.

But the message was of no use. He had said what he had to say, and Cynthia could not forget. She watched. She was afraid; as since her seventeenth birthday she had always been afraid.

CHAPTER XXIII

CYNTHIA ON THE HOUSE

On the morning after Parliament had risen the newspapers announced the marriage of Cynthia Daventry to Harry Rames. The ceremony had taken place by special license early one morning at a little church in Mayfair, with a girl friend of Cynthia's, and a member of Parliament named Robert Brook, as witnesses. A good many people were surprised; still more, however, declared that they had foreseen the marriage all along, and that of course it couldn't last; while Lord Helmsdale's mother simply remarked in accents of pity: "Poor thing! Double her age, isn't he? And she was so pretty, too, a few months ago."

On the other hand, however, a good many honest telegrams of congratulations reached the couple honeymooning in the woods of Fontainebleau; and when Harry and Cynthia returned to London, there were fresher incidents than their marriage for people to discuss. They settled down in Curzon Street to keep their bargain loyally.

If Cynthia's heart ached at times, as it had done amongst the trees of Fontainebleau, for a life struck to fire by passion, she gave no outward sign of her pain. She was to help forward the great career, and to the best of her powers she did. She threw open her house to her husband's party; she entertained; she attended social gatherings; she walked abroad in Ludsey with a good memory for faces; she spent many hours on the train. Harry, on his side, was assiduous at Westminster. He sat upon committees in the morning, and on one of the green benches below the gangway during the afternoon and evening, with an occasional rush home at a quarter to eight to take his wife out to dinner.

"Be there!" was one of Henry Smale's maxims which he had taken to heart. "Sit in the House. Never mind the library or the smoking-room, or the lobby, or the terrace. Sit in the House! However dull the debate, and however inviting the sunlight streaming through the high windows, sit in the House. All the great Parliamentarians have done it. The lawyers can't do it, of course. But you haven't their excuse. You can. It may seem a waste of time. You'll find that it isn't."

So Harry Rames sat in the House, and Cynthia, when she had no other engagement to detain her, came down to Westminster, dined with him there, and spent an hour afterward in the ladies' gallery. She became acquainted with many men of different calibre, and amongst them with Mr. Devenish, the Secretary for Agriculture, who was just beginning to do a little more than make a vociferous noise in the world. Mr. Devenish happened to pass through the dining-room when Harry and his wife were finishing dinner, and catching sight of them he turned off toward their table.

He was a brisk, smallish man, and Cynthia was astonished by his aspect. She had seen him often enough upon the floor of the House of Commons, and had taken him for a person of a commanding height. But it was not the first time she had made this mistake. The House of Commons, like the theatre, magnifies men to the galleries. Mr. Devenish dropped his hand upon Rames's shoulder.

"I want a word with you to-night, Rames," he said

"Why not now?" asked Rames. "This is my wife, Mr. Devenish."

Mr. Devenish bowed to her.

"I knew that very well," he said.

Cynthia disbelieved him. Also she had formed a dislike of him. There was something too acrid in his speeches. She thought of him as a man going about with a phial of vitriol hidden in the palm of his hand.

"I am not famous," she said coldly. "How should you know, Mr. Devenish?"

"I saw you in the lobby, and--I asked;" he smiled as he spoke, and she found his smile singularly disarming; it was so friendly and genuine a thing. Mr. Devenish turned again to Harry Rames.

"We want you to help us. A vote on account for the navy is coming up on Thursday. There will be a motion for the reduction of armaments. We want you to speak."

Harry Rames shook his head.

"I rather propose to leave those questions alone. I don't want to get the reputation of being a service member."

"I appreciate that," said Mr. Devenish. "But you are asked to speak in this debate by the government."

"On the general question?" asked Rames.

"Not so much on that. The point is the economy of the big ship. You can speak from practical experience. You know. You are here in Parliament to contribute your knowledge." Mr. Devenish turned to Cynthia, and again his smile illumined his face. "Persuade him, Mrs. Rames."

It occurred to Cynthia that Mr. Devenish did not trouble to inquire whether Harry Rames believed the big ship to be an economical thing. Harry was to support the government. The rest of his argument she agreed with. It was Harry's duty, since he was in Parliament, to contribute of his knowledge.

"Very well," said Captain Rames. "Of course if the government wishes it, I shall be proud to take part in the debate. Won't you sit down and have some coffee?"

"Yes, do!" said Cynthia cordially, and she was not altogether engaged in helping her husband on when she spoke. Mr. Devenish now puzzled her. She had begun by disliking him. He had spoken very few words to her, and yet she no longer disliked him. There was a charm in his manner of which he seemed quite unaware. At close quarters he lost the narrowness, which she had thought the mark of him. He seemed broadly human, comprehensively sympathetic. Yet he obviously wore no mask. He was simple, and he gave a pleasant impression of being a good fighter. Mr. Devenish drew up a chair and sat down.

"You come to many of our debates," he said to Cynthia. "What do you think of us?" and with an unaffected interest in the views of a pretty woman, he led her on to express her opinion.

"Well," she said frankly, "I think most of your debates are very dull."

"That's quite true," Mr. Devenish replied with a laugh at the little spurt of complaint in her voice. "Nine out of ten are dull, and if you were in the government you would wish the tenth was too. The debate which sparkles and amuses you in the gallery means keen opposition on the floor of the House. The debate which is dull means that the government gets its bill. And the government is there to get its bills."

"Yes, I suppose that's true," said Cynthia, and then Harry Rames intervened.

"It's curious," he said, "but I no longer find any debate dull. I used to be bored, I admit it, but I can sit through anything now and find it interesting."

"Yes," said Cynthia, nodding her head; "I have noticed that, Harry, from the gallery, and--I think it's a bad sign."

"The sign of the true Parliamentarian," said Mr. Devenish.

"Perhaps," said Cynthia stubbornly. "Still a bad one."

"Now why?" asked Mr. Devenish indulgently. Cynthia was certainly a very pretty woman. Let her talk! Cynthia colored and replied hotly:

"Because it means that the four walls of that little chamber are closing in on you. The game inside, with its pauses, its coups, its manœuvres, is becoming more important than the great interests and issues outside which you are there to decide. It means that in your thoughts the country and the constituency are growing smaller, and the green leather benches on which you sit becoming more and more important. If you don't find any debates dull, you are growing aloof from the country. You are becoming, as you say, a Parliamentarian. That means Parliament first, the country a bad second."

Cynthia stopped abruptly. She had allowed herself to be betrayed into delivering a lecture upon politics to a past-master in the art, a man who, out of his forty-five years, had spent twenty in the House of Commons. She flushed. "But you must think me a fool," she cried.

"I don't," Mr. Devenish exclaimed. "Yours is a definite point of view." He was not speaking seriously. For he was eager to learn so long as the learning came to him by word of mouth, and not from the printed page. "Tell me some more."

He was considering no longer the prettiness of the woman, the changing lights upon her face. He was conceding respect to her judgment. Cynthia was mollified. She continued:

"And here's something which to me makes many of the debates tedious and unreal. You all behave as if your ideal of a member of the House of Commons were a fossil on a shelf."

Mr. Devenish laughed.

"Why do you say that, Mrs. Rames?"

"Because if a man changes his opinions ever so little during a course of years, he at once has the reports of his old speeches flung at his head in scathing accents, as though he had committed the meanest of crimes."

"It's a party score," said Mr. Devenish.

"Yes, but why?" Cynthia insisted. "You must all know that a man who is any use at all does change his opinions as his experience widens. Surely that's true. What's the use of thought at all if it leaves you precisely where you were?"

"Mrs. Rames," said Mr. Devenish, "I cannot dispute it."

Cynthia had long been puzzled by this extraordinary childishness on the part of men of reputed intelligence. She was determined if she could to get at the truth. "Then why?" she asked. "Why, when one of the opposition proves that a member of the government has changed his view, does all the opposition shout with derision, and why do all on the government side look glum? Why must the minister labor to show that he really hasn't changed any views? Why does he rise so quickly to do it? And why, when he has risen, doesn't he say: 'Of course I have changed my views. I am a better man than I was two years ago.'"

"Well, upon my word, I can't tell you why," said Mr. Devenish honestly. "I suppose we haven't the courage. Don't you approve of us at all?"

"Oh, yes, I do," said Cynthia quickly; "and much more than I expected to do." She was induced to give her impression of the body of members.

"I had got an idea that everybody was in here to get something." She grew suddenly red, and in a flurry, which Mr. Devenish did not understand. She continued, "I suppose I got the idea from newspapers. I made a wrong inference. They are here, of course--the rich men who want honors to put a crown upon their wealth, the office-hunters, the speculator, and the financier, who use their membership to help their city business--But there are others one is apt to overlook, the silent people, who make no mark, and don't want to make one. You see them in the lobby, rather disconsolately busy about nothing. They are probably not particularly intelligent. Some of them, no doubt, are quite stupid. But one rather respects them, because membership of the House of Commons means to them a real daily loss. They would be more prosperous if they devoted the time they spend here to their business. But they seem to be here because they believe that some things want doing, some definite things, and that they can help to get them done by their votes. There is a lot of them. Then there are the country gentlemen who would be happier on their estates, and would be there but for their conviction that the solid judgment of the country gentleman is absolutely necessary in the council of the nation." She spoke with pomposity and a friendly mimicry of the class she described. "But I like them. I think they are of value because to them, too, membership here means a real loss."

"Well, I agree," said Mr. Devenish.

"You! You do?" asked Cynthia in surprise. "I thought that--" and she stopped.

"Well, what?" Mr. Devenish pressed for her opinion with a laugh.

"Never mind," said Cynthia. "There's another class, too, which attracts me. The failures. The ambitious men who just don't succeed, and fail by so very little, but fail completely."

"Yes," Mr. Devenish agreed, "their lot is not attractive. They can't bring themselves to admit failure. They drift along here until the time is past for them to do anything else. The four walls, as you say, have closed about them. They sit here, eating out their hearts, jealous of the others who succeed, and making a bitter pretence of contentment."

"They are the prisoners of the House of Commons," said Cynthia, and the phrase struck pleasantly upon Mr. Devenish's ears so used to the slipshod metaphors of the average speaker.

"Yes," he said with a quick look of interest. "Yes, that's a true saying. How did you think of it, Mrs. Rames?"

"I have sympathy with failures," she replied.

"Ah," said Mr. Devenish. "But it's easy to have that when one is married to success," and he turned genially to Captain Rames.

A junior whip hurried up to the table.

"You are wanted, Mr. Devenish, in the House," he said.

Devenish looked at his watch and sprang up. "I have stayed longer than I ought to. We can count upon you then, Rames, for Thursday," and he hurried away. Cynthia followed him with her eyes. He attracted her and he left with her an impression of power, which made his interest in her, obviously expressed, a subtle flattery. She turned back to her husband.

"I was mistaken in that man," she said, and as Harry Rames did not answer her, she continued: "You see, Harry, I am doing my best to help you on."

"You are indeed," said Harry Rames sulkily. Cynthia stared at him. The sulkiness in his voice set her blood tingling. He could be jealous then! She laughed out loud suddenly, with a girl's joyousness, and, as Harry lifted inquiring eyes to her, the blood mantled into her cheeks, and she sat in a pretty confusion. For a moment both of them were embarrassed, and neither could have told why. Cynthia broke through the embarrassment with the first words which occurred to her:

"I can't reconcile Mr. Devenish with his speeches," she said.

"Yet there's a continuity," replied Harry. "He is one of your instances of men big enough to widen out. But he's an enthusiast, and he has done in his day a deal of platform work so that the old phrases come trippingly to his tongue. He says, when he's carried away, more than he thinks now, but less than he used to think ten years ago. I fancy that's the explanation."

Cynthia looked toward the door through which Mr. Devenish had disappeared.

"Tell me about him, Harry," she said.

"I will, certainly," said Rames. His ill-humor had passed. He leaned toward his wife with a smile upon his face. It seemed to Cynthia that the moment of embarrassment so quickly gone had brought now as its consequence another moment quite as inexplicable--a moment during which she and Harry were nearer to one another than as yet they had been.

"The one thing I think to remember about Devenish is this," Rames continued. "As a boy he had always to walk in the road and he has not forgotten it."

The division bell began to ring before he could say another word to elaborate his sketch of the man. He led Cynthia out through the arches to the door where her carriage waited, and he left her to drive home puzzled by his phrase.

He spoke, as he had promised to do, on the following Thursday. Cynthia heard the speech from the ladies' gallery, not siding with it at all, nor against it, but simply attentive to its effect. He rose in a full House, which did not diminish as he spoke, and the space behind the bar grew crowded. He was brief; he worked his own intimate knowledge of the mechanism of a modern ship of war into the scheme of his speech. He was nervous, Cynthia knew, but he gave no outward sign of nervousness; he spoke with a quiet resonance of voice, as though he had the measure of that assembly; and he brought into play that remarkable gift of counterfeiting sincerity, which always astonished, and sometimes frightened her. It was difficult even for her to realize that he had no real opinion about the value of the big ship, one way or the other, and that he had merely crammed his subject diligently with her help during the last few days. He spoke, indeed, with telling effect. There were friends of Cynthia in the gallery who were quick to congratulate her. She herself was filled with admiration, but it was the admiration for the fine performance of an actor; and when she went down in the lift to join him after the debate was over, the cry was loud in her heart: "If only he believed one word of it!"

He met her at the gate of the lift, and she caught his arm and pressed it against her side.

"Thank you," said Harry. "That's better than words."

"It wasn't a congratulation," she replied. "It was an appeal."

Harry Rames spoke once more during that session, late at night, in a thin House, and to try himself in unprepared debate, rather than with any intention to arrest notice. But the moment was well chosen, for a speaker on the government side was needed; and when the House rose for the autumn, he took down with him to Warwickshire the reputation of a rising man. He had kept his bargain, Cynthia gratefully acknowledged it, and the fears which Isaac Benoliel had aroused in her began for a time to lose their substance.

CHAPTER XXIV

THE MAN WHO HAD WALKED IN THE ROAD

Harry Rames and Cynthia passed the autumn at the white house, and hardly a day passed but one or the other was seen in the climbing streets of Ludsey. Harry presided at the social gatherings of the city, the musical clubs, the horticultural society, and the rest. He was busy with his town clerk over a railway bill which the municipality meant to oppose. He made friends with his public opponents. Cynthia herself was hardly less active. She threw herself into the work of committees and councils, not from enthusiasm, but in a desperate search for that color which Mr. Arnall and his fellows had got from politics, and her own youth demanded for herself. And with the work, interest in it came, if color did not. They were establishing Harry Rames in his seat--that was certain, and she had her share in it. They were winning and, being a woman, she loved to win. Cynthia was a success in Ludsey--she could not but know it. For the demands for her presence and her time grew with every morning's post. There came to her a sort of exultation of battle. She was doing her work; she was helping to make the great career, and in the pleasure of helping to make, she lost sight of the essential emptiness of the thing she was making.

"Yes," said Harry one night to her. "You are making this seat safe for me, Cynthia, for the next election."

Cynthia looked at him with her eyes bright.

"Do you think so?" she asked eagerly, asking for praise, and Arthur Pynes, the young chairman of the association, who had been dining with them, corroborated her husband.

"We once had a candidate whose wife would sing at the public meetings. We couldn't stop her, and every time she sang she cost us fifty votes. We have always stipulated for a bachelor since. But you have changed our views now, Mrs. Rames."

"I am very glad," said Cynthia; and the trio fell to discussing plans for the next session. "We want to see you in office before three years are out," said Pynes to Harry Rames. "There's no reason why we shouldn't."

"Yes, there is," said Harry Rames. "A large majority. They want you to keep quiet and vote and, being strong, they would just as soon put into office men who have never opened their mouths in the House as not, and probably sooner."

"Then you must force 'em," said Arthur Pynes.

They discussed the government programme for the next session, and what opportunities would arise from it. But the changes and transitions of Parliament are rapid. However sternly the government may cling to its ordered sequence of legislation, great questions will arise which have not been foreseen, and the ballot will give to private members their opportunity of discord. Thus the man who sits next to you may be in hot debate with you to-morrow, and those who smiled at you from the treasury bench yesterday may see you stroll with a fine air of indifference into the opposition lobby to-day. Harry Rames was well aware of the pull of the undercurrents, but neither he nor Cynthia, nor Arthur Pynes had a suspicion that night that the next session was to see him in definite antagonism to Devenish, the man who had been forced to walk in the road.

It was not, indeed, until the session was more than half-way through that Cynthia herself learnt it. She had dined with her husband at the House. It was a warm night of early summer, and after dinner they took their coffee upon the terrace. A private bill was occupying the attention of a thin House, and the terrace was fairly full of members waiting for the resumption of public business. Amongst them was Mr. Devenish. He strolled up to the couple, and after shaking hands with Cynthia, turned to Harry Rames:

"I hear you are against Fanshawe's bill."

"Yes," said Harry Rames.

"It comes on next Friday," continued Devenish. "The government will accept the principle, and give the bill a second reading."

"It won't go further than that," said Harry Rames.

"Not this year. But next year we shall embody the principle in a measure of our own, and then--?" He looked inquiringly at Harry.

"Then," said Harry deliberately, "I suppose we must try to get it amended."

A beam of light pouring from one of the windows showed Devenish's face clearly to Cynthia. She saw it harden and narrow. When he spoke his voice was sharp.

"I shall be in charge," he said. "I shall not accept any amendment which strikes at the principle."

"I am sorry," said Rames. He lit his cigar. He had not the air of a man receding from his position.

Cynthia was leaning forward, her eyes travelling curiously from one to the other. She had noticed the quick snap in the voice of Devenish, the quiet indifference to it in her husband's. But she did not know on what point they disagreed. Harry Rames turned toward her and explained:

"Fanshawe is bringing in a land bill on Friday afternoon. I didn't think that the government would take it up or I would have told you about it, Cynthia, and talked it over with you."

Devenish looked quickly toward the girl. Since Rames consulted her, could he enlist her upon his side? Cynthia read the unspoken question in his face, and turned gratefully to her husband who had made it clear that she had her word in his decisions.

"Fanshawe proposes that the State should buy compulsorily so much land at intervals of so many years, split it into small holdings and lease them," Rames continued.

"And you disapprove?" said Cynthia.

"Yes. I am against the small holding. I think that's waste. I am in favor of the small farm. But I want the farm owned, not taken on lease. That's my chief objection. The State's a hard landlord."

"Is a bank a better one?" asked Devenish.

"I think so," returned Rames. "A bank's a business; the State's a machine. There's a big difference there."

"Well, I shall be interested to hear what you have to say on Friday," said Devenish, as he rose from his chair. "It would be a pity if we lost your support--a great pity." He spoke with a slow significance. The words were half a compliment, and the other half a menace. He turned at once lightly to Cynthia. "You must persuade him, Mrs. Rames, to be sensible, you really must," he said. "To create owners is a long, slow process, and I can't wait." A sudden violence flamed in his voice, and with a characteristic action he brought a clenched fist sharply down into the open palm of his other hand. He looked out across the Thames and leftward to the lights on Westminster bridge. He seemed to be assuring himself that he stood at last where he had always meant to stand, that the moment for which he had lived was surely coming. "No, I can't wait. I want to set about the land system in this country. With tenancies one can begin at once."

As he walked away from them Cynthia recalled the description of him which Harry Rames had given to her. "As a boy he had always to walk in the road, and he has not forgotten it." She began to understand the phrase now. Devenish's swift and bitter outburst had been an illumination.

He had been forced to walk in the road. Rames had shown a shrewd insight into a complex character when he coined the phrase. Devenish was the son of a small struggling tradesman, in a little town surrounded by land which was carefully preserved. Therefore he was chased out of the woods and off the grass. The game-keeper was his enemy, and an enemy always at hand. To feel the turf beneath his feet he must use stealth like a criminal. He lived in a good grass country, and all the share he had of it was the dust kicked up from the road by the wheels of carriages. In his boyhood he had brooded over his exclusion, and through the hard struggles of his youth his thoughts had been rancorous. Now, it is true, the rancor had diminished. At the age of forty-five he had reached high office, and with high office, for the first time, a regular and sufficient income. He was freed for a while, at all events, from the desperate endeavor to pay his way outside and keep his footing inside the House of Commons. He met men of diverse pursuits from the far corners of the earth. The world broadened out before him magically.

He entered late, as it were, upon his youth; the arts swept into his view, a glittering procession, and enchanted him. All was new to him as to a child. The natural charm of the man found an outlet; he had good-humor now, and a pleasant friendliness. Gradually the doors of great houses had been opened to him--and he had looked in. It was to his credit that he had only looked in. He had come away unspoilt, uncaptured. But though he recognized that for him the world had become wonderfully a place of amenities, he had not forgotten that as a boy he had been forced to walk in the road; and the dust of it was still bitter in his mouth. "For those who come after me," he had said to himself, "it shall not be so," and he was in a hurry to set about the change. To create peasant proprietors? There was a world of obstacles in the way. To create tenants of the State? A single budget would suffice. Fanshawe's scheme should be the chief item in the government programme of next year, and Captain Rames must look to himself if he stood firm to oppose it.

Captain Rames, on his side, had no intention to give way. He drove away from the House that night with Cynthia, and in the carriage he said:

"I shall put up as big a fight as I can, Cynthia, on this question."

"Against Mr. Devenish?"

"Yes."

Cynthia was silent, and Harry Rames turned to her swiftly with a question upon his lips. "You think it rash?" he was going to ask, but he never did. He saw her eyes shining at him out of the darkness, and in a low tone she said:

"You feel very strongly about it, strongly enough to risk your future. Oh, I am so glad!"

There was a throb of joy in her voice. She was still a girl. Though she professed to laugh at the enchanted garden of her dreams, there was still some yearning for it at her heart. The men with ideas had peopled it. It seemed that after all her husband, since at all costs he meant to stand up against Mr. Devenish for an idea, must be one of them. But a slight, almost an uneasy gesture, which Harry made, stopped her on the threshold of a great happiness. She lay back, chilled with disappointment.

If Harry had spoken, he would have said: "No, I don't feel strongly about it. I don't feel about it, at all. I simply recognize that it is my opportunity." And thus he would have spoken before their marriage, perhaps, too, during the first few weeks after it. But a change had inevitably come for both of them. The frankness which Rames had deliberately used, so that she might know him for what he was, no longer served. Always it had hurt Cynthia, even though she had welcomed it. More than once he had seen her flinch from it as from a blow. But now that they were so much together, a hint or silence had to take its place. Blunt honesty was all very well twice a week or so, but repeated every hour, it bruised too heavily. So, too, with Cynthia. Her business as a wife was to help, not chide. Their year of marriage had taught them the little diplomacies and managements which made life together possible for them. Frankness was to save them--so they had planned. What was saving them was reticence.

This time, however, Cynthia was told the truth by her husband's gesture. He was going to follow the old historic, dangerous road, the road of the third parties, the short cut to power which has lured so many ambitious men to disappointment, and advanced a very few before their time. And he had chosen William Devenish to tilt against, a man supple and quick in debate, sharp of tongue, with a gift of ridicule and a wealth of language; a speaker who hit with a nice discrimination just above the belt in the House, and just a little bit lower outside of it. To Cynthia it seemed that Harry must be gambling on his success; that he had cast his prudence from him like a cloak. Harry Rames answered some part of her thought.

"It's not so mad as it appears to be," he said. "In the first place the question of tenancy against ownership is an open one. You are not breaking away from your party whatever view you take. You may be breaking away from a minister, but that's a different thing."

Cynthia's fears were assuaged. In her relief she turned eagerly to Rames.

"But your minister is Mr. Devenish," she cried.

"I know," he returned. "A hard fighter. All the more gain then, if I can stand square to him, and remain standing. Besides, Devenish has a peculiar weakness."

"Yes?" cried Cynthia. "You can make use of it?" and she stopped, wondering at herself. She was startled to realize that for the first time she herself was keeping his eyes from lifting to the high path above.

"I have noticed it," Rames continued. "He can stand any amount of opposition from his opponents. If he gets heated, he remains master of his wit and tongue. But he cannot endure criticism from the benches behind him. It strikes some hidden string of arrogance in him. He loses his control. He says foolish things. He hands himself over a victim, if his critic has courage and skill enough to use his chance."

"I see," said Cynthia. "And the third point?"

"Oh," said Harry carelessly. "The question is an important one for the country. It must provoke discussion. Yes, I shall move the rejection of Fanshawe's bill if I get the chance."

He put down on the notice paper, with some twenty members on the opposition side, a motion for rejection. He rose on the Friday, immediately after Fanshawe had sat down, and was called upon by the Speaker. He was content with two objections. But either of them, if established, was fatal to the bill. He argued against the small holding, which he regarded as the pastime of the well-to-do tradesman in the neighboring town, rather than as a serious method of settling a genuine peasantry on the land; and he pleaded for the farm of sixty or seventy acres. It is a matter nowadays of ancient dispute, yet he managed to say a new thing about it, not parading his knowledge--for there were too many in that House who had made land the study of their lives--but suggesting it with a deference, which took his audience. The great farm, he maintained, was a modern product, due to quite other causes than natural development. It came from the vanity of the eighteenth century, its love of spaciousness and show. The monstrous porticoed houses and the huge farms were the symbols of its parade. But in the seventeenth century, when agriculture really prospered, the small farm of seventy acres was the rule. It was at a return to this condition that policy and legislation ought to aim.

He passed to his second argument. Tenancy under the State was bad. For the State was a hard landlord, and could be nothing else. It took no account of bad seasons or the shortness of money. It had to collect its revenues and rents within the year. Moreover, the idea was petty in its conception. (Here Mr. Devenish turned an outraged head toward the orator.) Legislation should aim at something beyond the immediate benefit it conferred. Otherwise let them commit the fortunes of the country to a parish council, and themselves go home.

"There is to my mind one question by which all legislation can be tested," said Rames, "and that question is not: 'Does it supply an immediate need?' but 'Does it help to strengthen the character of the race?'"

The bill failed according to that test. For it meant no more than the substitution of one landlord for another, and left the tenant pretty much where he was. If Mr. Fanshawe had taken a bold course and produced a just measure, with the object of creating owners, then the bill would not have failed. For the desire to possess land was the surest sign of a sound and healthy race. It was that desire in men which good legislation would try to keep alive. This bill merely fobbed them off with a miserable makeshift, and shut the door against ownership. Ownership with its obligations and its responsibility, and its response to the most primal and most durable of all ambitions, was the only policy worthy of a great Parliament.

Mr. Devenish replied later in the afternoon, and quite briefly, He did not, he said, propose to enter into the discussion, but simply to state the intention of the government. It would give the bill a second reading, accepting thus the two principles of small holdings and tenancies under the State; and next year it would introduce a measure of its own, based upon those principles, and press it through until it was placed upon the statute-book. Mr. Devenish studiously refrained from any reference to Captain Rames, and as soon as he sat down, the hands of the clock then pointing within a minute of five, Mr. Fanshawe moved the closure, and the Speaker accepted the motion. The closure was accepted without a division, and the main question was put.

In the interval, while the division bells were ringing, a slim, middle-aged man, with a moustache which was beginning to grow gray, and a handsome, ineffective face, passed into the House from the lobby, and took a seat on the bench by Rames's side.

"What are you going to do, Rames?" he asked.

"Vote as I spoke," said Harry.

"Then I'll go with you," said his companion. "I didn't hear your speech, or indeed anything of the debate. But I am sure Devenish is wrong."

Harry Rames laughed.

"That sounds like a good working rule. Thank you, Brook. Let us go and vote."

The two men, alone of their party, strolled into the opposition lobby, and that was the beginning of the great cave. It was a Friday afternoon in summer, the weather was very hot, the House very thin and Mr. Devenish and his under-secretary the only men present on the treasury bench. No one paid any attention to the revolt; the newspapers next day had the briefest reports of the debate. Cynthia herself, who had come to the House to listen to a fierce and tingling discussion, was disappointed at the gentle apathy which overlay the proceedings of that afternoon.

But Harry said: "Wait a little, Cynthia"; and Mr. Brook, who from that time began to drop in frequently at their house in Curzon Street, chuckled like a man with secret knowledge.

"Eight men on our side," Harry explained, "had met several times in one of the committee rooms before Friday, to decide what course they should take to resist this bill. I did not know of their meetings at the time, and they agreed to do nothing until they were sure of the line the government was going to take. Had they suspected that I was going to move the rejection of the bill, they would have attended and voted with me."

CHAPTER XXV

COLONEL CHALLONER'S REVOLT

"We will have to make a great stand next year, Rames," said Robert Brook. "We must organize. We have time, thank goodness. There are ten of us now. A lot more will join us."

"But will they vote? That's the point," returned Rames. "Will they vote against the government's bill on its second reading?"

"Oh, yes," Mr. Brook replied enthusiastically. "There are a lot of discontented people in our majority. We'll have voters--Challoner, for instance. Besides, you have friends."

Rames laughed.

"Yes, I know the kind of friends--fellows who come to you in your seat after you have spoken, pat you on the back, whisper that they are with you, and then troop like tame mice into the government lobby against you. I've watched them."

Brook, however, was not to be damped. He threw himself for the rest of that session into the work of organization. A halting speaker and an ineffectual personage, he had sat for twenty years in the House of Commons and was not tired of it. He was without distinction, he was the confidant of no minister, he was never caricatured, he was never the chairman of a committee, he rarely spoke. The recruits of each new Parliament took almost its duration before they assigned individuality to his features or honored him with a name. He was mediocrity's last word. But he had charming manners and won to a kind of friendly pity those whose acquaintance he gently made. He was born for private life, but the House of Commons had caught him as in a net. He had no other interests, he had no wife, he did not any longer even aspire to office. To be busy in the House of Commons--that was lifeblood to him and a renewal of youth. His chance had come now. He hurried from man to man, discreet and furtive. He arranged private meetings. He hooked his little wagon to Rames's star. He approached Colonel Challoner.

Challoner, the party hack, was instinctively outraged. Was the list of ministers closed forever? No! But as he was about to repel Robert Brook's advances, the very holder of the office which he coveted stung him into revolt.

It was quite toward the end of the session. Colonel Challoner was walking through the division lobby late at night when he saw the Under Secretary for Foreign Affairs, Mr. Charles Bradley, in front of him. There was some stir at the time because certain Indian emigrants had suffered in one of the disturbances of southern Persia. Colonel Challoner hurried officiously to Mr. Bradley's side.

"Bradley," he said, "don't you think it would be good policy to repatriate those Indians at our expense. What?"

Mr. Bradley, a florid gentleman, youthfully middle-aged, with a sweet voice, a pompous manner, and perhaps a bare sufficiency of brains, turned to the colonel with condescending kindness.

"As a member of the government," he said importantly, "I can no longer speak freely. Ah, my dear Challoner, I tell you I regret day after day that corner seat on the front bench below the gangway, and the opportunity of supplementary questions. But that happy time has gone. You might, if you like, raise the question on the adjournment or the Appropriation Bill next week. I could then reply to you."

Mr. Bradley smiled benignantly upon Colonel Challoner as from heights of sunrise, and passed on. He had grown very lordly since his elevation to office. Still, a few paces further on it seemed worth his while to stop until Challoner rejoined him. He did not notice that the colonel had grown rather red in the face.

"If you do raise the question, Colonel Challoner, could you introduce into your speech 'Civis Romanus sum'? I should like to hang my speech upon that. Thank you."

Even a party hack will turn if he be sufficiently trodden upon by minor ministers, and Colonel Challoner did now.

"Mr. Bradley," he asked with a most elaborate politeness, "have you ever calculated how many Under Secretaries of State, past and present, there are alive to-day? Or how many of them have names which are even faintly familiar to the public?"

Mr. Bradley gasped and stared. This was Challoner--old Challoner--talking! Bradley was quite unprepared to cope with so unparalleled an outrage. The colonel actually went on, and in accents of raillery:

"'Civis Romanus sum.' Now, why quote a phrase so banal. Surely, Mr. Bradley, it has had its day. We can do better than that if we put our heads together. Civis Romanus sum! God bless my soul! But I am willing to help you with a tag of Latin. I will introduce another sentence. Balbus shall build a wall--upon my word he shall--and you can hang your speech onto that, and be damned to you."

Mr. Bradley, however, had suffered enough of this unseemliness. He hurried forward and passed between the clerks who recorded the votes with a heightened color. Colonel Challoner followed him. But he waited at the door for Robert Brook to emerge, and then drew him by the arm into the outer lobby.

"I have been thinking over what you proposed, Brook," he said. "Certainly, certainly we must make a stand against Fanshawe's bill. We have a duty to our constituents. We must show the government we are not to be trifled with."

Robert Brook responded with warmth.

"I thought that upon reflection you would look upon it that way. You will be a pillar of strength to us, Challoner."

"That's very good of you," said Challoner. After all, there were some, it seemed, who knew his worth. "We must meet in the autumn--just those on whom we can depend--and arrange a plan of campaign."

"Yes," said Brook. "But where? We want, don't you think, to mask our batteries until the time comes for opening fire. We might meet at Rames's house--but it is known that he is opposed to the measure." He looked invitingly at his new ally.

"Yes, I see, I see," said Colonel Challoner a little doubtfully. There was a proposal in his mind--he was not quite sure whether he would make it. It was a bold one--it was the burning of his boats.

"Well, why not?" he suddenly said. "Why not meet at my house in Dorsetshire? I have some partridges. They will provide the excuse. Let us meet in October. Let me have the names and I'll quietly ask the men before the session ends."

Mr. Brook was delighted. He called mysteriously upon Harry Rames.

"We have got Challoner," he said. Rames shook his head.

"He'll back out."

"I don't see how he can. He is asking us all to meet at Bramling in the autumn."

Harry Rames sat back in his chair.

"How in the world did you manage that, Brook? We must go, of course."

Challoner spoke to Rames that evening. "It's to be quite an informal little party," he said with a wink, and took Rames and Brook each by the arm. Now that he had tasted the delights of revolt, Colonel Challoner, too, was a different man. He lost his dreariness. No longer he moulted; no longer he dripped melancholy on all who stood near to him. He passed ministers with a high head and an arrogant smile. "We'll show 'em," he said. "Yes, sir, we'll show 'em." And as he saw Bradley approaching him, "Here's Civis Romanus," he cried in tones loud enough to carry to the Under Secretary's ears. The Under Secretary flushed and hurried on. Colonel Challoner had told his story freely, and Civis Romanus Mr. Bradley remained for the rest of that Parliament. Colonel Challoner resumed: "We'll meet on the eighth of October. A little partridge shoot, eh? Just a few of us, jolly fellows all. You'll bring your wife, Rames, won't you? The others will."

That was a precaution which had been suggested by Brook.

"Some one is sure to let out that we are meeting at Bramling," he said. "If the men go without their wives, the gathering will have the look of a conspiracy. With them it will just be an ordinary autumn shooting party."

"Quite so," said Rames.

The House rose at eleven o'clock that night, and when Harry went home, he found his wife just returned from a dinner party. She came with him into his study and while they sat and talked he told her that she, too, was to be included in the visit to Bramling. Cynthia's face clouded.

"I would rather not go," she said. "I don't think there is any need that I should."

"The other men will bring their wives."

"There will be enough then. It won't matter if one wife doesn't go."

She was looking at Harry Rames directly, but with a great disquiet in her eyes. Harry, however, persisted.

"I think you are wanted, Cynthia. We have a difficult job to keep these men together and agree upon a line of concerted action. Some women could be very useful at a juncture like this. You are one of them."

Cynthia rose with a quick movement to her feet. She stood before him, her broad forehead troubled, her lips mutinous, and by her attitude she made all the more plain his need of her. The room was Rames's own study which had been lined with mahogany, and against the bright dark panelling, in her white dress, she gleamed slim and fair and beautiful as silver. Harry Rames looked her over with a smile. She was, as he put it to himself, exquisitely turned out. She had the grace and delicacy natural to a family nursed in good manners through a century, and with all her beauty she had simplicity and a desire to please.

"Yes, I want you, Cynthia," he said, and the blood rushed hot to her face and throat. She turned from him swiftly and went out of the open window onto a balcony which overhung their tiny square of garden. Rames's eyes followed her curiously. Something had gone wrong; that was clear. He could see her leaning over the rail in the darkness, her face between her hands.

Rames's survey of her had brought back to her recollection that distant morning by the wheat-field in South America when her father had looked her over horribly from head to foot and had valued her for a market. There had been just a touch of appraisement in her husband's look now. Almost she traced a resemblance in the two men's thoughts, the two men's examinations.

Harry left her to herself for a few minutes. Then he followed her:

"I think I understand, Cynthia," he said gently. "Of course it isn't a very high and lofty business we're engaged on. That's right enough. And when you consider the sort of people our party's going to be composed of--the dissatisfied, the ambitious, the timid, and just a few who believe Fanshawe's bill a bad thing--the manœuvre doesn't look very pretty. So if you don't want to go, don't."

But Cynthia had changed her mind.

"No. I'll come, Harry," she said. "It's too late to be half-hearted now. I'll certainly come."

She turned back into the room, and picking up her gloves from a table went upstairs. Harry Rames had no doubt that he had hit upon the reason of her disinclination to go to Bramling. But as Cynthia ran up the stairs she kept saying to herself nervously like one who would frighten fear away with words:

"Perhaps no one will notice it. Very likely no one will notice it. And if they do, they will think it an accident."

She had not been considering at all the worthiness of these autumn manœuvres. She had been thinking of a picture by Romney which hung in the dining-room of Bramling, a picture which she had never seen, but which yet she knew to be a portrait of herself. She had, however, promised to help in the making of the great career and this was one of its critical moments. It was, as she had said to Harry, too late to be half-hearted. If she failed him now, she failed him altogether. She must take the risk that others would notice the resemblance--and amongst the others, perhaps even her grandfather Colonel Challoner himself. To one determination, however, she clung. She would admit no kinship with the Challoners. Nothing should persuade her, neither the old man's loneliness nor his disappointed hopes. She held the name and the family in horror, though the name and the family were her own.

CHAPTER XXVI

THE PICTURE AT BRAMLING

Bramling is the very house for a conspiracy. It lies in Dorsetshire, hidden away at the back of the grass-walled town of Wareham on the road to no where. A stream runs past its door down to Poole Harbor, and its windows look across grass meadows to where the sea-cliffs lift against the sky. Hither through one October day came in old-fashioned flies and private motor-cars the inhabitants of the Cave--Cynthia amongst the last of them with a foot which hesitated to cross the threshold. There were thirty in all assembled in the drawing-room when the dinner-gong sounded, eighteen men and twelve women. Colonel Challoner, to Cynthia's satisfaction, had to give his arm to Lady Lorme, the wife of an ex-Under Secretary of the home office who had quarreled with his chief and resigned. She herself was taken in by Robert Brook. Reluctance and curiosity struggled for mastery within her as she entered the dining-room, and took her seat. She would not look up at the walls, yet she could hardly but look up, and she sought furtively around the dinner-table whether any noticed the picture and her resemblance to it. But no one was looking at any picture at all. Not a remark was made or a glance thrown to show her where it hung. She looked more boldly at her companions, and coming to a greater ease began with enjoyment to laugh at herself. Not one person at the table was devoting a thought to her at all. They were all very busy, drinking their soup and talking rapidly like uncomfortable people who fear that if once their speech flags they will never find anything more to say. They were in truth an uncongenial company, held together by a single link, their eagerness to harass their own government. Even Robert Brook, who knew Cynthia well, was talking to her with incoherence in his agitation lest the gathering at Bramling should fail. She heard Sir Faraday Lorme, a big red-faced man of sixty with a bull-neck, say across the table to Charles Payne, one of the eight who genuinely thought Fanshawe's bill a bad experiment:

"Of course, as a rule, you know I don't act with you, but--" and the rest of the sentence was lost to her ears, but it seemed to her that fully half of those present might have said as much to their neighbors. Further along the table she caught sight of Mr. Andrew Fallon, a dark white-faced man who had only joined them because his wife had been signally and publicly snubbed by the wife of a Cabinet Minister. Cynthia could see the wife on the opposite side of the table, a portly over-dressed woman with an overbearing voice; and on behalf of all her sex she felt grateful to the Cabinet Minister's wife.

A singularly gentle voice drew her attention. She turned away from Robert Brook, to find at her other side Mr. Howard Fall.

"We have spoken in the lobby, Mrs. Rames," said Howard Fall timidly. "Captain Rames was kind enough to introduce me."

"Yes, indeed," said Cynthia. "Oh, I am glad that you are here."

To her Howard Fall was, with the exception of her husband, the most interesting man in the room. She welcomed his presence whole-heartedly. He was intellect, he was modesty. Even now at her implied compliment he was blushing like a young girl and his eyes shone with dog-like gratitude. Howard Fall was then about fifty years of age; and though he was but a contemporary of Harry Rames in the House of Commons, he had already acquired there a special place of high distinction. Of too acute and logical a mind to be a good party-man, he harried with a pleasant voice and most destructive criticism, now his own party, now his opponents. He had one great quality in common with Cynthia, he was quite without affectation. He would make a brilliant speech with extraordinary diffidence. But he made it, and a genuine word of praise or thanks delighted him, as a schoolboy is delighted with a sovereign. With the mild manners of a curate he combined the courage of a soldier. If he had ideas to express--and he generally had--no thought of prudence could hinder him from expressing them. Indeed, he drew a gentle contentment from the knowledge that as a rule they were troublesome to those whom he nominally supported. Cynthia had heard him more than once from the ladies' gallery, and had admired his honesty and his courage. For the moment she was enheartened by his presence. It put confidence into her. With him to help, Harry might indeed put up a fight against Mr. Devenish.

"I didn't know," said Howard Fall, "that Captain Rames was going to speak against Fanshawe's bill. Otherwise, of course, I should have been in the House to support him;" and the "of course" struck all Cynthia's comfort from her. It was so significant of the man. He was born predestined always to revolt. Any party of two had him for a third. Cynthia glanced disconsolately to where her husband sat at the end of the table. But he showed no sign of misgiving. He was talking energetically to the four people nearest to him, and he only paused when her eyes rested upon his face. She turned away again and there above the head of Colonel Challoner, who was sitting exactly opposite to her, she saw at last the portrait glowing upon the wall.

For the moment she had forgotten it. Now it caught away her breath. She sat and stared at it. It was the portrait of a girl of seventeen, dressed in white from the big straw hat with its flapping brim to the shoes upon her feet. There was but one touch of color, a broad shining ribbon of bright blue looped about the crown of the hat, and thus dressed, the girl stood in a field of sunlight and corn, looking straight out from the picture, with a great curiosity and eagerness in her dark-blue eyes. She seemed to be looking upon the gates of a world of wonder--gates which with a most tantalizing tardiness were slowly opening to let her through.

Was she herself indeed like that? The question rushed into Cynthia's mind. As pretty as that? It was impossible. Yet she had been recognized because of it. Just so then she must have looked that morning when, after sending her neglected telegram to Captain Rames, she had stood at the edge of the wheat on the Daventry estancia. Yet nobody recognized her now. She had the features of the girl in the portrait, the broad forehead, the straight, delicate nose, the fair hair, the big dark-blue eyes. Yet nobody recognized her. Perhaps, however, she had gone off. She was getting old. A gentle melancholy descended upon Cynthia. The fear lest her likeness to the girl in the picture should be remarked had quite gone since she had seen the picture. She was now rather hurt and indignant that no one had noticed it.

Lady Lorme gave the signal a little while afterward, and the ladies rose and left the men to their cigars and their discussion. Colonel Challoner opened the proceedings with a pompous, unnecessary little speech. He welcomed his guests, and he reminded them at considerable length of the object of the gathering. He concluded with a question as to whether any honorable member present had any views as to the best procedure to be adopted.

"Yes," said Harry Rames, "if I may make a suggestion. There are eighteen of us here. I propose that we now go carefully through the list of members and consider how many more we can get to join us, upon whom we can count. I have Vacher's list here;" and he drew out from his pocket the familiar little paper-covered book with the names and addresses of the members.

"I think that's the first thing to be done," a man agreed from the other end of the table. He was a Mr. Edgington, a little, square, bald man with short side-whiskers, who seemed a cross between an attorney and a stable-boy. He was one of the many men in the House who have a subject. He had mastered the Housing question; he really knew the facts, he had the figures at his fingers' ends, and he had counted upon his knowledge to take him straight through the doors of the Local Government Board. But the doors had remained closed, and he had turned gadfly in consequence--a gadfly that trumpeted but had no sting. "To be sure about the men who will stand out against the pressure of the Whips, who will not be frightened into line by their local associations, who retain, in a word, some self-respect and some veneration for the independence of the House of Commons--that is our first requisite," he said floridly.

The company then went carefully through the list and marked off twenty fresh names as the names of men who might be inclined to join the revolt. It was arranged that discreet letters should be written to them on the following day, and Robert Brook was appointed secretary by an unanimous vote.

"Of course we shan't get them all," said Lorme.

"And of those we do get, some will shirk when the division bell rings," added Howard Fall.

"No doubt," said Rames. "But if we can carry thirty men into the opposition lobby on the second reading, we shall have made a demonstration which will go far to kill the bill. It will mean sixty on a division. It will leave the government with a comfortable majority. We all want that of course,"--a chorus of approval, more or less sincere, greeted the remark--"But it will also mean that the government will hardly be able to force the bill through its committee stages by a drastic use of the closure."

"Exactly," said a tall, bearded man with a strong Scotch accent, who up to this moment had held his tongue. He represented a northern town of Scotland, and was one of the eight who were opposed to the measure first and last because they believed it harmful to the country. "Exactly. The demonstration is very well, but if the bill is to be killed, we will have to kill it in committee. And to prepare for that must be our chief work here, Colonel Challoner."

"Yes," said Rames. "Mr. Monro is right. We must go word by word through those clauses of Fanshawe's bill, which we are fairly certain Devenish will incorporate in his measure. We must formulate amendments, and we ought, I think, to agree, to some extent, upon the speakers to move them. It will, of course, have to be a provisional arrangement--" and he was interrupted by a strident voice which belonged to a sandy-haired hunting-man with a broad red face who would have seemed totally out of place in any conspiracy.

"Yes. Devenish may sell us a pup. He's a deuce of a clever fellow is Devenish. Let him get wind of your partridges, Challoner, and he'll sell us a pup for a sure thing."

"All the more reason we should keep our gathering quiet," said Challoner. He looked round the table with an impatience which had been growing upon him during the last half-hour. "I think that's all we can do to-night."

"About all," said Monro. "There is just this suggestion I would like to make. I know a man whose business is land, and he is most experienced in it; and I thought that if you would like, I would send him a telegram to-morrow, and we could employ him to help us in framing these amendments. He is a partner in Beevis and Beevis, the land-agents in Piccadilly."

"By all means, do," said Challoner. "We all agree to that, don't we? And now let us join the ladies."

He sprang up and opened the door like a man in a great hurry. When he entered the drawing-room, he crossed it at once to Cynthia's side.

"I was sorry, Mrs. Rames, that I couldn't take you in to dinner to-night. I would have liked very much that on your first evening at Bramling you should have come in with me. For, as you know, I somehow associate you with this house."

He looked at her with a very direct inquiry in his eyes. But Cynthia would not respond to it; and he sat at her side with a wistfulness in his voice and his words against which she had a little trouble to protect her heart. But she did, for she was alarmed. When she had met him before he had spoken rather as though he wished that they were related. To-night he spoke as if he suspected that they were.

Mr. Beevis arrived the next afternoon, and for the rest of the week, while the morning was given to the partridges and the amusements of the country, the afternoon and the evening found the Cave busy upon the bill. Amendments were formulated and shared out amongst them, whilst it was by general consent left to Rames to raise the question, first of all, on the Address at the beginning of the session and then to move the rejection of the bill later on when it came before the House upon its second reading. Good progress, in a word, was made, and, to the delight of all, no whisper of this conspiracy crept into any of the daily papers. They were examined anxiously every day upon their arrival at eleven, and laid down with relief. Cynthia could not but laugh.

"I never would have believed that you could have found so many members of Parliament reluctant to see their names in the papers," she said to her husband.

"Yes, it's astonishing what modesty they can develop," he replied.

But though Cynthia laughed, the work, the concealments, the sort of restrained excitement which was diffused through the house, began to have their effect upon her. She was getting color into her life at last, she assured herself, even if it was only a dingy color. Moreover, she had the opportunity to compare her husband with his rivals in the career. Indeed, he had but one real rival in that House, Howard Fall. And though he lacked the subtlety of his intellect, he had a swifter initiative, a more telling vigor of phrase. As for the rest he stood head and shoulders above them all, and they knew it and looked to him to lead them. If he did not share the strong convictions of the honest men, he overtopped them by sheer ability, and as to the others he knew nothing either of their malice or their fear. Thus they all came hopefully to the last day of their visit; and then at one o'clock in the day the thunderbolt fell.

It was a Sunday and the whole party had just settled down to luncheon when the whir of a motor-car floated into the room. It was followed by the sound of a door opening and shutting, a pleasant and familiar voice was heard to inquire for Colonel Challoner, and the next moment, ushered in by the butler, Mr. Devenish entered the room. Consternation ran round that luncheon table like a wind across a field of corn. Colonel Challoner sprang up hastily with every sign of discomfort.

"My dear Devenish, I am delighted to see you, I am sure. You are just in time for luncheon." He called to the butler to lay another place at his side. "I didn't know you were in the neighborhood. You should have let me know."

"I didn't mean to do that," said Devenish dryly. He ran his eye from face to face with a twinkling glance. Cynthia herself could hardly restrain a laugh. The independent members of the nation's Parliament looked so singularly like a set of school-boys' caught by a master in the planning of a rebellion.

"Quite a large party, eh, Challoner?" he said with a smile.

"Yes, yes," replied the colonel. "The partridges, you know."

"Ah, the partridges, to be sure. But I didn't know that Howard Fall shot at anything but ministers. And even they only get winged, eh, Fall?"

Mr. Devenish strolled round the table and shook hands with Fall. Fall, however, was one of the few who was quite undisturbed.

"Yes, but I am looking to practice to improve my shooting," he said.

A place was now laid for Devenish. Colonel Challoner called to him.

"Will you come and sit here, Devenish?"

"Certainly," replied the smiling minister. "But I should first of all like to shake hands with all my friends;" and quite slowly he walked round the table and shook hands with each of the men present and those of the ladies whom he knew. He was in the best of tempers, and he had a cordial word for every one except for Captain Ramos. To him he merely said:

"Ah!" and the accent of his voice had in it no note of surprise. It was the ejaculation of a man establishing something which he had suspected. Then he walked to his place and sat down.

"There are eighteen members of Parliament, Challoner," he said pleasantly. "I hope that I have forgotten no one. Let me see!" Again his eye ranged round the table, obviously registering in his memory the identity of

Challoner's guests. "No, eighteen members of Parliament. Have you got a partridge left?"

Rames leaned forward and met smile with smile.

"We have just left one for next year," he said, "and we have been making a careful note of the piece of land on which we think we shall get him."

Howard Fall was delighted. For he loved courage. But the others of that company were more than ever confused and disconcerted.

"He's giving us away," said one of the weak-kneed in an indignant whisper to Andrew Fallon. Fallon's white face was twisted in a grin.

"He's cutting down the bridge behind you, my friend. And I don't think he's a bad judge."

Meanwhile Devenish returned the direct gaze of Captain Rames. There was no pretence between these two. Their eyes met; they challenged each other, Rames with perfect good-humor, Devenish with a certain grimness in his smile. He nodded his head toward Rames and tightened his lips. There was not a man at that table who could not construe the gesture into words.

"You are the leader here, Rames. Very well, we'll see."

Mr. Devenish turned to his neighbor. It was Cynthia, and even to her he talked for a little while with reserve. Rames had been correct in his diagnosis of the man. A good-humored fighter as a rule, he lost his good-humor when the attack was made upon his flank. He had begun his own political career with side-shots at his leaders from the front-bench below the gangway; but he did not rejoice when the same disposition of battle was planned against himself. However, luncheon and the proximity of a beautiful woman appeased him as they should. He began to talk freely; his smile lost its grimness, his natural geniality flashed bright.

"Tell me one thing," he said suddenly.

"It depends--" said Cynthia warily.

"Very well then. Tell me another thing. Why does your portrait hang in this house?"

Cynthia's cheeks flamed. She looked swiftly across Devenish at Colonel Challoner. But he was giving no heed to them.

"Do you think it's like me?" she asked.

"It *is* you," he replied.

"No one else has noticed the resemblance all this week," said Cynthia.

Mr. Devenish glanced along the table.

"Well, look at 'em," he said contemptuously, and they both laughed. Lady Lorme rose at that moment from the table, and Mr. Devenish, pleading the distance he had to travel, took his departure.

"I have enjoyed myself very much, Challoner," he said as the colonel came out with him to-the doorway. "I can't tell you how glad I am that I thought of dropping in upon you for luncheon. I am going back to London now. Good-by."

He mounted into his car and drove gaily off. In the dining-room behind him, the sandy-haired man was saying over and over again to the dismayed conspirators--

"He'll sell us a pup. He'll sell us a pup. I'll bet you a monkey, he'll sell us a pup."

That night, when the men went upstairs, Rames passing from his dressing-room into his wife's bedroom found her still up and sitting by her fire.

"We go back to-morrow, Cynthia. It has been a long week. I hope you haven't been bored."

"No," she said. "I haven't."

"What do you think of them? Will they run away when the fight comes?"

"Not all," said Cynthia. "But even of those who stay with you, there's not one who is a match for Mr. Devenish."

She spoke with some warmth in her voice.

"You like him?" said Harry Rames.

"I think he's a big man," she replied.

Rames, who was standing looking into her mirror, suddenly swung round.

"Shall I tell you why you say that, Cynthia?"

"Yes."

"Because he's the only man except myself who has noticed your likeness to that very pretty girl on the wall of the dining-room. I heard him mention it to you at luncheon."

He burst out into a laugh as he spoke; and in a moment or two Cynthia joined in the laugh. So Harry Rames too had noticed the resemblance. She laughed and her eyes laughed with her lips.

"After all," said Harry Rames, "we get some fun out of it, don't we, Cynthia?"

"Yes," said Cynthia and her laughter died away. "We get some fun out of it, Harry. That's just what we do get"; and her eyes turned away from him to the fire.

CHAPTER XXVII

DEVENISH REPLIES

Captain Rames had arranged to travel by a train which ran directly into Warwickshire through the outskirts of London. It left Wareham at mid-day, some two hours later than the fast London trains, and though Cynthia had wished to escape in all the hurry of the general departure, she had found no sufficient reason. She and her husband were thus the last of that company at Bramling, and when all but they had gone, Colonel Challoner turned from the front door whence he had been speeding his guests, and invited her to walk with him in the garden. Cynthia in a flurry began to search for excuses, and before she found one realized that the moment for excuses had already gone. She turned and walked with Colonel Challoner into the red-walled garden where his fruit and flowers grew. The half-hour which ever since the first evening at Bramling she had intended to avoid was, after all, upon her.

"There is not very much to see now, Mrs. Rames," said the colonel, and without any change of voice he added, "I learnt just before the session ended that you had come from South America."

"From the Argentine," said Cynthia.

"But you are English-born, of course?"

"Oh, yes, of course," said Cynthia. "But I never came to England until five years ago. I was brought up partly in Buenos Ayres and partly on the Daventry estancia two hundred miles to the south-west of Buenos Ayres. My name was Cynthia Daventry."

Cynthia rattled off her story to spare herself his questions, and for a few minutes he walked by her side in silence. But he was not altogether to be deterred.

"I had a son in South America," he continued. "He went out under--rather unhappy circumstances. He took a young wife with him. She ran away to join him. They went to Chile. There a daughter was born--my granddaughter."

"On the other side of the Andes," said Cynthia.

"Yes," said Colonel Challoner. "You were never in Chile, I suppose?"

Cynthia answered without any hesitation and in a voice schooled perfectly to indifference.

"Oh, yes, once. I have seen Valparaiso."

Colonel Challoner was deceived by her indifference. To him, with the particular intention of his question filling his mind, it was as though she had said she had never been in Valparaiso at all.

"I knew nothing of what my boy was doing, Mrs. Rames," he continued, "nor that he had a daughter. He left England under a cloud. I gave him what money I could afford and--I had done with him. Perhaps I was harsh--I did not think that I was. But--well, it's not so easy to have done with people when they are your own flesh and blood, and after a time I began to make inquiries. I heard of the daughter then."

"Yes?" said Cynthia. She looked up into his face inquiringly. She had dreaded this half-hour of acting lest the changes of color in her face, and the unevenness of her voice, should betray her. Yet now that the half-hour was here she played her part with ease.

"I heard that Jim and his wife and his child had all perished in one of the earthquakes, eighteen years ago. And there was I, you see, alone again, but alone for life now."

"I am sorry," said Cynthia.

"But the news was wrong," the old man continued with a sudden violence. "My son--died," and he plainly substituted that verb for another, "only five years ago. I received a cutting from a newspaper. I sent out again at once to South America a man whom I could trust; and I discovered that Jim was not killed by the earthquake, nor was his daughter. He carried her up the valley toward the Andes--tramped away, since Valparaiso was ruined, with his daughter in his arms. He wouldn't leave her behind. No, he must have carried her across the Continent. There was good in Jim, after all, you see--only I, his father hadn't the sense to see it."

Colonel Challoner was not aware that it was just the weight of the little daughter in Jim's arms which had made his journey across the Andes possible and profitable. Cynthia left him all the comfort of his delusion, and all its remorse, since the remorse was so completely outweighed by the comfort.

"That's the last I have been able to find out," Colonel Challoner resumed. "They disappeared up into the mountains together, and years after Jim--died--in the Argentine. As for the daughter, I have come upon no trace of her. She may have lived. She may have died. Had she lived she would have been just about your age, Mrs. Rames."

"Indeed?"

"I suppose that you never heard of her?"

"What was her name?"

"Even that I can't tell you. There was a daughter. That's all I know."

Colonel Challoner waited with his eyes upon Cynthia's face. He longed, yet he hardly dared to hope for an answer. It would be such a wonderful thing for him if the girl facing him in his trim brick-walled garden had when a child eighteen years ago been carried in Jim's arms over the stupendous passes of the Andes. Surely if it were so, she must admit it now out of gratitude for Jim's devotion. But Cynthia made no reply and he moved slowly to the door of the garden and held it open for her to pass out. She went from Bramling with her secret still her own, though some remorse was now her penalty for keeping it. She could not quite get rid of the picture of the old man at the open door in the high red-brick wall waiting wistfully for an answer to a question which he could only suggest. But she had made her plan and with a certain stubbornness--almost a hardness which marked this phase of her life--she had abided by it. If Colonel Challoner had said clearly and formally that he made no claim upon her, that he did not ask her to take her place in the family of Challoners, then she would have acknowledged what he plainly suspected. But he had imposed upon himself no such condition. On the contrary she had been led to believe that he would claim her; and that was intolerable to her thoughts. She did not argue or reason; she recollected. And what she recollected was a night of horror when her father had claimed her for the ruin of her body and her soul. When she stepped into the train she made a silent vow that she would never come to Bramling again.

"It's a strange thing," said Harry Rames as they were travelling across the country, "that two strangers to Bramling, Devenish and myself, noticed your extraordinary likeness to that picture on the wall, and Challoner who has sat beneath it most nights of the week for years didn't. It had become so familiar to him, I suppose, that it had ceased to have definite features."

"That's how things happen," said Cynthia, and this time she uttered the phrase with relief. "When you know people very well, you cease to notice the changes, you lose count of how they look. But when we first met at Ludsey he did claim to recognize me, though he could not fix upon the place or time. I have no doubt it was because of that picture."

Harry Rames agreed. None of Colonel Challoner's suspicions had even occurred to him. He drifted off to the great subject.

"Devenish won't be idle, Cynthia," he said.

"No," answered Cynthia. "He gives me the impression that even on his death-bed he would be quick about it."

And on the Tuesday morning, the very day after they had reached home, the *Times* brought Harry Rames news which sent him out of his study in search of his wife.

"Look, Cynthia," he said and he handed to her the paper. Cynthia read the paragraph at which he pointed.

"Mr. Devenish returned to London on Sunday evening and putting off two deputations which had been arranged for Tuesday left London hurriedly on Monday afternoon to join the Prime-Minister in Scotland."

Cynthia laid down the paper with a genuine sense of consternation. She was astonished to realize how much she now longed for the success of Harry's rather dingy plot. Fear was written upon her face.

"That means--?" she said.

"That we must look out," replied Rames. He laughed a little as a man will when the joy of battle is upon him. "Lucky Devenish can't get at my constituency. I don't know that he would try to in any case. But he can't."

"You have Arthur Pynes with you."

"Yes. And I pledged myself before I was elected to resign at once if any responsible number of my supporters objected to any action I thought it my duty to take in the House. Do you see, Cynthia?" and he laughed again. "That pledge is my safeguard. I thought it would be when I made it. If any one tries to put pressure upon me, I can always point to that pledge. I can always ask whether they would like me to resign."

"Suppose they said yes," cried Cynthia in alarm.

Harry Rames grinned.

"I'd get in again if they did. I'd keep nine-tenths of my own people and get a good lot of the other fellow's because of my independence. But they won't! No one wants a by-election at Ludsey. Ludsey is too busy."

"I suppose that's true," said Cynthia with a smile of relief. Once more she had occasion to recognize the accuracy of her husband's foresight. But there was a little change. The recognition was no longer accompanied with regret that the foresight was not being used in a higher cause. She was simply relieved that on this side at all events the great career was not open to attack.

Rames took a turn across the room and stopped at the window.

"But I wonder what his next move will be," he said.

In a month he knew. The movement was swift and dramatic. Rames was summoned to London by a letter from the Prime-Minister. He travelled up from Ludsey in the morning; he reached home again in time for dinner.

"They are raising Lamson to the peerage," he said to Cynthia. "That means the Under Secretaryship of the Local Government Board will be vacant. It was offered to me."

Cynthia was radiant.

"That's splendid," she cried.

"I refused it," said Harry Rames.

Cynthia stared at him. Here was a definite step onward, a step refused.

"Why?" she asked in her perplexity.

"It would have meant the end of me, had I accepted it. It was offered to me to make an end of me, to break up the opposition to Devenish's bill, to show me a traitor to my friends, and an enemy who could be silenced by a bribe. If I had taken it, not merely the government, but the House, the whole House, would have despised me. I should have been done for. I should be an Under Secretary for a year, two years, three years--after that nothing and never anything so long as I lived. I refused it, Cynthia;" and he bent over the table toward her.

"You mustn't blame me. I am not failing you. I was thinking of you, my dear, when I refused office. An Under Secretaryship? You remember Challoner's question to Bradley? I should have failed you had I taken it."

Cynthia was almost conscious of disappointment. She liked definite things and here was a tangible sign of Harry Rames's advancement. But she received confirmation very soon that he had been right in refusing it.

It was at the reception at the Foreign Office in January which marked the beginning of the session. Mr. Devenish himself came up to her with a smile. For a moment Cynthia felt an awkwardness at meeting him, but he was quick to put her at her ease.

"Captain Rames did well to refuse office," he said. "I congratulate you, for I suppose that you had some share in the decision."

"No," she replied honestly. "To tell you the truth I was a trifle disappointed."

Mr. Devenish shook his head.

"His whole reputation was at stake. It's character which counts in the House of Commons. If he had taken that Under Secretaryship, he would have been pigeon-holed. We should have had the measure of him. We should not have troubled our heads about him again. For once, Mrs. Rames, you were wrong; he was right."

Cynthia looked at him, her great eyes full of a gentle reproach.

"Wasn't it a little unkind of you to offer it then. You are a friend of mine, aren't you, Mr. Devenish?"

There was no anger in her voice, only a wondering melancholy, a kind of piteous despair that she was living in so graceless a world. Mr. Devenish stared, then he smiled, and he looked at Cynthia with enjoyment.

"It wants a woman to use that argument, Mrs. Rames. No man alive would have the nerve. You are out for a fight with me. Yes, but I am a friend of yours, so I mustn't defend myself." He shook his head. "The House of Commons isn't a nursery, Mrs. Rames. You have got to stand by yourself if you're going to stand, neither being kind nor expecting kindness. Captain Rames stands--and he stands to fight me. Very well--but you can't expect me to prop him up."

"I quite understand," said Cynthia in her iciest manner. "I am not at all hurt or offended. You mustn't think that, Mr. Devenish," she bowed to him distantly and sailed off with great dignity. But she had humor enough to appreciate her discomfiture, and, even as she turned her back, her lips were twitching into a smile which she did not mean him to see. But ten minutes later in another of the rooms she came face to face with him again. He looked at her whimsically, and with a blush and a laugh she made friends with him again.

"Tell me," he said. "Your husband refused the post with decision after the merest pause for thought, though the offer surprised him. I know that. Was he troubled about his decision afterward?"

"Not at all," said Cynthia. "He slept perfectly; he ate his dinner with absolute contentment."

"Now I am afraid of him," said Mr. Devenish gravely, and he added a shrewd saying to explain his fear. "Here's the great difference which makes art and politics incompatible. The men who succeed in politics are the men who don't worry. The men who succeed in art are the men who do. Yes, I am afraid of him now, and if I hit hard, Mrs. Rames, bear me no grudge. I shall hit hard because I must."

Cynthia's heart warmed to him. She laughed joyously.

"I'll bear no grudge, Mr. Devenish."

"By the way, why isn't he here to-night? He ought to be."

"He was here," Cynthia replied. "But a telephone message was brought to him. Some one had called at our house who was urgent to see him. So he went home."

Mr. Devenish saw Cynthia into her carriage and she drove back to Curzon Street. The visitor was still with Harry Rames in his study when she reached home. As she went up to her room she heard his voice through the door, and once she waked up from her sleep and in the small hours she again heard his voice. He was in the hall taking his leave of Harry Rames. Cynthia switched on the light and looked at her watch. It was three o'clock in the morning. Drowsily she asked herself who this visitor could be, but she was asleep again almost before the question was formulated in her mind.

CHAPTER XXVIII

WIRELESS

Harry Rames, however, told her who it was the next morning as they sat at breakfast. He had come down late and Cynthia looked at him with anxious eyes.

"You were kept late in your study?" she said, thinking of the critical week which lay in front of him.

"Yes."

Harry Rames laid down his Sunday newspaper.

"Walter Hemming was here."

"Hemming?"

To Cynthia the name was quite unfamiliar. There had been no Walter Hemming at Bramling.

"He was one of my officers on the *Perhaps*. He has got together some money, has bought the old ship and is off to the South."

"He takes up your work?"

"Yes. I never saw a man so enthusiastic. Suppose he reaches the Pole, what then?" Harry Rames laughed contemptuously.

"Aren't there discoveries to be made, maps to be drawn of that continent and something to be learned from the soundings?" asked Cynthia, recollecting Harry Rames's own book upon his voyage. He shook his head.

"That's all trimmings, Cynthia. You have got to surround your expedition with a scientific halo. It gets you money, and official support, and the countenance of the learned societies. But the man who goes south into the Antarctic goes with just one reason--to reach the Pole. Why? You can't give a rational answer to that Cynthia. No one can. Such men are just driven on by a torment of their souls."

No stranger watching Harry Rames as he speculated with an indulgent smile upon the aimlessness of Walter Hemming's long itinerary could have imagined that he had once himself led just such an expedition. Even Cynthia found the fact difficult of belief. By so complete a dissociation of spirit he was cut off from the race of the wanderers.

"Let a man become insane in the East," he continued, "and he's looked upon as a holy man, touched by the finger of God. The fellows who go South and

North are our holy men of the West." He turned back again to his newspaper, and then uttered an exclamation:

"They have offered that Under Secretaryship to Edgington!"

"Of course he'll refuse it," said Cynthia.

"He has taken it. There's the first defection."

"A traitor. I never liked him. He was thinking of himself all the while," said Cynthia, with a heat which made Harry look toward her curiously. She had not been wont to side so heartily with him and his plans in the days of the contest at Ludsey. He became suddenly aware of the remarkable change which had come over her character since that date. She who had blamed him with all the enthusiasm of a romantic girl because he would not take the high road, now walked the low road herself with her eyes concentrated, even more closely than his, upon the pathway at her feet. A pang of remorse made him wince.

"I shouldn't wonder," he answered drily, "if Devenish says the same of me."

But his comment fell upon inattentive ears. Cynthia's eyes had been caught by the blank, cheerless look of the street outside. It was a morning of black frost. There was no fog, but there was no glint of sunlight, either. London lay unburnished, like an ill-kept yacht, and the emptiness of Sunday made it dreary beyond all words. The chill of that day and the fevers of the week to come caused Cynthia's heart to sink. A vision rose before her eyes with unexpected vividness of another place where life ran occupied with smoother matters. Not in Warwickshire, but over far seas. She thought with a sudden poignancy of longing of the Daventry estancia where to-day the golden leagues of corn would be rippling to the sun and the cattle searching for the rare blades of green in the burnt pastures. Remorse came to her as it had come to her husband. So seldom had she thought of that spacious and wide place which had lain so close to her adopted father's heart. He had prayed her to go thither from time to time. Greatly she wished that she were there now.

"It's a pity Mr. Hemming stayed so late," she said.

"Oh, that's all right," replied Harry. "My amendment can't come on before Wednesday. It may not be chosen at all. And there's always the possibility that the Land Bill may not be mentioned in the King's speech. However, that's not likely. We shall know to-morrow."

The Land Bill was mentioned as one of the principal measures of the session, and Harry handed in at the clerk's table his humble prayer to His Majesty that no solution of the land question would be found lasting or real which did not provide opportunities for the acquisition of small farms as freehold properties. Thursday was set aside for the discussion of Rames's amendment, and the fact that it was deemed of sufficient importance to take precedence of a host of other amendments was in itself regarded as a triumph by his adherents.

"Go your own way over it," Robert Brook advised in an agitated voice. "Don't sink your personality in a conventional speech. You must strike a special note on Thursday. The third bench below the gangway and the corner seat. That will be the best place for you. You command the House from there. And we'll be all together around you. It's a great thing to have some voices to cheer you at your elbow. Howard Fall will speak in support of you. He always gets called." Robert Brook ceased from his stage-managements to whisper with a lengthened face, "By the way, have you heard?"

"What?" asked Harry.

"That Challoner's weakening. Yes, it's true. The whips have been getting at him, I expect. At all events he came to me pleading that the amendment need not be pressed to a division if we get anything like a friendly reply."

Harry Rames smiled.

"We shan't get that. I'll take care not to get it. So you can agree with Challoner. We can't afford to let any one break away now. I'll speak to him myself."

The colonel strenuously disavowed any faintness of heart. "You must go to a division, Rames, unless you get a satisfactory reply. That's understood. We've got to stick to our guns. I think we all know that. Edgington's example isn't one any of us would care to follow. No. All my idea was that perhaps the government might be willing to take our view, but unable at this moment to say so publicly. However, don't you worry about us. Think of your speech, Rames. We look to you to do something unusual on Thursday."

Harry went away to his study and from his documents and blue books labored to hammer out some spark of his own which should set fire to the Thames or to that portion of it at all events which flows under Westminster Bridge. He woke at five o'clock on the Thursday morning, and lying in bed repeated his speech word by word to himself. Then he dismissed it into the chamber of his memory to wait until it was needed. But the knowledge that the day was to be one of supreme importance to his career hung over him all that forenoon. The labor was over and therefore the strain upon him was the heavier. His nerves had free play and he wandered restlessly from room to room, calm outwardly except for some spasmodic movements which people unacquainted with him would never have remarked, but inwardly a creature in torment. He had pitted himself against his own government. The enormity of his presumption grew with every lagging hour. Failure to-day would cover him with ridicule. He saw himself as one of those bubbles ripe for pricking with which the House of Commons is perpetually iridescent. Before twelve o'clock he was already looking at his watch lest he should be too late to fix before prayers the card in the slot at the back of his seat which would reserve his place for him during the day.

Cynthia, with a covert fear, watched his fever, but said never a word, either of comfort or inquiry. It was her part to notice nothing of his agitation. She had claimed, when he had asked her to marry him, her share in the troubles and the terrors which went before the public success. But married life had taught her that much of her share must come to her by guesswork, by intuition, by observation, by any means except those of question and answer. So she said little and left Harry Rames mostly to himself, only coming upon him now and again on some indifferent errand, when they would speak for a moment or two, he chiefly at random and upon any chance subject which came uppermost in his mind. Thus once he said abruptly:

"There was a stamp struck. Did you ever see it, Cynthia?"

"No," she answered; "you must show it to me."

"I will; I have a specimen somewhere. I'll look it out."

"Do," said Cynthia in a voice which conveyed that it would be a particular joy to her to see that stamp.

But she was quite in the dark about it. She had no notion at all that he was speaking of that great territory which he had discovered far to the south, beyond the ice-floes, beyond the open blue water. It had no inhabitants but the penguins; yet since Rames had spent a winter of darkness on its inhospitable shores and had annexed it for Great Britain, a penny stamp had been struck and postage duly established. The recollection passed in and out of Harry Rames's head, with a hundred trivial thoughts and memories. And it was the mark and consequence of his agitation that his mind acquired an extraordinary and unnatural lucidity so that his thoughts became swift visions of things with a small but surprisingly clear definition, as though he saw them through a diminishing glass.

In this supersensitive spirit he walked down Parliament Street at half-past one in the afternoon on the eastern side of the road; and when he had come opposite to the Horse-Guards, he suddenly stopped. Behind the Horse-Guards' Arch and a little to the north rose the great red building of the Admiralty where Cynthia and he had been made acquainted with one another. But it was not of the first meeting nor of the quarrel which ended it that Harry Rames was thinking. He was not looking at the main mass of the Admiralty Building, but only at the three grayish-blue domes which surmounted it. From these domes rose three tall spars at the points of a triangle, each of them rigged and dressed with wires to which were attached curious little hoops and contrivances of cane like Catherine wheels set for a night of fireworks. He was gazing at the mechanism of wireless telegraphy.

He had passed those poles either just here or on the other side of the Horse-Guards' Parade in St. James's Park on every day when Parliament was in session; and no doubt he had often enough lifted his head and seen them with the blind eyes of a man for the landmarks he habitually walks by. But this morning his imagination was made acute by a night of wakefulness and the tension of his nerves, and he was sensitive to all the suggestion of that aerial toyshop of contrivances. He stopped. He almost fancied that he heard--so keen was the lucidity of his senses--the messages of distant ships, here tumbling on seas of storm there upright on seas of sunshine, whizzing homeward to the dim smoke-wreathed city, crowding the air. He almost fancied that he saw them, the myriad bright spokes of an illimitable wheel which hung poised roof-high over all the world. His thoughts were swept quite away from England, and the roar of Whitehall died from his ears. He saw the big roadsteads of the East and West Indies and anchored vessels mirrored in waveless seas. He saw the meetings of ships in the narrows of the great trade-routes, barkentine and schooner, tramp and liner, and in and out amongst them like the gray shadows of sharks seen beneath the water, the long cruisers of the fleet.

He walked on like a man in a dream. He left the busy harbors and the great trade-routes behind him. The stately procession of vessels receded and now he saw only one--a little, full-rigged, black-hulled ship quite alone on a silent sea, the *Perhaps*, reeling down with all her canvas drawing, from her sky-sail to her spanker, reeling down with the water breaking from her broad stern bows into the mists of the south. The picture was so vivid in his mind that he could see the brightness of the binnacle and the wheel spinning in the helmsman's hands. He paused again to consider why, and paused with a curious sense of comfort. Once before, on the occasion of his maiden speech, the vision of a ship had risen before his eyes. But then it was fear which had evoked the picture. He had longed to be safely upon its bridge doing the thing he knew how to do. Now he had no such fear. He was nervous, but he had no desire to run away, he had no terror that the necessary words would fail him, he had no longing to stand upon the deck of the *Perhaps*. He was strung up for the contest of the afternoon. He walked slowly on and turned in at the gate of Palace Yard, and still the *Perhaps* fled southward before his eyes.

CHAPTER XXIX

IN THE LADIES' GALLERY

An hour later Cynthia drove down to the House of Commons, anxious and yet expectant of triumph. For on this afternoon Harry Rames should particularly excel; the occasion was so confederate with his gifts. In debate he was as yet too inexperienced to shine with any brilliancy. His success had been made with prepared speeches. He had not as yet the art to handle words with such precision that he could express vividly in an argument across the floor just what he meant, and no more and no less. He was not at ease with his vocabulary when a sudden call was made upon it, and his lack of ease became manifest and spread, as it always does, discomfort. He was in a word on the way to becoming a polished debater but as yet he was at school. This afternoon, however, he had not to reply, not to intervene in the middle of a discussion; his business was to make the set speech which set the debate going. And here he was on his own good ground. He could prepare the vivid phrase and, a quality perhaps still more important, he could speak it. He had an invaluable gift which had stood him in good stead when he had delivered his maiden speech. He was able so to deliver a carefully concocted speech as to give the impression that he was thinking aloud. He gained his effect by an apt breaking off of sentences and a recommencement, by a sudden drop to the homeliest of colloquialisms, by a seeming deliberation in the choice of his words, so that the picturesque and living sentence, which had been so carefully thought out, appeared to leap new-minted from a furnace of conviction. He had been shrewd enough to recognize with his own unflattering estimation of his powers that an amendment to the address provided him especially with a rare opportunity.

When Cynthia reached the ladies' gallery she had some trouble to find a place whence she could command the House. The gallery was full, since it was the beginning of the session. For the same reason the House itself was not. Even though questions were being asked of the ministers, a time when the House is seldom less than crowded, there were to-day vacant spaces on the benches. The real business of Parliament would not begin until the debate on the Address was concluded. Members still lingered in the country or the south of France. Rames's amendment was considered rather as a dress-parade than an engagement. It was not expected that he would press his views to a division. At the last moment suave words from a Cabinet Minister would no doubt dissuade the recalcitrant as they had done a thousand times before.

But his supporters were there clustered close below the gangway on the three back benches; Howard Fall two seats away from Harry Rames, chirruping gently and rubbing his hands together with delight; beyond him the sandy-haired man from the Shires with an eye on Devenish upon the treasury bench, and prepared at any moment for the production of that threatened pup which the Minister for Agriculture was sure to sell them; beyond him again Colonel Challoner and the timid spirits all trying to look unconscious and most of them pretending that they only occupied these particular seats by the merest accident. But they were in full view. Robert Brook had seen to that. They were labelled plainly and legibly, and if some of them shirked at the last moment, they would still get the credit of having shared in the revolt. In front of all were the earnest men who believed the policy of Devenish to be dangerous. Behind all under the shadow of the gallery were the young bloods, all as convinced as their graver seniors in the front, but still youths spoiling for a row and totally unawed by the frockcoats of the treasury bench. Their business was to cheer and to ejaculate, not to speak. Thus had Robert Brook disposed his forces for the battle. He himself sat between Harry Rames and Howard Fall, and, looking about him, was proud of the array.

Before questions had come to an end Cynthia had squeezed herself into a place on the first row of seats behind the stone grille. She had now from her aerie the whole group within her view, or rather, the tops of all its particular heads. She waited impatiently. Every now and then a sudden fluttering like the waving of little flags ran with a crackle of sound along the benches below and showed that another page of the question paper had been turned. Questions must now be coming to an end surely, she thought in her ignorance. Her mistake was colossal. The Speaker had only this moment come to the questions of the Irish members, and there was a postmaster in Ballymena who had last week committed the hideous crime of refusing a registered letter at two minutes to eight by the church-clock. Upon this important matter, by question and supplementary question, the Imperial Parliament was forced to concentrate its attention till the hands of the clock above the door pointed to a quarter to four. Then the Speaker rose, a buzz of talk mounted to Cynthia's ears, a few members called upon by name came forward from behind the Speaker's chair to the clerk's table with private bills, others drifted out into the lobby and the tea-room and the smoking-rooms. Then once more the Speaker rose. His canopied chair was just beneath Cynthia. She could not see him but she heard his voice quite clearly.

"Captain Rames."

Rames rose amidst vociferous applause from his own group and some cheers from the opposition. The personal question flashed into Cynthia's mind.

"Will he look up toward the gallery in which I am sitting?"

He threw his head back. It seemed that he did look up. Cynthia leaned forward as though across that distance her eyes could answer and sustain him. She forgot that the only light in the gallery was fixed against the wall behind her, and that nothing more individual of her was visible upon the floor of the chamber than the wide sphere of her hat.

He was not so nervous, she realized at once, as he usually was. Nervousness gave to his voice a peculiar vibration which was not without its effect in arresting attention. Cynthia missed it now. But the sentences which she already knew by heart followed one behind the other spaced and regular as the waves of a calm sea. She forgot that little significant omission of manner. She followed the argument as she knew it, and it was developed step by step as it had been prepared. Harry Rames had spoken for five minutes when a lady on Cynthia's left whispered in an audible voice to her neighbor on the right:

"I thought you told me that Captain Rames was a brilliant speaker."

"Not I, dear," came the reply. "These men of action are seldom effective in their speeches. I shouldn't expect him to do better than he is doing."

Cynthia moved indignantly. The poor woman must be off her head. But if she did not know what good speaking was, she might at all events hold her tongue. She looked down again into the well of the House and became perplexed. The benches were actually emptying. The double doors opposite to her which led from the chamber to the lobby were swinging silently backward and forward with a perpetual motion as the members passed out, and the space just in front of those doors where members may stand and where she had seen them stand packed on other days while Harry spoke, was almost empty. There were just one or two standing there, but they were obtaining orders for the galleries from the sergeant-at-arms. Then the voice at her elbow spoke again in an accent of resignation.

"He is very, very dull."

Cynthia clenched her hands. She would have dearly liked to have boxed her neighbor's ears. Was he dull she asked? And the dreadful continuous buzz of voices, which always rises when a speaker has lost the attention of the House, rose from the benches below to answer her. With a sob only half suppressed Cynthia was forced to admit the truth. The incredible thing was happening. Harry Rames at the crisis of his fortunes was signally failing.

"If he fails it's partly my fault," she thought. "I helped in the preparation of the speech."

For it was word for word the prepared speech which he was delivering, the very phrases chosen for their simplicity and their force were uttered in their due place. Yet the effect was dreary beyond measure. Even the ardent spirits beneath the gallery had ceased to applaud; they sat back in the shadow, all their enthusiasm quenched. A still worse sign, Mr. Devenish had laid his writing pad and his fountain-pen on the table in front of him; he took no more notes, he leaned back with his arms folded and his eyes closed, a typical picture of a Cabinet Minister, a man inured to patience and the bed-fellow of boredom.

"Why is Harry failing?" Cynthia asked of herself despairingly. And the answer came from her neighbor.

"You know, my dear, I don't believe that what he's saying is nonsense if one only had the necessary concentration to follow it. But his delivery's so bad that he makes attention impossible."

Again Cynthia was constrained to admit the criticism. The chosen sentences were uttered, but no conviction winged them. Harry's gifts of speech were that afternoon quite hidden. He was as one delivering a recitation which by constant repetition had become at once meaningless and automatic. His voice trailed away into lassitude. There was no spirit behind any word.

The buzz of conversation increased, a protesting voice called "Order, order," and then Harry faltered and stopped, stopped quite noticeably. A general cheer rose to encourage him--for the House of Commons can be generous, especially to those who are dropping out of the race--and twisting his hands together suddenly, almost with the air of a man waking from a dream, Harry Rames staggered on again. Cynthia's heart went out to him in a rush of pity. What he must be suffering! He had staked so much upon this afternoon. So much had been expected of him. Cynthia's thoughts went back to the week at Bramling. With what high hopes that company had counted upon his leadership!

"If he would only finish!" she prayed. She looked upon him as a man in torment. She leaned her elbows on the rail in front of her, closed her ears with her thumbs and shut her eyes. She took at once with the exaggeration of her years the blackest view.

"He has attacked his own government and frightened no one. His career will be affected, perhaps ruined. A really bad mistake may take a man years to overcome in the House of Commons. Who was it said that? Mr. Smale. This is a really bad mistake. The debate itself may collapse. That would mean ruin."

So she reasoned until in a clap the truth of the mistake came upon her, its cause, its meaning.

"I ought to have foreseen his failure," she murmured. "It was bound to come. Sooner or later it was bound to come. For his heart is never in the theme but always in the career."

She might indeed have looked upon it as a retribution, a just retribution.

"And a year ago I should so have looked upon it," she reflected, and sat back in her seat amazed at the change which two years had wrought in her. The magnitude of it was now for the first time revealed to her. Success following success, each in its anticipated sequence, had sealed up from her the knowledge of herself. It had needed the failure to reveal it.

She leaned back in a confusion of her emotions. She heard no longer any word of the debate. For a little while the House of Commons vanished and was not. She glanced swiftly backward across the months of her married life and detected one by one the indications of the change. Gradually she had ceased to clamor for ideas, she had come to look only at the man and she had desired him to tower above his fellows, because that was his desire. And the reason for the change? She jumped to it with her heart on fire. She loved him.

But while she thus began to make her account with herself a perfunctory cheer and the Speaker's distinct pronouncement of another name broke in upon her reckoning. The voice of her neighbor brought her back to earth.

"Mr. Howard Fall. I hear he's quite a favorite speaker."

The turn of the words recalled irrelevantly to Cynthia Harry's indignant story of the elector who had told him that he was well patronized in Ludsey. The recollection brought a smile to her face. But the smile faded as her anxieties came home to her. Would the debate collapse?

Howard Fall was already upon his legs seconding the amendment; and in a little while she saw members enter through the doors, stand for a moment at the bar and then as though here was matter worthy of their attention, slip into places upon the seats. Cynthia's first feeling was one of relief. Yes, the House was undoubtedly filling up. Then, as a burst of laughter followed upon one of Fall's sallies against Devenish, a sharp pang of jealousy pierced her. The lady at her elbow incensed her by a laugh of approval--a ridiculous snigger Cynthia termed it.

"Yes, now *he's* really brilliant," she said, and Cynthia had to hold herself in, so impelled was she to explain to the lady exactly what she thought of her judgment and her manners and her family and of everything which appertained to her. But she did not. She remained outwardly calm, though inwardly she seethed.

"Mrs. Rames," a quiet voice called to her from behind. She turned and saw Robert Brook. She left her seat and went to him.

"What's the matter?" she asked anxiously, her heart leaping with a fear of calamity.

"Nothing," Brook reassured her. "Your husband asked me to look after you. He can't well leave the House." Another burst of laughter intermingled with applause rose up to them. Devenish had petulantly interrupted Howard Fall, and interruptions Howard Fall thrived upon. "Isn't he in splendid form?" cried Brook with enthusiasm.

"No doubt," said Cynthia, eyeing him coldly.

Brook looked at her quickly.

"Perhaps you would like some tea Mrs. Rames. Shall we go? The debate will tail off for a bit after Fall has finished."

He led the way to the lift. Cynthia hurried after him.

"Why?" she cried. "And what do you mean by tailing off?" There was an impatience in her voice with which Brook was unfamiliar. "Do you mean that the debate will collapse?"

"Oh, no," he replied. "But the big-wigs won't speak until later. The subject is much too important to drop for want of argument. Indeed, there are enough men eager to speak to carry the debate well over to-morrow, if that were possible."

They came out from the lift and walked down the long corridor toward the lobby between the rows of books protected by their frames of gilt wire. Robert Brook continued cheerfully:

"Rames, to be sure, wasn't at his best in opening the debate. But no man is always at his best. There's not a soul in the House who doesn't know that."

"Then this afternoon won't put him back?"

"Why should it? It was he who had the shrewdness to recognize the opportunity which this question affords, and to select this particular line of attack. He engineered the whole movement. That's known. And if he carries his own people into the division lobby with him, and the opposition into the bargain, he will have established a fine reputation for Parliamentary capacity. That counts, Mrs. Rames, take the word-of an old hand. That counts here more than speech-making."

"Does it?" cried Cynthia, smiles breaking through the tragic gloom of her countenance. But the smiles vanished. She shook her head wistfully. "You are merely saying this because you see that I am troubled."

"But it's none the less true. This House has a corporate life which is rather difficult for those who are not members of it to understand."

Robert Brook certainly seemed very well contented. Cynthia, however, was not satisfied.

"But will he carry his people with him into the division lobby--now?" she asked. "Won't they a little have lost faith?"

"Not a bit. You see Howard Fall has quite saved the situation," Brook replied cheerily, and Cynthia suddenly stepped on ahead. The name of Howard Fall was beginning to exasperate her. She stopped, however, as they came into the round hall of the lobby.

"On the whole," she said, with the loftiest impartiality, "I liked my husband's speech a good deal better than I did Mr. Howard Fall's. Perhaps on a second thought you will too, Mr. Brook."

She surveyed him steadily with a pair of cold blue eyes, and then her face suddenly dimpled to a smile of appeal.

"You really mean that I can't see him?"

"The man who starts a discussion must hear it out. That's a sound old rule, and if it's not so religiously kept as it used to be, the House of Commons is the worse."

"I can send him a little note at all events."

"Certainly. Write it and I'll give it to a messenger."

"A messenger!" said Cynthia doubtfully. "Will it be sure to reach him? It's rather important."

Brook smiled.

"Very well. I'll take it in myself, Mrs. Rames."

Cynthia took a little diary from the bag she carried, tore out a leaf, scribbled hastily:

"You did splendidly. Everybody thinks so. Cynthia;" and having calmly perpetrated that obvious untruth, she twisted up her message and handed it to Brook. The sandy-haired man from the Shires was drifting about the lobby. Brook called to him. "Look after Mrs. Rames for a moment, will you?" he said, and hurried off through the swing-doors.

It seemed a very short time to Cynthia before he came back, though in that short time she had not so much as addressed a word to her companion. She looked at Robert Brook's hands. They were empty and a shadow passed over her face.

"Did you give it him?" she asked.

"I passed it along the bench and saw that it reached him. I didn't wait for him to open it."

The shadow passed from Cynthia. She was disappointed now, but not hurt; and in a second the disappointment passed too. This was not the day on which small things should be allowed to sting.

"Now you'll have some tea," said Brook.

"No, I don't think I will stay any longer to-day, Mr. Brook," she replied. Now that her fears were dispersed she was in a hurry to get away and be alone with her new secret. "I am keeping you from the House, and you are our Whip, aren't you?"

The flattery did not compensate Mr. Brook for his loss. The privilege of parading a pretty and well-dressed woman before the envious eyes of less fortunate colleagues is one which no member of Parliament, not even its sedatest representative of non-conformity, would forego without regret; and in a remote philandering way, Robert Brook was a kind of lady's man. Cynthia was wearing a trim coat and skirt of dark velvet, and from a coil of fur about her throat her face rose like a summer flower, and was framed in the wide border of her blue hat.

"My duties are light just now," he protested, but Cynthia lifted up her hands in her great muff appealingly and coaxed him.

"You will let me go now, Mr. Brook, won't you?" Her eyes besought his permission as though without it she could not go, and Mr. Brook was duly reduced to subservience.

"Good-by," said Cynthia, and she swung off, the long ends of her stole swinging about her hips, and her step indescribably light. Robert Brook watched her pass down the corridor to the rails where the visitors waited, and sighed in a melancholy fashion. It seemed to him for the moment contemptible to be a bachelor. For there was something strangely appealing about Cynthia, to-day--a winsomeness, a warmth. She seemed all a-quiver with youth. A swift variety of moods swept across her face in lights and shadows, and gave to her vitality. Her feet moved with a dancing buoyancy. All that Robert Brook felt the sandy-haired man from the Shires summarized in one reflective sentence:

"I should like to kiss that girl," he said. "It would do me a great deal of good."

CHAPTER XXX

THE LETTER

Cynthia ran down the broad flight of steps into Westminster Hall, and skimmed across the historic flags of the ancient building without a pause. What at this moment was Charles the First to her, or even Mr. Gladstone? She came out into Palace Yard and drove home through the dusk just as the lamps in the shop-windows were beginning to bring some gleams of cheerfulness into the black February streets. She sat back in the corner of her car with her muff tightly held against her breast as though to cherish close some knowledge treasured there. When she reached her house she let herself in with her key and walked with secret steps into Harry's study. Once there she locked the door and with the firelight dancing upon the walls to keep her company, she sat down to make her reckoning with herself. But in truth the reckoning was already made.

The great bargain, on her side at all events, was a bargain no more, could never again be a bargain. A veritable revolution had taken place in her that afternoon. She knew it from the depth of her sympathy with Harry in his failure--above all from the surprising sharpness of her disappointment when Robert Brook had returned with no answer to her scribbled message.

For the failure as a factor in their fortunes she cared not a straw. Indeed, she welcomed it, since it was that which had wakened her. She had believed herself to be defective in the quality of passion, and her sense of the defect had hurt her like a bitter humiliation; she had envied wistfully the other women who possessed passion, even the wantons who flaunted it. Now the humiliation was gone. She rejoiced. She leaned back in her chair with her eyes closed and sailed over magical seas which were joyous and golden. She loved. She was like some lady of old Italy lit to swift flame by the first kiss from her lover's lips. Only it was a trivial irony in closer keeping with our modern days that what had kindled her who had demanded ideas, was a failure due to nothing but the lack of them.

Cynthia rejoiced; for she loved. That pain and disappointment were in store for her she did not doubt. But she ran forward to meet the pain. She was young. Sooner all the pain in the world than the placidity of years without fire or inspiration. She recognized frankly that though upon her side the bargain was no longer any bargain at all, it still was just a bargain to her husband. A sign had been given to her that afternoon, a little sign, yet great in its significance. She had pleaded to herself as she sat in the ladies' gallery that when Harry rose, and just before he began to speak, he had looked up to where she sat, as though he were conscious of her presence, as though he drew strength from it. But he had not looked up. Even at the time she had known that he had not.

"I merely pretended to myself that he had," she frankly admitted now. "His movement was nothing more than the natural muscular action of a man bracing himself for an effort." She herself, Cynthia, had not been, she felt sure, at that moment, in the remotest of his thoughts.

"If Harry had changed toward me as I have toward him," she argued, "he would have looked up, not only because he wanted to, but because he would have remembered what I had said to him on that very point the afternoon when he asked me to marry him."

But in spite of her conviction she rejoiced. Some kinship she could claim with Juliet. For all her longing was to give and to give, and still to give. She had sought desperately for color in her life. She had welcomed politics in the hunt for it. She had it now and to spare--enough to daub the world. The handle of the door was tried and through the panels her astonished maid told her the hour. Cynthia sprang up and unlocked it.

"I shall dine at home to-night," she said. "The cook must get me some dinner, anything."

The maid reminded Cynthia that she had arranged to dine with some friends and visit a theatre. "I know," said Cynthia. She had made the plan so that she might not spend in loneliness the anxious hours of this evening. But since she had made the plan the world had changed its hues.

"You must telephone and say that I can't come," said Cynthia, remorselessly, as she ran upstairs.

Whilst she dressed she considered what she should do with this wonderful evening. She meant to spend it alone--yes, but that did not quite content her. Somehow it should be made memorable. Something she must do which, but for this day of days, she never would have done. Something which must not merely mark it as a harbor boom marks a turn of the channel, but must be the definite consequence of it. Cynthia, in a word, went down to her solitary dinner much more akin than she had ever been since to the girl who, eager for life with the glorious eagerness of youth, had run down the stairs on the morning of her seventeenth birthday into the dining-room of the Daventry estancia. Half-way through dinner the thing to do, in order fitly to commemorate the day, came to her in a burst of light.

She went back to Harry's study and sitting at his writing-table, composed with great care a letter of many pages. The hours passed as she wrote and rewrote, and glancing at the clock before the end was reached, she saw that it was already past eleven. Then she hurried. The division at this moment was being taken. Within the hour Harry would have returned; and indeed she had only just folded her letter in its envelope when his step sounded in the hall.

She heard the door open and shut. He was in the room. But she kept her head bowed over her letter lest her face should betray her over much. Nor for a moment did she speak, since she did not quite trust her voice. It was Harry who spoke first.

"You have come back? I did not expect you so soon."

"I never went. I stayed at home."

"Oh! You are not ill, Cynthia?"

"No. But I felt that I had been rather hard and cruel----"

"You?"

"Oh, yes, I can be." Cynthia was stamping down her envelope with an elaboration of care which almost suggested that it was never meant to be opened. "I was in this case. So I stayed at home and wrote a letter to make amends. I should very much like it to be posted to-night, Harry. The servants have all gone to bed. I wonder if you----"

"Of course. You are afraid that you might change your mind about it in the morning."

"Not at all," replied Cynthia with a laugh. Harry Rames walked over to the table.

"Give it to me, Cynthia," he said; and at last Cynthia raised her head and rather shyly her eyes sought his face. At his first glance she stood up quickly and she did not give him her letter. Harry Rames was standing, his face white and drawn and harassed. He had been answering her vaguely, as though the words came from him by reflex action rather than through a comprehension of what she said. For a moment Cynthia was afraid to speak. The beating of her heart was painful. Then she laid her hand upon his arm.

"Something has happened, Harry?" she faltered.

"Something terrible," he replied, and walking to the fire he warmed his hands at the blaze like one smitten with a chill.

"The debate collapsed? Your people didn't follow you into the lobby? Oh, Harry!"

She went to his side.

"No. That's not the trouble. We did better in the division than I had anticipated. Of course we had the labor party solid against us. But that we had reckoned on. On the other hand, some of the Irish members came along with us, and it had been expected that they would all abstain. No, we ran the government majority down to thirty-one. Devenish is shaken, I can tell you. He passed me after the division was over, without a word and white with passion. No, Cynthia, we did very well." He moved away from the fire and sat down in the chair at his writing-table. "I took all my people into the Division Lobby with me--except one."

Cynthia put out a hand and steadied herself against the mantel-piece.

"Except one?" She turned toward him, her face troubled, her eyes most wistful. "One failed you--one alone. Oh, Harry, it wasn't Colonel Challoner?"

But though she asked the question, she did not need the answer. Her foreboding made her sure of it.

"It was," replied Harry, and Cynthia turned again to the fire. A little sob, half-checked, burst from her. Then she tore the letter which she had been at such great pains to write, across and again across, and dropped the fragments into the fire.

"The Challoners are no good," she said, in a voice curiously distinct and hard.

"Don't say that, Cynthia," Harry Rames answered gently.

"I do say it. I ought to know."

The words were uttered, and only then she realized what she had said. She looked quickly toward her husband, but he gave to her cry no particular significance. His brain seemed to register her words, not to comprehend them. Cynthia was conscious of a great relief. Loud at her heart rose a hope, a prayer that in all things, all qualities, even to tricks of manner, she was her mother's child, and had nothing of her father. Never would she acknowledge her relationship with that family. Never would she admit her name. Her first resolve and instinct had been right. The Challoners were no good.

"No, I should not say that, Cynthia," Raines repeated. "He's dead."

Cynthia turned swiftly upon the word. Her dress rustled as she turned, and when that sound ceased there was absolute silence in the room. Cynthia stood by the mantel-shelf still as stone. Her face was white, and a look of awe overspread it. With her lips parted and her eyes troubled and wondering she watched her husband. Harry Rames sat with a large silver paper-knife in his hands, looking absently straight in front of him. And in a little while he broke the silence by absently tapping with the blade of the paper-knife upon his blotting-pad. The sound roused Cynthia. She moved to a low chair close to the writing-table.

"Dead? Harry, I don't quite understand."

The tapping ceased.

"His heart was wrong. He died in the Division Lobby--actually while the division was being taken."

"In the Division Lobby? But you said you didn't take him with you."

"I didn't. He was in the Government Lobby."

Cynthia's face contracted with pain. A low moan burst from her. "He was actually voting against you!"

"Yes."

Harry added reluctantly:

"Our revolt killed him." Cynthia sat down in the chair.

"Tell me everything, will you, Harry?" she entreated, and thus the story was told her.

"The Whips got at Challoner. You know Hamlin, don't you? But you don't know his methods, Cynthia. He doesn't bully you if you revolt. He doesn't threaten. He takes you affectionately by the arm and makes you feel a beast. His round brown eyes survey you with a gentle and wistful regret. You leave him, convinced that he personally will be dreadfully hurt if you vote against the government. You are glad to be rid of him as you are glad to be rid of a man whom you have injured; and within the hour he is at your elbow again, pursuing the same insidious, amicable strategy. That's how he worked on Challoner, and Challoner was not the man either to withstand him, or to tell us boldly that he was going to--"--"rat" was on the tip of his tongue, but Rames caught the word back and substituted "change his mind." "So, do you see, he stayed with us to the last minute. It was arranged that the division should be taken at eleven. As soon as the Speaker rose to put the question, Challoner, who had been standing at the bar of the House slipped out through the lobby and down the stairs to a little smoking-room on the opposite side of the passage to the big strangers' smoking-room. That room is very often quite deserted. Few people, indeed, use it at any time. In a corner of that room he sat behind a newspaper all of the ten minutes during which the division bells were ringing."

"To avoid meeting any of you?" asked Cynthia.

"Yes, I suppose so."

"But how do you know he was there?"

"He was seen by one or two of the Irish members who did not intend to vote at all. They went into the room while the bells were ringing and saw him."

"I understand."

"As soon as the bells stopped, as soon, in a word, as he was quite certain that we should be all in our lobby, he started up quickly. There is just a little time between the moment when the bells cease ringing and the moment when the lobby doors are locked. But it is only a little time. If you want to vote you have to hurry. Challoner was a good distance away, and he had a flight of stairs to ascend. He hurried, he ran; I expect, too, that he was agitated. His courage had failed him. He must prove his loyalty to his official leaders at all costs. He reached the lobby in plenty of time. Monro, you remember him, the Scotchman? He was at Bramling."

"Yes," said Cynthia.

"He saw Challoner. He was standing by the entrance door of our lobby. We were in the 'No' Lobby, for the question we had to vote upon was that the original words of the Address 'stand part,' and to enter the 'Aye' Lobby a man must pass our entrance door and traverse the House. Monro saw Challoner hurry past the door, and thinking that he had mistaken our lobby and was under the impression that the question he had to vote upon was that the amendment be substituted--in which case, of course, we should all have been in the 'Aye' Lobby--he called to the Colonel. Challoner didn't hear, or wouldn't hear. He hurried on, and once inside the Government Lobby, collapsed onto the bench which runs along the sides. He died within a couple of minutes."

Harry Rames ceased. The shock of this swift calamity had driven from Cynthia's thoughts all her indignation against the Challoners. She pictured to herself that old, unhappy, disappointed man, dropping at last between the shafts, the pack-horse of politics. Not even the insignificance of an Under Secretaryship had come to requite him for his tedious years of service. And it never could have fallen to him. That she recognized. Again the silence was broken by the tap-tap of the paper-knife upon the blotting-pad.

"It's a Juggernaut, that House, isn't it? You said that once, Cynthia," said Rames.

"I did? I don't remember."

Cynthia was perplexed by his distress. Sensibility was not to be counted amongst his qualities. Yet he sat there with trouble heavy upon him, and every now and then a shiver of the shoulders, a shiver of repugnance.

"This has shocked you terribly, Harry," she said.

"Yes. I have known death before now, but never death without any dignity. That's what I find terrible." He paused for a moment and then said in a low and distinct voice:

"I am to blame for it, Cynthia."

"You?" she exclaimed.

"Yes. I ought to have left him alone. I ought never to have taken advantage of his disappointments. I dragged him into the revolt to serve myself--yes, that's the truth, Cynthia. We both know it. I dragged him in without giving him and his character a thought. He was the real party hack. To him the men upon the treasury bench were as gods walking the earth. A nod from one of them in a passage, a hand-shake in a drawing-room, a little private conversation with a Cabinet Minister in the Division Lobby--that was the kind of food which sustained him through how many years! And he was a good cavalry officer once, I am told." Harry Rames suddenly swung round toward his wife. "That's strange, isn't it? Very strange. He must have come into the House of Commons twenty years ago a very different man. But I suppose the walls closed round him and crushed the vitality out of him. You had a phrase about such men--the prisoners of the House of Commons. He was one of them. I did a cruel thing when I enlisted him. For I might have known that he must desert. I am to blame for his death."

"No," Cynthia protested.

"Yes."

"Even if you might have known that he must desert, you couldn't have foreseen that he would hide from you till the last moment."

"That's just what he would do."

"Even so, you didn't know, Harry, that he had heart disease."

"Would it have made any difference to me if I had?" And that question silenced Cynthia.

Harry Rames fell again to tapping with his paper-knife upon the blotting-pad. He tapped aimlessly, the silver handle flashing in the light, the ivory blade striking and resounding. But gradually an intention seemed to become audible in his tapping. The taps came quickly, three or four together, then were spaced, then streamed swiftly again like sparks from an anvil. The noise began to jar on Cynthia's nerves.

"Don't do that, Harry, please," she said.

"I won't," said he, throwing down the paper-knife.

"You might have been sending a telegram."

"By wireless, eh?" he said with a smile, and then a curious look came into his face. "I was," he said slowly. Cynthia drew back in her chair with a queer feeling of uneasiness.

"Not to--?" she began, and stopped short of the name. She glanced furtively around the room. She was suddenly chilled.

"To Challoner? No," he answered. He had hardly been aware of what he was doing, and he wondered now why the idea to do it had thus irrelevantly entered his head. No doubt an instinctive desire to get relief from the obsession of the sordid tragedy of Challoner's death had prompted him. But, whatever the cause, he had been tapping out, in accordance with the Morse code, a message to the little, black, full-rigged ship far away upon Southern seas.

He sprang up from his chair.

"There's a letter you wanted me to post, Cynthia. I had forgotten it. Give it to me."

"It dropped into the fire," said Cynthia.

Harry looked into the fire; a torn fragment or two had fallen into the grate.

"I dropped it into the fire," said Cynthia. "For I had already changed my mind about it."

The long letter which she had torn up at the first news of Colonel Challoner's defection, the letter which was to commemorate that evening, had been written to Colonel Challoner, and admitted that she was the daughter of his son.

CHAPTER XXXI

M. POIZAT AGAIN

"There is a man at the door, madam. He says that he is a Ludsey man, and that he worked for Captain Rames during the election."

It was midday. Cynthia had her hat on and was at the moment buttoning her gloves.

"Tell him that Captain Rames is at the House of Commons now, and that he will be back at home by five," she said.

"The man asked for you," said the footman.

"For me? Did he give a name?"

"No. But he said that you would know him."

Cynthia shrugged her shoulders.

"Very well, Howard. Show him in."

Visitors who would not give their names but claimed to be citizens of Ludsey were not infrequent while Parliament was in session. They usually came with the same request--the loan of their fare home, where they had relations to look after them; and they were usually impostors, who had not so much as seen the spire of St. Anne's Church. But, on the other hand, there was always a possibility that the case might be genuine, and Cynthia made it a rule to see them. She had already got her purse out of her bag when the door was opened. But she dropped it when she saw her visitor.

"M. Poizat," she cried, and she held out her hand to him.

M. Poizat, however, did not take it.

"You have been kept waiting. You should have sent in your name."

M. Poizat shook his head.

"Would you have received me if I had, Mrs. Rames?"

"Of course."

"You are very kind."

Cynthia looked at him with a closer scrutiny. Certainly the M. Poizat who confronted her was the merest shadow of the sprightly inventor of Lungatine. The elasticity had gone from his wonderful legs. No longer he danced when he walked. His arms hung loose at his side, and the potency of his elixir had quite failed him. He was now a really old, small man. Indeed, he seemed to have diminished in stature and to have shrivelled in breadth; and his eyes were red, as though he had lately wept. Thus much had been taken from him. Yet something had been added, the dignity of a man whom calamity has overtaken.

"Why am I very kind to receive you?" Cynthia asked gently.

M. Poizat stared at her incredulously.

"Then you do not know what has happened to me?"

"No! Sit down and tell me."

But M. Poizat remained standing.

"I have no longer a friend in the world. I have no longer a house. I have no longer a wife. All is gone."

"I don't understand."

"Ah, I know. Ladies do not read their newspapers very carefully. If the men, too, were like you! But all the same you will have heard of a case which a few days ago was making a great stir in Paris--the Jobert case."

"Of course."

"But you have not followed it in detail."

"No."

The intricacies of that gigantic case of fraud were indeed difficult to follow even for those who gave to it their attention. Nor did Poizat do more than give to Cynthia a necessary outline. Monsieur and Madame Jobert, the latter being the protagonist of the conspiracy, had borrowed over a course of years immense sums of money on the strength of securities which were supposed to exist in a sealed safe. The case could not be opened since a fictitious action by claimants, whom Madame Jobert had invented, was perpetually being deferred in the courts of law. At the last, however, the creditors of the Joberts had obtained authority to break the seals, and a safe which was absolutely empty was exposed. The Joberts alleged a theft, but they were arrested and prosecuted.

"You see, Mrs. Rames, the one hope of the Joberts upon their trial was to establish the existence of a great sum of money which the securities supposed to be stolen could represent. What was this money? How was it come by? And when? Who bequeathed it? Madame Jobert was examined upon these questions by the juge d'instruction week after week, during a whole year. Lie after lie she told. Each explanation she put forward was sifted and proved a lie. At last she cried:

"'It is true. I have lied. I do not wish France to remember what she should forget. I have not told my secret. But, if I must, I will. The great fortune exists. I will tell its origin when I am on my trial; but I warn you, Monsieur le Juge, the revelation will convulse France from the Mediterranean to the Channel.' That is what she said. No one believed her. In Paris, indeed, they had already begun to laugh. Almost they loved her. She was a criminal but magnificent in her crime.

"'La Grande Clothilde,' they named her. What *blague* would she have ready for the Cour d'Assizes? No one was alarmed, least of all I, a little restaurant-keeper in a city of the Midlands. Yet this last lie of hers ruined me."

"Ruined you?" cried Cynthia.

"Yes; it is strange, is it not? A great trial like that in Paris, a woman in the dock snatching at any defence or delay; she tells a story so ridiculous in its application that it sets all Paris in a delighted roar of laughter; and that story which could not save her, drags into the light a little man of no importance, who has been hiding his head in a foreign country for thirty years."

"Yes, but if the story is a lie?" cried Cynthia.

"Its application was the lie. It did not explain that fictitious fortune of the Joberts. But the story itself was true," said M. Poizat. He sat down in a chair in a queer, huddled attitude, with his knees and his feet together, his hands joined upon his knees and his chin sunk upon his breast. He seemed to have composed himself to be hit at. "I am amazed," he said. "It seems that one has never quite finished with anything one has done until one is dead. Here is a part of my life which I had buried. Then come thirty years, each one adding its layer of oblivion. Then comes La Grande Clothilde, who has never seen me, nor been seen by me. Look! I was laughing with everybody else. We take in the *Petit Parisien*. I read the trial in the evening, day by day, to my wife. We both amused ourselves by wondering what will be the great secret which La Grande Clothilde has to reveal. Then comes the day of the revelation, and in Ludsey my newspaper falls from my hands and my wife, who has been my wife for twenty years, looks upon me as a stranger."

Cynthia's face changed. The gentleness and the pity vanished. She drew in her breath sharply as though alarm knocked at her heart.

"Something out of your past life has come alive, quite unexpectedly after all these years, and has snatched you back," she said slowly, as if she were comparing the words with others she had once heard spoken. "Quick! Tell me!"

She bent forward with her eyes intent upon M. Poizat's face, and fear growing in them more and more visibly.

"You remember, Mrs. Rames, the night before the election at Ludsey. You were all having supper in the hotel after the meeting. I came in and was asked by Captain Rames to join you. There was a man who claimed to know me."

"Yes, yes, Colonel Challoner," cried Cynthia, with a rising excitement. She remembered that supper-room at Ludsey, and the queer moment of sensation when Colonel Challoner, gaunt and menacing, had recollected, and M. Poizat, in a panic, had denied the recollection. Some vague notion, too, of the defence which Clothilde Jobert had made a week ago returned to her. She began dimly to understand the disaster which had overtaken her little visitor.

"He remembered that he had seen you--Wait! Now I have it-- In a long corridor, in Metz, in '71."

M. Poizat nodded.

"The corridor of the Arsenal. Colonel Challoner--it's so you call him?--he was right. More than once I went along that corridor. I went to see the Marshal Bazaine."

"Yes," replied Cynthia. "And Madame Jobert accounted for the origin of this great sum of money which the prosecution declared to have no existence, by stating that it was the price paid to Bazaine by the Germans for the betrayal of Metz."

"That is so. No such sum of money came that way into Clothilde Jobert's hands. But details of her story were true."

"For instance?" asked Cynthia.

"That a small farmer, a Frenchman on the outskirts of Metz, called Henri Poizat, was the go-between in the negotiations between the Germans and Bazaine."

"That was true?"

"Yes. I am Henri Poizat. With the money I was paid I came to Ludsey and opened my little restaurant. I did well. I returned to France and married, and brought my wife back. Then suddenly this news! My wife is of Lorraine. Her father was of those sturdy ones who would not live under the German rule, but left their homes in Lorraine and began anew in France. Conceive to yourself how she looked at me when she read that statement in the paper, and I could not deny it. She has gone back to her own people. I have had a letter from her brother. I am not to come near them. In Ludsey I was pointed at in the streets as the man who sold his country. My restaurant suffered. My trade began to vanish. I sold it, goodwill and all, two days ago. As I say, I have no longer any house."

He buried his face in his hands. Cynthia watched him uncomfortably. She could not blame the wife. Rather she applauded her. She could find no sincere words of comfort for M. Poizat.

"I think you had better come back at five," she said, "and tell my husband your story."

"But of course he knows it already," cried M. Poizat.

Cynthia shook her head.

"He would have spoken of it to me if he had."

M. Poizat, however, was equally positive.

"But it is in the Ludsey newspapers. Captain Rames takes them in, and reads them of course."

"Of course," said Cynthia.

"Then he must know. Such news is not tucked away in the corner of a local paper. No, indeed. It was printed on the first page."

"Still you had better see him," said Cynthia. She rose as she spoke, and she spoke a trifle absently, as though her thoughts had been suddenly diverted from the consideration of M. Poizat's calamity. "Come back at five. He will advise you."

She rang the bell. She was in a hurry now to get rid of the little Frenchman. Something much more important to her had occurred than the revelations of La Grande Clothilde. Doubts had flashed into her mind--doubts which she was in torture to resolve. As soon as Poizat's back was turned she went quickly into her husband's study. Upon a side-table, carelessly heaped, with their wrappers still gummed about them, she counted a dozen of the local papers of Ludsey. They took two a week, one of each political complexion. It was six weeks then since Harry Rames had taken the trouble to glance at a newspaper from his own constituency.

She stripped off the wrappers to make sure. Then she turned to the calendar upon the top of his writing-table. Six weeks just took her back to the date when Harry Rames had emptied the House with a speech, and had brought home the tragic news of Colonel Challoner's death.

Harry's omission on the surface was trivial enough. But to Cynthia it was significant and disquieting. For it was not in accordance with the deliberate prudence which used to mark the conduct of his political career. To nurse the constituency, to be familiar with its events and its needs, to respond to it, this had been his first care. Now for six weeks he neglected even to inform himself about it. And the omission did not stand alone.

"He will be home at five," Cynthia argued, "he who made it a rule to sit in the House however dull the course of public business."

Often of late he had left the House as soon as questions were over and the usual vote taken upon the suspension of the eleven-o'clock rule, and had only returned thither upon the stroke of eleven on the chance of coming in for a division. Cynthia remembered, too, how indifferent he had been, on the day after he had made his failure, to the criticisms which the failure had evoked. Mr. Devenish had put in some biting and effective work in his reply, which should have been gall and wormwood to the ambitious Harry Rames. But he had not seemed to mind. The newspapers which supported the Government too had not spared him. Conceit and presumption were the least of his failings. The *Piccadilly News* had published a cartoon of him as Humpty Dumpty. Yet he had remained unmoved, though Cynthia had cried her eyes red over the castigation.

Certainly some change had come over him, she reflected, and once more she was conscious of fear and a sinking heart. For the story which she had heard this morning from M. Poizat linked itself up in her mind with the warning of Mr. Benoliel. Poizat's history was not quite an illustration of the warning. That she recognized. Mr. Benoliel had bidden her beware of latent tendencies of character, latent cravings and ambitions, taking their origin from the years in which she had had no share. It was a definite act which had sprung into being in the case of M. Poizat. Still Poizat's disaster was a proof of the clutch of finished things, and of the continuity of life; was an instance that to turn over the new page and begin to write afresh as she and Harry Rames had proposed to do, is beyond man's reach. Two lines of verse, gathered she knew not whence, rang in her brain and would not be silenced:

"Our past deeds follow us from afar
And what we have been makes us what we are."

After a year's respite Cynthia was again afraid. Mr. Benoliel was magnified by her fears into the semblance of a prophet of old.

CHAPTER XXXII

THE CALL

Cynthia went that night alone to a dinner party in Seamore Place. But she was ill at ease and as soon as she could get away she hurried home. She had not seen her husband that day. He had returned at five o'clock, had been closeted for a long while with M. Poizat and had then departed, leaving a message that a series of divisions would compel him to dine at the House of Commons. The couple, however, had made it a habit to reserve for themselves, whenever the House was not sitting late, an hour or so at the close of even the busiest day, and Cynthia was fairly sure that she would not have to wait long before Harry Rames came home. As a fact, he was already in his study. The door was ajar and through the opening the light streamed out into the hall.

Cynthia pushed the door open. Harry was sitting at his writing-table on the opposite side of the room and studying with a complete absorption a scroll which he held down unrolled beneath his eyes. Cynthia stood in the doorway for a moment or two watching him with a tender smile upon her face, and speculating idly upon the document which so riveted his attention. For the moment her trouble was quite driven from her thoughts. He was here, after all, in the house with her: he, the loved one: and with a sort of fierceness she was content. Then he looked up and saw her standing in the doorway. His face changed; he had the aspect clearly of a man at bay. He swept a pile of letters and printed papers over his scroll, spreading them out. He rose and stood between her and the writing-table, hiding it from her view.

"You are home early," he said.

"Earlier than you expected! Yet I am later than you."

"Oh, I paired at ten o'clock."

"I see."

The furtive movement of her husband increased her fears and at the same time wounded her pride. They were to be frank with one another. That was the pledge which each had given to the other. And here was the pledge broken, for Harry was definitely practising concealments. Cynthia, however, did not belong to the tribe of the clamorous. She stepped within the room and left him to continue the conversation. Rames spoke hastily to engage her attention.

"Poizat came to see me this afternoon."

"Yes?"

"He was desperate. We talked over his position. I recommended him to go to Tangier and settle there. He has a little money. He will find compatriots, and I should think it's the place where people will be least likely to trouble about him. I fancy that he will go there. But it's a bad business to have to start life all over again at seventy."

"Yes," said Cynthia.

She watched him as he walked up and down the room, making up her mind that on her side at all events the pledge should not be broken.

"M. Poizat said something to me which I think is true. That nothing one has ever done is ever quite done with."

Harry Rames stopped in his walk. He stood quite still for a few moments.

"Oh, surely that's not true," he said carelessly and resumed his pacing. But Cynthia was aware of a change in him. Before he had been thinking of Poizat and his destiny; now he was alert and waiting upon her words.

"I believe that it's more true than he knew. For even if nothing actual comes of the thing done, it's still there, recorded in the character. Harry, we are in the clutch of finished things."

Her voice rose in a low cry and brought Harry swiftly round upon his heel. Her words hit him shrewdly, but her aspect more shrewdly still. She was still standing close by the door. She was dressed in a gown of pale blue and gold with a bright ribbon of blue in her hair. Her cloak had slipped from her shoulders to her feet, her gloves were twisted in her hands, her eyes wide and dark with trouble looked out from a face which was piteously wistful. She made unconsciously a poignant appeal to him. The delicate loveliness of her youth and the gay panoply of her attire contrasted so strikingly with the quivering misery of her face.

"What makes you believe that, Cynthia?" He crossed the room to her side and shook her arm with a friendly gesture familiar to her. "Poizat's case is not enough to build a world of theory on."

"Nor do I," replied Cynthia. "I was adding to that case another." Harry Rames flinched.

"What other?" he asked with an effort.

"Years ago in Argentina I once listened at a door," she began, and in Harry's eyes shone a great relief. "What I heard frightened me. I lay awake in terror all that night. I have lived in fear ever since. I could not shake fear off even after I knew there was no longer any cause for fear. I can find causes anywhere. Fear's the truth of me. Most of the things which I have done have been done from fear."

"I never understood that, Cynthia."

"I never spoke of it before."

"Fear even prompted your marriage?"

Cynthia looked him frankly in the face.

"Yes. You were so frank, so honest about yourself. I felt safe with you. And after we were married--I escaped from fear. I was reprieved."

"Thank you," said Harry with a quiet sincerity. Then he moved away from her to the fireplace and turned again.

"Why do you tell me this for the first time tonight?"

"Because fear's awake in me again to-night," she answered simply. "I have had another visitor today besides M. Poizat."

"Who?"

"Howard Fall."

Harry Rames's voice hardened.

"He came to complain of me, I suppose."

"It wasn't complaint; it was regret. He thought it would be such a loss if you ceased to be interested in Parliament. He was afraid that Colonel Challoner's death had been a shock to you."

Harry Rames looked curiously at his wife.

"And what did you say?"

"That I knew you well enough to be sure that wasn't the case. He said you had not spoken once since the debate on the Address and that the organization against the land bill was tumbling to pieces."

Harry's face cleared.

"There's a very good reason for that. The government programme is overloaded and Devenish's bill won't come on this year after all. Our opposition shook their confidence in it besides. No, it won't come on."

Cynthia moved swiftly forward to the fireplace.

"You know that?"

"Yes. Hamlin told me in confidence."

"When, Harry?"

"A month ago at least. We can always whip up the opposition to Devenish's bill when it becomes once more a practical proposition."

Perhaps after all the Government's change of plan was the simple explanation of the change in her husband. Cynthia sank down into a chair. Before now, she remembered, she had tortured herself with unnecessary fears.

"Oh, I am glad. I am glad," she cried. All her heart was in her voice and tuned it to a note full and low and wonderfully sweet. Harry was moved by the music of it. There was a joy, a tenderness, which he had noticed more than once of late, but which had never rung so clear as it did to-night. He planted himself in front of her with a wry sort of smile upon his face.

"Cynthia."

"Yes."

"You want me to go on--just as I am going? You are satisfied? There have been times when you have wanted more----"

But Cynthia broke in upon him. She shut her eyes upon her ideals and her dreams. They were for the girl steeped to the lips in romance, not for the woman made real by love. Something had come between them. Something secret. Something which threatened even such community of life as they had. She was in revolt against it.

"Yes, yes," she cried passionately. "I do want you to go on. I want you to make a great career. I want my share in it, my pride in it. I shall be satisfied. I shall be thankful. Oh, my dear, are you blind?" She rose abruptly and stood in front of him. "What I want and all that I want is to keep you." If she had never spoken the words, the eagerness of her voice and the prayer of her clasped hands would have uttered them for her. But she had spoken them deliberately. She knew very well the danger for a woman in telling a man who does not love her, that she loves him. But she accepted the danger. She was playing for a great stake that night, and great stakes are not to be won without great risks. She laid her reticence aside and made her appeal. But it seemed that her appeal failed. Harry Rames stood watching her, at a loss for words, with a face which concealed carefully all his thoughts. Cynthia stooped and gathered up her gloves which had fallen to the floor.

"I shall go up now," she said.

Yet she waited; and Harry still was silent. A moment of passion had caught him unprepared with any words.

"What are you thinking about, Harry, so profoundly?" Cynthia asked in an indifferent voice. His silence was a rebuff most bitter to her. But she would not betray herself a second time. Her eyes and her hands were busy with some imaginary fault in the fit of her dress.

"That you have never shown me yourself before," he said, moving toward her. She stood quite still as he came close. He put his arm about her and she asked quietly:

"Wasn't I wise, Harry? It's a little disconcerting, isn't it, when a woman shows you something you know nothing about. Just a little disconcerting, isn't it?"

She left him standing in the room and went upstairs. She had made her plea with all the frankness which had been the condition of their marriage. She would not ask for a like frankness in return. It was for him to give it. She had made it quite plain that on her side she wanted frankness. More she would not do. Not for anything would she ask what secret thing he had hidden under the papers upon his table. But she knew that there was a secret thing and her feet dragged as she mounted the stairs.

She had been in bed according to her reckoning for about an hour when she heard a noise of the shutting of a door. And the door was the front-door of the house. Cynthia sprung from her bed and lifting the blind looked out from the window. It was a dark night, but there was no fog. By the light of the street lamps she saw a man crossing the road toward the corner of South Audley Street. He had the look of her husband. She flung up the window and the sound of his footsteps made her sure. Her eyes gazing into the tempered darkness of a London street might well have deceived her, her ears could not. There was no one else walking in Curzon Street at that moment; the sound of his footsteps reverberated unmistakably, diminishing as the distance between him and the window increased. The man who now vanished into South Audley Street was Harry Rames.

Cynthia switched on the light and looked at her watch. It was one o'clock in the morning. She wrapped a dressing-gown about her and sat down trying to think calmly, seeking to discover, if she could, some other reason for his departure than the obvious one. But the obvious one recurred again and again in her thoughts. It explained everything, fitted in with everything, as no other reason did. His sudden indifference to his career, his furtive movement at his writing-table upon her appearance, his refusal to meet frankness with frankness could all thus be accounted for. His departure from the house was thus explained. He had not come up into his room next to hers; he had waited in his study for an hour; he had given her time to fall asleep; he had gone out. It was a woman then who had twisted the current of his life as she, Cynthia, could not, who had moved him to passion as she even that evening had failed to do. Cynthia raged in fury against herself for having so weakly betrayed herself. She sat in torture. Then her jealousy flamed up. *That*--no! Her pride must give way. If there was another woman in her story--why then the other woman must look to herself. Cynthia would fight. She hurried down-stairs into the study. She switched on the lights and tumbled hither and thither the papers on the writing-table for the one so swiftly hidden which should betray the other woman's name and her abode. But she found nothing to satisfy her. She looked round the room. From a drawer in a bureau against the wall Harry's keys had been dangling. That she had noticed; and the keys were gone now. She tried the drawer. It was locked. In that drawer then was hidden the key to his secret. So much knowledge at all events Cynthia was sure that she had gained. She went back to her room and lying in bed ran over all the names of her acquaintances, even of her friends. She was not in the mood to trust any of them, but she could not fix upon any of them either. One and all they were cats and treacherous. Cynthia was no longer afraid; she was simply furious; and her fury was not diminished when she heard the front-door open and shut once more, almost noiselessly--so much caution was being used.

But Cynthia, though she was right in her facts, had never been so mistaken in her conclusions. The scroll which Harry Rames had pushed beneath his papers was simply a chart of the Antarctic seas; whereon lines distinguished one from the other by the manner of their tracing recorded the journeys of successive explorers and marked each one's "farthest South." He stood for a little while after Cynthia had left him on the same spot half-way between his chart and her position at the door. Then he turned back to his writing-table and spread out the map once more. The call of the unknown places was loud in his ears that night.

"Come back! Come back!"

Six weeks ago it had been the merest whisper--flashed to the wireless poles on the roof of the Admiralty and heard by him one afternoon, a message very small and clear amidst the clatter of Parliament Street. But the whisper had gathered volume and vehemence, until the map before him seemed a mouth shouting it, and the room throbbed with it as though the walls would burst asunder.

"Come back! Come back!"

It seemed to him that the command was not to be denied or must ring in his ears forever; and that arena of the House of Commons, where man fought with man, became a trivial place of meanness and intrigue compared with the vast battle-ground in the South, where one fought in a grandeur of silence with the careless, stubborn elements of a wild and unknown world.

He bent over his map and across it, as across the table of a camera obscura he saw moving, in miniature and brilliantly defined, the ships of the men who had sailed to the South. James Cook's two vessels, the *Resolution* and the *Adventure*, crossed the Antarctic circle as it seemed underneath his eyes--the first, of all the ships that were ever built, to sail upon these waters. Bellingshausen of Kronstadt came next and dropped his anchor under the shelter of Peter I Island and gave to it its name. He was followed by the whaling captains, each choosing his own line, great navigators inspired by a great and spirited firm. Weddell and Biscoe in their brigs. Balleny in his schooner. The later ships of the scientific expeditions under D'Urville of France and Wilkes of Chesapeake Bay moved southward in the track of the whaling captains, and close upon their heels James Ross from England with the *Erebus* and the *Terror* burst for the first time in the history of the world through the ice-pack into the open sea beyond and sailed from west to east along the great ice-barrier. There were other lines where the *Challenger* had sailed, and the official expeditions; and there was yet another, the longest of all the lines upon the chart, a line stretching out to a harbor never visited before, and against that line in tiny letters was printed "Rames." He followed the course of his ship from his first harbor in the Antarctic continent with the wooden cross high on a hill above it, which marks the grave of a naturalist of a past expedition. He fell to speculating where the *Perhaps* lay now. Parliament had met in the first days of January. It was just before the opening of Parliament that Hemming had started on the mail steamer to New Zealand to pick up his ship in Lyttelton Harbor. Allow him five weeks for his journey. The second week of February would have come to an end before the *Perhaps* had steamed out past the headland. Hemming himself had recognized that he was late. The difficulty of collecting money to finance the expedition had detained him beyond his time. A fortnight out from New Zealand, where was the *Perhaps* now? She might still be in the stormy seas on the outer edge of Ross's pack with the petrels and the albatrosses like a cloud about her yards. Or she might have touched at one of the northerly harbors of the continent. Perhaps winter was coming early on to wrap her about with snow and ice. If that happened, Hemming's chance was gone, for he had only money for one year. He must reach the Pole this next summer or not at all. He must therefore winter well to the South.

Rames got up from his chair, trying not to hope that Hemming's expedition would fail. He looked up from this map to the spot where Cynthia had stood close to the door, and a smile came upon his face.

"She was wrong," he said. "We are in the clutch of the unfinished, not the finished things."

He carried his map over to a bureau which stood against the wall and opened a drawer from the lock of which his bunch of keys was dangling. There were other charts in the drawer, a barometer which had hung in his cabin in the *Perhaps* throughout the three years during which that ship had been his home, a shell or two dredged up from the depths of the sea, and a brown paper package tied up with a piece of string. The charts lying there were all the charts which existed of the Antarctic seas, arranged in the order of their making. He added to them now his map, the last of them all; the printed facsimile of his own chart. Then reluctantly he locked the drawer. The reverberation of the seas seemed to fill the room and through it imperative and loud rang the call of the South. Yet he was aware, too, of Cynthia standing in her delicate blue frock, subduing her pride, revealing herself in a passionate appeal. He was stirred to shame at the poverty of his own response. She had been friend, counsellor, wife in the normal way. They had jogged side by side along the low road of his endeavor. To-night she pleaded for more, she offered more. He could never quite look upon her as he had been wont to. For she had stirred him to shame.

He slipped the key off the ring and swung it round upon his finger. At all events he would keep his bargain.

"It's a queer piece of irony," he said to himself, "that the very thing which I would give my soul to do, she was urging me to do two years ago; and now I must keep my longing hidden. Our positions are quite reversed."

But he would keep to his bargain. Perhaps after all Hemming would succeed; and sooner or later no doubt the reverberation of the seas would die away in the porches of his ears.

He went out into the hall, carrying the key in his hand, and let himself out at the front-door. He walked quickly up South Audley Street, turned to the left, and crossed Park Lane into Hyde Park. He walked to the stone bridge which crosses the Serpentine. The night was quiet and dark about him, and from afar off the never ceasing roar of the London traffic came to him like the roar of distant seas. He leaned over the parapet and stretching out his hand opened it. He heard a tiny splash in the water beneath the bridge.

He walked back more slowly than he had come to where the glare of the sky indicated the houses and the streets. As he crossed Park Lane again two men arm-in-arm passed him and one of them stopped.

"Is that you, Rames?" asked a friendly and solicitous voice.

Rames recognized it at once as the voice of Hamlin the chief Whip.

"You had paired for to-night," Hamlin continued, "hadn't you? You didn't miss much. But I want to be able to rely on you for Thursday. We know, of course, that you are against us over Devenish's land bill. That's all right. But you are with us on the rest of our policy and we want your help."

"I shall be there on Thursday," answered Harry Rames. "It's quite true that I have not been so much in the House this session as I used to be. But you will see me in my old place to-morrow. Good-night."

He walked on and Hamlin rejoined his companion.

"It was Rames," he said. "We're not going to lose him. I am glad. He's marked out for a great position if he doesn't throw it away."

But Rames through the roar of the traffic, carriages rolling home, wagons lumbering in to Covent Garden, heard louder than ever the boom of Southern seas and the wind whistling between the halyards of a ship.

CHAPTER XXXIII

A LETTER FROM ABROAD

The session passed, and Devenish's land bill, as Rames had foretold, was postponed. It figured again in the Address at the beginning of the following year, but as late as March no definite date had been assigned for its introduction. On a Saturday morning of this month Cynthia and her husband were breakfasting in the dining-room of the white house, when the morning's letters were brought in by the butler. Harry Rames tossed one or two aside.

"Circulars, pamphlets," he said. He opened some of the others, taking them from the top of the pile. "Here's one from the Chamber of Commerce--railway rates. I'll answer that this morning. Here's another--the committee of a school wants a grant from the treasury. Here's a third--" and as he was beginning to tear open the envelope, his voice suddenly stopped.

Cynthia looked up from her own letters and saw that while he was holding the third letter in his hand he was not looking at it. His eyes were fixed upon that one which was now uppermost on the heap. He sat and stared at the envelope for an appreciable time. Then dropping the letter which he held, he picked up this new and startling one and carried it swiftly over to the window. Cynthia followed his movement with her eyes, just curious, but nothing more. Her eyes indeed travelled beyond him and noticed the sunlight in the garden, the yellow and purple crocuses and the first of the daffodils, noticed them with an up-springing lightness of heart. Then the stillness of her husband's attitude caught her attention. She saw something in his face which she had never seen there before, which she had never thought to see there at all. He wore the look of a man quite caught out of himself. He was as one wrapped in visions and refined by the fires of great longings. It seemed to her that she saw a man whose eyes, brimful of light, looked upon the Holy Grail.

He turned back to her. He brought her the letter still unopened and placed it in her hands. Cynthia received it as though written upon its cover she would read the revelation of his secret. Yet she saw nothing but a soiled envelope with a foreign stamp. She gazed up at her husband mystified.

"Look at the stamp, Cynthia!" said Rames in a queer voice.

Cynthia looked. It wore the head familiar to English people. But the lettering about the head was strange. She spelled it out.

"Rexland."

With a start she turned to him. "That is the country you discovered."

"Yes. A stamp was struck to commemorate my discovery of it."

"A stamp?" cried Cynthia. "Wait a minute, Harry! You once spoke of a stamp to me before. Yes, on the morning of the day when you were to deliver your speech--the speech which failed. It was this stamp of which you were speaking?"

"Yes."

"You remembered it on that morning, even when your thoughts were full of the speech you were going to deliver."

"I remembered it by accident," he said sharply. "I can't think why. It had been out of my thoughts for so long. Yet it was that stamp." His voice softened. "It is issued by the post-office--for a penny. Just think of it! A penny stamp brings a letter from the Antarctic seas to us here in Warwickshire."

"Mr. Hemming sent it?"

"Without a doubt. When he came to see me in London fifteen months ago, he told me that if I intended to go out again he would not use my harbor."

Harry was standing just behind his wife. Cynthia was not looking at him any longer. But she was listening with a curious intentness as though the words which he spoke were of less importance to her than the accent with which he spoke them. She put questions to him to make yet more sure of it.

"And you gave him permission!"

"Of course. I had not the right to refuse it. I was never going South again. Nothing was further from my thoughts. I told him to use not only my harbor, but the depots of food I had made along my sledge-route from the harbor toward the Pole."

"You think that he reached the harbor?"

"I am sure of it. Otherwise he would not have used this stamp. He must have wintered there. I did not think that he would reach it before winter closed in upon him. The summer last year must have been very late."

Cynthia nodded her head.

"Yes."

Her attention was relaxed. Harry Rames had been striving to keep from his voice any note of regret, to speak in the ordinary level tone suitable to a matter of only ordinary interest. But in spite of his efforts he was not sure that he had succeeded. Cynthia handed to him the letter. He took it and turned it over in his hand.

"He has had time since he wintered in that harbor. One summer would be enough. He may have done it--if his dogs lived. There's always that condition. If his dogs lived! Mine didn't. Perhaps--perhaps--" He broke off abruptly and thrust the letter back into Cynthia's hand.

"You open it! You can tell me what he says."

Harry Rames walked again to the window and stood with his back to the room. Cynthia's eyes followed him and travelled past him once more to the garden. She was sure that she would never forget those daffodils and the purple crocuses waving in the sunlight for one day as long as she lived. A minute ago she had noticed them; now she noticed them again; and within that minute had been revealed to her the great secret Harry Rames had been at so much pains to hide. She knew her rival now, and was appalled. "Such men are driven by a torment of their souls." It was Harry himself who had said that. The wish came to her, "If only this man has succeeded." She tore open the envelope.

Harry Rames stood at the window waiting for the letter to be read to him; and it seemed to him that he waited for an eternity. He had heard the tearing of the envelope. The letter was open in Cynthia's hands. Yet she did not speak a word. Rames's heart sank.

"Then he has reached the Pole?" he asked with a studied carelessness.

"I don't know," Cynthia replied in perplexity.

"Read it."

"There is nothing to read."

Rames turned round and came swiftly toward her.

"He must have forgotten to enclose his letter. There is nothing but this," said Cynthia. She was holding a single blank sheet of note-paper in her hand. She turned it over. "No, there's not a word written anywhere. Do you understand it?"

"Yes. He has failed."

There was no doubt left to her of her husband's joy. The cry which broke from his lips was not to be denied. It was a real cry of exultation. Cynthia turned pale as she heard it. But she would not acknowledge that she understood it, nor would she look into Harry's face lest she should see the same exultation blazoned there.

"Poor Hemming," said Rames. "That's bad luck. The disappointment must have hit him hard."

"You can understand that," said Cynthia steadily.

"Yes. He would have written, you see, if he had taken it more lightly. He has nothing to say. That is what his blank sheet of paper means. That is what it must mean. Well, I must go and write to the Chamber of Commerce, Cynthia;" and gathering up his letters he went out of the room.

As for Cynthia, she remembered that the North Warwickshire met that morning at eleven o'clock four miles from the house. She rode to the meet and followed the hounds over a good grass country flying her hedges on a big horse which old Mr. Daventry had given to her on the very first day when she had hunted over six years ago. It had always been her experience that when troubles and fears overburdened her, a hard day's hunting was her best medicine. It smoothed out the creases of her mind, whipped up the blood in her veins, set her pulses dancing with the joy of living and unrolled her courage like a banner. The sunlight, the swift rush through the air, the rhythm of movement, the keenness of the animal beneath her, the flight over hedge and ditch, had never failed her up till now. It always seemed to her that by some process, of which she was quite unconscious, the direct and simple thing to do emerged from the confusion of her thoughts and shone out unmistakably. And it shone out to-day. But she could not bring herself to accept it. As she rode homeward through the lanes she was at her arguments again.

"No! With time contentment will come to him. He will be subdued to the matter he works in. And I cannot let him go."

Mr. Benoliel's warning obstinately confronted her.

"One party doesn't keep the bargain or keeps it half-heartedly as an irksome thing and day by day the separation grows more complete until you are living with your enemy or living quite alone."

But she would not be convinced; she battled against it. "There was a saving clause. 'Unless on both sides there is love.' In that case a way could be found. And on both sides there may be love."

She had treasured up little acts of thoughtfulness on Harry Rames's part, the merest small things which women are quick to notice and to build upon; such as having a cloak ready for her shoulders almost before she was aware that she was cold. She ran these trifles over in her mind, clutching at them for proof that the longed for change was coming--nay, perhaps had come. There had been a constant watchfulness, a constant care for her shown by her husband during this last year. It might be of course that a certain remorse was stirring in him--remorse that he was only keeping his side of the bargain in the letter and not the spirit.

"But I cannot let him go," she insisted. The perils, the hardships, the dangers of snow-storms and cold and shipwreck and famine which had all seemed so trivial to her in her days of romance now loomed up before her terrible and dark. It was no use to argue that other men had gone that road and had come back. This one might not. She reached her home with her distress as heavy upon her as when she had set out; and was told that Mr. Benoliel was waiting to see her.

She went at once into the drawing-room and gave Mr. Benoliel some tea.

"Will you tell Mr. Rames," she said to her butler, "that Mr. Benoliel is here."

"He's not in the house," said Benoliel. "He's in Ludsey. I asked for him when I heard that you were out. I am glad. For I should like to tell you my news first."

The butler left the room and Mr. Benoliel became at once mysterious and omniscient.

"Sir George Carberley is going to resign," he said.

Cynthia looked at him in surprise.

"The member for our division?"

The white house was not within the borough limits of Ludsey. It stood in the Hickleton Division of the county of Warwickshire and Sir George Carberley, an important unit of the opposition, was Harry Rames's representative in the House of Commons.

"Yes," said Mr. Benoliel. "He has sat for the division for forty years now and he is tired. He intends to resign when this session is over."

"Are you sure?" asked Cynthia. "How do you know this?"

"Ah!" said Benoliel with a smile. "You mustn't ask me that, Cynthia. Indeed I am not quite sure that I ought to have told you the news at all. But I thought that it was so important for you to know it at once that I stretched a point of confidence."

"Thank you," said Cynthia. "But what I don't understand is why it is so important for us to have the news before the others?"

"Captain Rames is on the executive of your association, isn't he?"

"Yes."

"Then he will have a voice in the selection of the candidate who will fight the seat from your political point of view."

"Of course."

"Very well," said Mr. Benoliel. "If he has a candidate ready when the news of the approaching resignation is published, and if that man is willing to follow not simply the Government's policy, but also your husband's policy as regards Devenish's land bill, don't you see what a chance he gets? If Rames can secure the selection of his man as candidate and then can win over the seat, he strengthens his position with the Government enormously. He has put his views about Devenish's bill to the test of an election, and he has won."

"Yes, I see that," said Cynthia doubtfully. She was considering the prospect Mr. Benoliel held out to her from a quite different point of view. If Harry succeeded in this plan, his victory would be one more link in the chain of obligation which bound him to his present life. If he failed, his failure would be another disappointment weakening it.

"But can we win?" she cried. "The seat's supposed to be impregnable."

"That's one of your advantages. More seats are lost by over-confidence than by bad candidates. Besides, the mere fact that one man has held a seat for forty years is against the probability of another man of the same color succeeding. There are lots of people who will be ready to say 'It's time we gave the other fellows a look-in.' Your husband has only got to throw himself heart and soul into the fight and he will stand a very good chance. No doubt of that."

Cynthia reflected. "Why did you wish to tell me this news before you told it to Harry?" she asked, bending her brows upon Mr. Benoliel in a steady frown which had before now warned him to walk with circumspection.

"I wasn't quite sure," he explained, "that you would wish him now to undertake a further obligation of political service."

"Indeed!" said Cynthia icily. "And why shouldn't I wish it now, Mr. Benoliel?"

Mr. Benoliel had no intention to allow himself to be browbeaten by a slip of a girl for whose happiness he was in a measure responsible.

"Because, my dear Cynthia," he answered, "it has seemed to me on the last few occasions when I have met your husband that he was feeling the strain of a Parliamentary life. He has looked worn and tired. I could almost fancy that he was disheartened."

Cynthia's thoughts did Mr. Benoliel some injustice at this moment. Certainly he was suggesting to her that his neglected warning had been justified, that Harry's Parliamentary ambition had been a mere phase in his life, which was now passing or had already passed. But she went further and assumed in him a kind of triumph at the accuracy of his diagnosis. Right underneath his sympathetic words she seemed to hear the whisper of a question:

"Am I not a clever man?"

The whirr of a motor-car grew loud and ceased. Harry had returned from Ludsey. Mr. Benoliel sat patiently in front of her, awaiting her decision. Was he to break his news to Harry Rames or was he not? Cynthia felt that Harry's destiny and hers were in her hands. She must make her choice and by that choice it seemed to her they would be both inextricably bound, their happiness or their misery allotted to them for the whole span of their lives.

She sat with her chin propped in the palm of her hand and her eyes brooding darkly on Mr. Benoliel. A door was shut somewhere in the house. She rose and pressed the bell.

"Howard," she said to her butler, "was that Mr. Rames?"

"Yes ma'am."

"He is in his study I think?"

"Yes."

"Will you show Mr. Benoliel in to him?" And as Benoliel rose, she said to him, "Will you come back after you have told your news? You will have an opportunity of reconsidering your judgment. I should like to hear whether you still think him disheartened."

Cynthia was in her most aggrieved and stately mood. She usually was when she knew herself to be in the wrong. She would not admit Mr. Benoliel's sympathy or affection for her. She had an epithet for him very near to the tip of her tongue at this moment. Mr. Benoliel was officious. With a distant bow she dismissed him.

She had the satisfaction half an hour later of hearing Mr. Benoliel's complete recantation.

"I was quite wrong, Cynthia. He was in the best of spirits. He was elated. The look of strain had gone if it was ever there. I have been mistaken. I am happy to admit it."

Cynthia relaxed from her frigidity. But her satisfaction was a poor one and had little life in it. She had merely tricked Mr. Benoliel into the belief that his insight had been at fault. For in truth, as she knew very well, it had never been more shrewd. What had led Mr. Benoliel into error was his ignorance of the letter with the "Rexland" stamp which had arrived at the white house by the morning's post. Hemming's failure was a kind of reprieve for Harry Rames. In a sudden revulsion he had been lifted out of his discouragement. His exultation had remained with him all that day. Cynthia had counted upon it when she had sent Benoliel to his study.

CHAPTER XXXIV

THE CONVICT AT THE OAR

A long account of Hemming's expedition, sent by a New Zealand correspondent, appeared in one of the morning papers the next day. Hemming had travelled a couple of hundred miles further south than Harry Rames. Then he had been compelled to return. But it was Harry Rames who had made it possible for him to get so far. For he used Rames's depots of provisions and was able to save his own for the stretch of new ice-covered country.

Harry lighted upon the account unexpectedly when he opened his newspaper at the breakfast table, but the moment he saw the head-line he folded the sheets quickly again and pushed the paper away from him. He shrank from reading it, hardly daring to trust himself, and he began to talk over with Cynthia the names of suitable candidates for the Hickleton Division.

"The Whips, of course, will have a man ready who will be pledged to swallow the whole of the Government policy, land bill and all. We must be beforehand with them. What do you say to young Burrell, Cynthia?"

"Sir James Burrell's son?"

"Yes. His father is anxious that he should do something," said Harry with a laugh.

"But isn't he rather young and rather insignificant?" asked Cynthia.

"Youth's a good quality in the House of Commons. The older men become suspicious of change and want life stereotyped as it is. And young Burrell isn't without brains. I don't say that he's a flyer, but then, like the Government, I prefer docility to brains in my followers. I think that I will run round to Sir James when we go back to town on Monday."

But though Harry Rames neglected his newspaper at the breakfast table, he came back for it at eleven in the morning. He could keep the drawer in his bureau locked upon his charts, but he could not quench his fever to read the details of Hemming's expedition. For an hour he tried to occupy himself with the business of Cynthia's estate, and then he gave up the attempt. When and how Hemming failed, how far he had travelled with his sledges, what new lessons were to be learnt from his experience--here were questions which he could not silence. He got the paper and read the account through. "The dogs gave out," he said to Cynthia. "The dogs are the trouble. You can't carry enough food for them and for the sledging-party as well. Of course, it's bad luck on Hemming. But I doubt if he followed the highest traditions of British exploration."

"Why?" asked Cynthia.

"He should have chosen a different base, converged upon the Pole from a different angle, and covered ground altogether new. Then, whether he failed or not, he would have brought back a hundred new facts of interest to the scientist and the geographer. As it is he adds very little I should think to our knowledge."

Cynthia was silent for awhile after he had finished. Then she said in a low voice, bending over some embroidery at which she was working:

"And if you were to go back, Harry, where would you make your base?"

"I?"

Harry Rames sprang eagerly up.

"Oh, I should search for a harbor a long way to the east of my old one. At least," and he caught himself up, "I think that is what I should do. I am speaking at random, of course. But I should at all events have considered that possibility carefully, if I had been going out again."

Again a spell of silence followed upon his words and Cynthia did not raise her eyes from her work. She was wearing a hat with a wide brim and Harry Rames could see nothing of her face.

"Won't you get your charts out and show me?" she asked. She had mastered her voice so that there was no sound of effort in it.

"I haven't got them here," said Harry, with a fine indifference. "They are in London I believe, somewhere or other."

Cynthia's needle stopped.

"In London," she said. An idea had occurred to her. "Locked up?"

"Very likely. I may have locked them up. I have done with them altogether, you see."

"Of course," said Cynthia.

This time it was Harry who did not at once reply. The finality of that "of course" brought a flush of anger into his face. He almost blamed her for her blindness, though all his efforts aimed at keeping her blind.

"I will ride into Hickleton this afternoon," he said, "and make sure that the chairman of our association has no pet candidate of his own."

"That will be a good plan," said Cynthia; and with a glance at the crown of that broad hat and a surprise at the obtuseness of the head which it so effectually concealed, he went out of the room. Not until the door was closed did Cynthia lift her face from her work. Her eyes were brimming with tears and she let her hands lie idle on her lap while the tears overflowed and ran down her cheeks. She was not much given to tears, but to-day they had their way with her. She was wretched. Their marriage had been a mistake. From first to last Mr. Benoliel had been right, but she would not listen to him and be warned. Even this afternoon he had accused her--for so she now looked upon his words--with his pitiless truths. It was true that Harry was discouraged, that his face had grown thin and worn, that despite the brave show which he was making, he was utterly unhappy. Harry's words, "The men who go South are driven on by a torment of their souls," lived with her night and day. They were written in fire upon every wall of her house. In that torment Harry Rames was now tossing and must toss, enduring the anguish of his longing silently--just as silently as she herself was weeping in the empty room.

She was afraid of herself and dissatisfied with herself. Afraid, because she had been perilously near to one wild outcry, "Since your heart is set on it, go!" Dissatisfied, because she had stifled the words before they were spoken, because she could not bring herself to speak them, and never would.

From that day a change came over her. She flung herself with a veritable fever of energy upon those opportunities which enable a woman to identify herself with politics. The work she had undertaken in Ludsey, she undertook in London on a wider scale, and with infinitely greater effort. She was elected upon the central committees of the various women's associations connected with her husband's party; she travelled far and wide throughout the country on the business of organizations; she made speeches; she sought the presence of Cabinet Ministers at her dinner-table; she lost her color, her buoyancy. What she did was done doggedly. To go to bed each night tired out, that was her ambition.

"If Harry wears himself out, why should not I?" she said when any of her friends remonstrated with her, but not one of them was allowed to guess that the secret of all her energy was remorse. She was seeking her rest in fatigue. For her remorse grew. Night after night Harry sat faithfully, as he had promised to Hamlin, in his seat on the front bench below the gangway. He took his part in the debates, he recovered the ground which he had lost. He was once more a man marked for high office. But it was all labor now, and unloved labor. And the strain of it was visible. He went out and in without that happy mien of confidence which once Cynthia had been wont to resent, but for which she vainly hungered now.

There was one Friday evening toward the end of June when she was impelled to approach the dangerous subject of her own accord. She and Harry had been dining with the Prime-Minister in Downing Street. All that week the House had been sitting into the small hours. The Prime-Minister himself had taken her aside and given her a warning. They returned home soon after eleven, and as they sat over a final cigarette in Harry's study, Cynthia could not shut her eyes to his restlessness, the nervous flickering of his fingers, the unsteady intonations of his voice.

"Aren't you doing too much, Harry?" she asked.

"Not more than you, Cynthia," he replied as he poured himself out a whiskey and soda.

"Much more. And women who are doing what they want to do can stand a great deal more than men who are not."

Harry looked across at her quickly.

"But, of course, I am doing just what I have always planned to do, just what you are helping me to do--just what I sought your help to enable me to do."

"Sure?"

"Of course."

Cynthia had crossed the room to his side and was standing with a hand upon his shoulder. She was in a mood of indecision and the touch of her hand revealed her mood to Rames. A change came over him. She felt a tremor of his body, a sudden quickening of the muscles beneath her hand. He became intensely expectant. She could read the question in his mind. Was she by some wonderful inspiration going to release him from the torment of his soul? But the mere sensation of his movement was enough for Cynthia. She withdrew her hand. She repeated unconsciously words which he had once used to her.

"After all we get some fun out of it, don't we, Harry?" she said; and Harry rose quickly from his chair.

"We get much more out of it, Cynthia," he said with a face which had suddenly grown very grave and tender; and the next moment she was in his arms, held there tightly, clasped against him. Cynthia was carried out of herself. She was swept away unexpectedly upon a swirl of passion.

"Harry! Oh, Harry!" she whispered in a low voice of happiness. His right hand touched and stroked her hair. Then he tilted her chin backward and he looked into her eyes and a smile transfigured his face.

"Oh, much more, Cynthia," he cried, and he bent his head and kissed her. He put her away from him and looked her over from her delicate feet to the fair crown of her hair. She wore a satin gown of white with her diamonds in her hair, and a rope of pearls about her neck.

"There! That's that!" he said, and Cynthia with a laugh and the blush of a girl answered, "Thank you." Harry Rames lit a cigarette and Cynthia's eyes followed each movement and followed it with incredulity. The change so ardently longed for by her had come then? He loved--he actually loved!

"Since when?" she asked gently.

"Do you remember one evening when you stood there by the door, very wistful, and told me something about yourself which I did not know?"

"Yes, I remember. I was unwise."

"You were not. For it began then."

"Really?"

She went up to him, and he caught her hand in his and held it tightly clasped.

"I looked at you to-night as we sat at dinner. There was no one but you at the dinner-table. How on earth you could have brought yourself to marry me, I can't think."

"I told you," said Cynthia, "I was afraid," and there was a note of exultation in the confession as though now at last she was freed from fear. Harry Rames lifted her suddenly from the ground and held her close to him. She hung inert in his arms.

"That's over," he said.

"Quite."

"I love you, Cynthia."

Cynthia threw her head back and closed her eyes, giving to him her face, her throat.

"I wanted to hear you say that," she whispered. He carried her over to the sofa and laid her down.

For a week or two after that evening Cynthia walked in a dream. The great trouble which had weighed upon her thoughts incessantly was altogether gone. Mr. Benoliel had been right in his conjectures. He must still be right, she reasoned. He had foreseen the trouble accurately. "You will be living with your enemy or living quite alone." But he had added a saving clause. If on both sides there was love, then salvation would be found. Cynthia did not enquire very deeply into Mr. Benoliel's meaning. The salvation would come automatically, following upon love. She was content to think that and she walked in a world of roses as in the days of her girlhood in the estancia before James Challoner had come to claim her.

But after a fortnight she waked from her dream. Life was different: it was intensified. There was a little more sunlight on a sunny day, a little more sparkle in the summer, one walked to music. But the trouble was not gone, in spite of the fact that on both sides there was love. For with love, contentment had not come to Harry Rames. He watched himself, but she watched him closer and she knew. His sleep grew disturbed. The torment of his soul was not appeased. Daily he became more and more the convict at the oar. There grew up between them a loving enmity.

A morning came in the middle of July when to Cynthia the strain became intolerable. She was riding under the trees in the Row. It was not yet half-past nine and the air was still fresh with the dews of the night. A light haze hung near to the ground, the sunlight touched the green alleys of trees to gold, and far off across the Park soldiers were marching to the drums and fifes. She had reached the cross-road which leads to the Albert Gate when an impulse seized her. Mr. Brook was riding at her side, dilating enthusiastically on the importance of their group in the House of Commons, while Cynthia from time to time said mechanically "yes," and again "yes," and wished with her whole heart that all the bores in London would not take their exercise at half-past nine in the morning. Mr. Brook was in full swing when Cynthia abruptly reined in her horse.

"Good-by," she said, "I am afraid I have something I must do," and to Mr. Brook's astonishment she turned and cantered quickly back to Hyde Park Corner. Thence she rode to Grosvenor Square, gave her horse to her groom, and burst into Mr. Benoliel's dining-room where he sat breakfasting delicately amidst his silver and flowers. She waved the butler from the room and sat down at the table at right-angles to Mr. Benoliel.

"I am very unhappy," she said. "I was riding in the Park. It seemed ridiculous to be unhappy on a day like this. Yet I am. So I put my pride in my pocket."

She spoke with a kind of petulance, like one aggrieved and surprised at the contrariness of things. But Mr. Benoliel recognized that her distress was very real. His face clouded over; he laid his hand upon her arm.

"Have some breakfast, Cynthia."

"Food!" cried Cynthia in contempt. Then she changed her tone. "Well, I haven't had any breakfast. Perhaps--yes."

She was a girl with a healthy appetite and very unhappily she ate a big breakfast.

"Now light a cigarette and tell me about it."

He pushed over a silver box lined with cedar wood from which Cynthia took a cigarette. She tapped the end upon the table and lighted it. Mr. Benoliel's cigarettes were famous for their freshness and the delicacy of their aroma. Cynthia inhaled the tobacco and was a little comforted.

"No," she said. "I can't tell you all about it. I just want to ask you a question."

"Yes?"

"You remember the warning you gave me at Culver when you didn't know that I was married?"

"Quite well," said Mr. Benoliel regretfully. "It came too late."

"I am glad that it came too late," Cynthia observed quietly. "For I might have taken it."

Mr. Benoliel looked perplexed.

"Yet you are unhappy, Cynthia?"

"Very. None the less I wouldn't go back. But I don't want you to ask me questions. I will tell you at once that you were right--quite right up to a point. And the happiness both of Harry and myself depends upon your being right all through."

Mr. Benoliel's eyes flashed into life.

"There is a chance then?"

"Oh yes! If you are right."

"Let me hear!"

Cynthia put her question.

"What did you exactly mean when you said that even if the change you feared should come and some latent ambition should spring to life and snatch him back, separation need not follow, provided that on both sides there was love?"

A gravity overspread Benoliel's face.

"I meant, my dear, that sooner or later," he said gently, "after much tribulation, much revolt, one of the two will make the necessary sacrifice, and will make it whole-heartedly."

Cynthia was silent for a little while.

"Yes," she said at last in a low voice. "Of late I have begun to think that that is what you meant."

She dropped her cigarette upon a plate and rose. "Thank you, Mr. Benoliel," she said, and she walked with a trailing step to the door. At the door she paused.

"And is it always the woman who must make the sacrifice?" she asked; and Mr. Benoliel lost in a moment all that second-hand aspect of the dilettante which habitually cloaked him.

"Always," he said, with a ringing gravity of voice. "That is the law of the world, and neither man nor woman shall change it."

Cynthia opened the door and went out.

CHAPTER XXXV

THE LITTLE BIT EXTRA

Yet that August when Parliament had risen, Harry Rames and Cynthia were cruising in the Solent and no word had been spoken by her to remedy their trouble. It was Cynthia who had proposed this holiday and Harry had fallen in with her plan eagerly. They had chartered a small steam yacht of a hundred tons. Rames navigated the boat himself and slipping their moorings one afternoon, they left Cowes behind them and steamed away through the north channel of the Shingles to Poole. Cynthia had ceased to wrestle with herself. She was content to lie in her deck chair and put into and out of the harbors of the West.

"This shall be the perfect holiday," she had said. "Whatever the future may hold for us, we will have this month together without visitors, without any shadows."

They were tossed in Portland race; they steamed across the West Bay over a sea smooth and bright as a steel mirror. They dropped their anchor at Dartmouth. They rounded the Start on the next day and crossed the Bar of Salcombe harbor under the shadow of Bolt Head on just such an evening of sunset as that which the poet fixed in a few lines of deathless verse. Cynthia stood with her arm through Harry's, as very slowly with the lead going in the bows he set the boat over the shallows.

"Sunset and evening star," Cynthia quoted.

"And one clear call for me," Harry Rames continued and abruptly broke off like a guilty person who has spoken without thought. Cynthia walked to the end of the bridge. After all, this cruise had made a difference to Harry. She consoled herself by the reflection. He had recovered something of his buoyancy of spirits since he had trodden the planks of this little yacht and looked down from its flimsy bridge onto its narrow deck and tapering bow. He was interested in the boat, quick to induce her to give him of her best, and her brass shone like a woman's ornaments. They put out from Salcombe the next day, and keeping clear of Plymouth and Polperro and Fowey, heard the bell upon the Manacles in the afternoon and dropped anchor between the woods of Helford River. They stayed there for a day and made a passage thence to Guernsey on a night of moonlight. Cynthia sat late upon the bridge while Rames in his great-coat kept the boat upon her course. Toward morning he came to her side and stooped over her.

"I thought you were asleep."

"No."

"Aren't you tired?"

"No."

"You were lying so still."

"Yes," said Cynthia. "I am storing this night up."

The swish and sparkle of the water along the boat's sides, the rattle of the chain as the helmsman spun the wheel, the quiet orders of her husband, the infinite peace of sky and sea, and the yacht like a jewel hung between them, were indeed to dwell long in Cynthia's memories. For their holiday was at an end. A sailor was sent ashore at Guernsey for the ship's letters and he brought them on board whilst Harry and Cynthia were at breakfast in the deck cabin. There was one for Rames with the Hickleton postmark stamped upon the envelope. Harry tore it open reluctantly.

"Carberley has resigned," he said. "There will be a meeting of the executive on Friday night to adopt young Burrell."

Cynthia looked out across the harbor.

"We ought to go back, oughtn't we?" she said slowly.

Harry glanced at his letter.

"It is not expected that the election will take place for five weeks," he answered.

Cynthia shook her head.

"We shall want all that time, Harry." Then she cried with a sudden vehemence. "You have got to win this fight, Harry. So much hangs on it for you and me."

"I know, Cynthia," he answered.

"More than you know."

Harry rose from his chair.

"I'll give orders. We will steam back to Southampton at once. But it's a pity, isn't it? Old Carberley might have waited for another month. I am sorry."

"So am I," said Cynthia. Her eyes had wandered from him and were once more fixed upon the shipping in the harbor. Her face had grown white. "More sorry than you can know."

A little white dinghy, gay with a sailor in a white jersey and a red cap, was just leaving the side of a big yacht moored across the water. The picture of that little boat was fixed for life in Cynthia's recollections. It had nothing to do with her, she never knew who sailed in the yacht, or on what business the boat put off to shore. But the picture of it was vivid to her long after important memories had grown altogether dim.

The fight for the Hickleton Division was memorable in the political history of that year. From first to last it was Rames's fight. The candidate was young, and a halting speaker, and unknown to the constituency. But he lived in Rames's house and when he appeared upon a platform he appeared with Rames at his side. When he spoke he uttered the words which Rames had prepared, and when he had finished Rames was on his legs to fill up the deficiencies and whip the assembly to a fire of enthusiasm. From the great guns of his own party no assistance came. Indeed, most of them would have been well pleased had the seat not been won. For in the forefront of his programme Mr. William Burrell put hostility to the land bill. The two men left the white house early in the morning to return there late at night. For five weeks the lights of Rames's motor flashed on the hedges of the country roads in Warwickshire, and the constituency was won. The result was declared at noon, and half an hour later Mr. William Burrell, M.P., a slim, fair young gentleman with a small gift of flippancy, made his one memorable speech in the big room of the club.

"Gentlemen," he said, "the British public, as a whole, is indifferent to politics. It wakes up to be sure at the time of an election. But if I were asked to define politics in relation to the British public I should define it as a spasm of pain recurring once in every four or five years. What, then, is it which arouses the enthusiasm of which I am a witness? What is it which achieves these triumphs? Need I say? It is personality. Character--that's what you want in public life--and now, gentlemen, you have got it."

The speech was received with a very tornado of laughter. Rames turned to his wife who sat by him on the little raised platform at the end of the room.

"I told you he wasn't a fool," he said, and Mr. Arnall, who had come over from Ludsey, cried out with a chuckle of delight that he had now a companion speech to match the famous one of Taylor the democrat.

"You won't go back to London until to-morrow, will you?" said Rames to young Burrell. "It's best not to hurry away the moment you've won the seat."

They returned accordingly to the white house, and when the two men were left by Cynthia to their wine after dinner, Rames turned inquisitively to his guest.

"I have noticed a change in you, Burrell, during these five weeks. You came into the contest as though it was a joke, didn't you?"

"Yes, I did," said Burrell, blushing.

"And though you laughed at it again to-day, as a matter of fact it ceased to be a joke very quickly."

Burrell agreed. "Very quickly."

Rames fetched a box of cigars from the sideboard.

"Now light a cigar," he said, "and tell me just as clearly as you can what brought about the change, and what this election really means to you."

Mr. William Burrell, M.P., shied at the proposal.

"Oh, I say, Rames," he began, but Rames cut him short.

"I really want to hear," he said earnestly. "I ask for a particular reason."

Burrell lit his cigar. The contest had impressed him deeply. But like most men he was shy of revealing any strength of feeling. The eager eyes of Rames, however, kept him to his task. He looked back over the five weeks, gathering up his little sheaf of recollections.

"What remains in my mind," he said with hesitation, "is not the excitement, nor the applause, is not the difficulty of making speeches about subjects with which one is not half acquainted, nor the fear of being asked questions for which one has no reply ready, but something quite different. It is the memory of little bare raftered school-rooms, hot with gas-light, crowded with white faces, faces so hopeful, so--intolerably hopeful--the faces of people who look confidently to candidates and Parliaments for so much more than it seems to me Parliaments and candidates can ever do."

"Ah!" said Rames curiously. "You felt that too. I remember that I did."

Burrell leaned forward.

"Did you too, though you shouted yourself hoarse with the rest, feel a little ashamed?"

Rames reflected. "No," he said; "never." Then he added with a smile, "but I think I should now."

"I did," said Burrell. "There were times when I wanted to stop my speech in the middle and cry out, 'Don't look at me with such high hopes. It's no use! It's no use!' But I held my tongue. For there's always the little that governments can do. That's the consolation, isn't it?" Burrell was finding it easier to speak out his thoughts now. The false shame with which he had begun had quite left him. His words tumbled out hot from his soul. The strangely curious, almost envious, look with which Harry Rames, his tutor and leader, waited upon him encouraged and urged him on.

"The fight, the excitement, the victory--oh yes, they are worth having, even though one owes them to another, just as I owe them, Captain Rames, to you. But now, after the victory, there's still the little which can be done; and there's still the memory of the raftered school-rooms, the hot gas-light, and the rows of eager, hopeful, pallid faces to help one on to do it."

He stopped and leaned back in his chair. The shame of a young man who has let his tongue wag before his elders and masters seized hold upon him.

"But why did you lead me on to talk this sort of blatter to you?" he asked in an aggrieved voice. "All that I have just learnt you knew long since."

Harry Rames shook his head.

"Your opposition to Devenish's land bill shows it," Burrell insisted. "Oh, we'll have a real policy of land reform, not an act of revenge."

Harry Rames leaned across the corner of the table toward young Burrell. To the youth's eyes he looked at this moment extraordinarily haggard and old.

"I'll tell you, Burrell, why I asked my question. I wanted to recapture from you if I could something of a man's enthusiasm at his first political victory."

Burrell looked at his leader with astonishment. Of the man of fire who had blazed through the constituency from corner to corner with clear ringing phrases and an inexhaustible good-humor there was now nothing left. He was burnt out. He sat with brooding eyes and a white face all fallen into despair. The tale of his years was suddenly written large upon him. Burrell had wit enough to understand that fatigue did not explain the change. A mask was withdrawn; he saw misery like a cancer. Rames sat and betrayed himself like a man in his cups.

"You tell me you felt ashamed in the school-rooms. I never knew anything of such shame. To win, to win, to win! That was all I thought about. That was all the desire I felt. That was what I hoped you would help me to recapture to-night. But you haven't helped."

Rames's eyes dwelt angrily upon his colleague.

"No. You have made me feel ashamed too." Then his face relaxed and he added in a friendlier voice: "I believe that I have helped you--really helped you. Oh, not to win a seat in the House of Commons. That's nothing to be so proud about. But to find your vocation."

"Where you have found yours," said Burrell firmly.

"Not a bit of it," said Rames, and then he woke from his moodiness to a savage outburst of contempt. "Oh, I am going on with it. Don't be alarmed, Burrell. I'll lead you. We'll put up a fight. We'll make the fur fly. Very possibly we'll pull the whole Government down with a run. But--" and drawing his chair nearer to the youth he changed his tone. "I'll tell you the truth about the House of Commons. It's the place where the second-rate gets the finest show in the world. In no walk of life does second-rate intellect reap so high a reward or meet with such great esteem. But it won't lift you to the very top. Nor will first-rate intellect either. Remember that!"

"What will then?" asked Burrell in perplexity, and Harry Rames shrugged his shoulders.

"The little bit extra. Character, perseverance! I don't know. Something anyway. It's the same everywhere now. There are too many clever people about. Faith in a cause, I think will do it. That's why the sentimentalists do so much harm in public affairs. They get their way, because they believe. They are not playing the political game. Cleverness is twelve for a penny nowadays. To get up to the top you must have the little bit extra. Now in the sphere of politics I haven't got it. I don't say office is out of my reach. It isn't. I have been offered it. I have refused it. But I haven't got the little bit extra. Outside politics--in quite another sphere--I believe I have. But that's all done with. I was warned when I went into politics--warned by a shrewd, wise man. But I wouldn't listen, and so some day amongst the second-rate Right Honorables half a dozen lines will announce my death in the *Times*."

Young Burrell had no great experience of the intenser emotions, and the bitterness with which Rames spoke appalled him. He saw a man in torture, and he listened to a cry of pain grown intolerable. Then in a second all was changed again. Rames was on his feet replacing the stoppers in the decanters, taking the shades from off the candles, performing the little conventional acts of a host in his dining-room. The chasm in the ordinary level surface of things which had yawned for a moment and given Burrell a glimpse of the pit where misery gnawed had closed up.

"We will join my wife," said Rames. He stopped at the door.

"Were you ever at Toulon?"

"No."

"There's a statue on the quay there, at the water's edge, overlooking the harbor. A great bronze figure, extraordinarily alert, with a light upon its forehead, the Genius of the Sea. And on the open pages of a bronze book in the front of the pedestal, the names of the great sailors are engraved. Cook and the rest of them. The list ends with D'Urville, I remember. I only saw the statue once. My father showed it to me when I was a boy. I don't suppose that I have ever thought of it until to-day." He repeated softly as though speaking to himself:

"Yes the list ends with D'Urville." Then he roused himself. "Bring your cigar in. Cynthia doesn't mind. By the way," and a smile of tenderness transfigured his face, "not a word of this to her. She thinks I am going to be a great man. She's wrong, but I don't want her to know before she needs must." Burrell consented at once. He followed Rames from the room with all joy in his victory quite overcast. He looked beyond the surprising revelations of his host and obtained a glimpse into a new side of life. He was the spectator of one of the grim comedies of marriage. Here was the wife--so it seemed to him--believing joyfully in the great destiny of her husband; and the husband laboring in torment to sustain her belief, while all the while he knew that his destiny was thwarted and that the true current of his life ran through other fields.

They went along the passage into the drawing-room. It was a warm night of September and the windows stood open upon the garden. Cynthia was not in the room. Harry stepped out onto the lawn. The night was dark and he could see no one. But the light in the drawing-room had revealed him as he stepped out, and whilst he was standing peering into the darkness Cynthia came softly over the grass to his side.

"You'll catch cold," he said. "The dew's heavy."

Cynthia took his arm. "Hush," she said. "Listen!" and through the still air the chimes of the great clock in Ludsey steeple floated with a silvery and melodious sound to their ears. A tune was struck out by the bells, then another.

"I heard that," said Cynthia in a whisper, "on the night my father died. I was sitting alone with him in the darkness while his life drifted away. It was winter."

Harry put his arm about her and pressed her to his side.

"I heard them again," she continued, "one night when I was waiting for you to telephone to me, Harry. Do you remember?"

"Yes."

"I waited a long time for you that night, Harry," and there was a catch in her voice. "Ludsey chimes have meant very much to us. Let us hear them out!"

They stood together in the darkness until the last distant note had died away. It seemed to Rames that Cynthia listened as though she were taking a farewell of them.

CHAPTER XXXVI

THE TELEGRAM

Harry Rames and Cynthia travelled up to London the next day. Cynthia was restless and excited.

"Let us dine at a restaurant and go to a theatre, Harry," she said. "I can't sit still and stay at home to-night."

"Very well. What shall we go and see?"

"Oh, something with bright colors and movement and music."

But there ran through the piece she chose a melody of a haunting wistfulness and Harry Rames, happening to glance at his wife in the darkness of the auditorium, saw that the tears were raining silently down her cheeks.

"What's the matter, Cynthia?" he asked in a whisper.

Cynthia smiled at him through her tears and laid a hand upon his arm.

"Hush!" she answered. "It's all right, Harry."

As the curtain descended at the end of the act she said, "Let us go now quickly, do you mind? Before the lights are turned up."

They were, fortunately, near to the end of their row of stalls, and they were able to slip out while the curtain was still ascending and descending upon the lighted stage, and the auditorium still dark. Rames left Cynthia in the lobby while he went in search of his carriage. When he returned he found her standing with her face carefully turned to the wall in front of a commonplace engraving, which seemed to be demanding from her the most meticulous study.

"Have you found it?" she asked, and she hurried with him across the pavement. "Let us go home, Harry. It was nothing except nerves. I was stupid. We have been doing a good deal lately, haven't we?"

"That's all right, Cynthia. You poor little girl," said Rames as he crossed her cloak over her throat. He knew her too well to make the mistake of plying her with questions, and they drove to their home in silence.

"You had better go to bed, Cynthia," he said. "I'll send your maid to you."

"No. I am all right now," she answered. "I have something to say, Harry."

She went forward to his study--that room with the mahogany panels where both had faced the hardest crises of their lives, had known the worst of their sorrows, the sweetest of their joys. Harry followed her, turned on the lights, and closed the door. Cynthia was already standing by the fireplace with a foot upon the fender; and she shivered as though she were cold.

"Yes, it's chilly," said Rames. "Ill light the fire."

He struck a match and set light to the paper. The wood crackled, the flames spurted up. Cynthia threw off her cloak and, crouching before the fire, warmed herself. Harry Rames drew up an arm-chair for her.

"Won't you sit here, Cynthia, and be comfortable?" he asked, and his voice seemed to rouse her from a gloomy contemplation. She stood up and walked over to his bureau.

Harry's eyes followed her movements closely. With a growing consternation he saw her grasp the handles of a locked drawer and try to open it.

"What do you keep in here, Harry?" she asked.

"Oh, some old forgotten things."

"Your charts?"

"My word, yes. I believe they are there," he said with an air of surprise.

"Will you show them to me?" Cynthia asked. "I should like to see them."

"I don't know where the key is. It's lost."

"Are you sure?"

"For all the chance I have of finding it, dear, it might just as well be at the bottom of the Serpentine."

Harry had not moved away from the fireplace. Cynthia, her back toward him, had been playing with the brass handles of the locked drawer. Now she swung round suddenly. Often she had wondered what errand had taken him from the house at one o'clock of the morning after she had revealed her heart to him in this very room. Now she guessed the truth. It was on that night that he had begun to build up his dykes against the encroachments of his longings. She faced him; her eyes burned steadily upon his face, thoughtful, but betraying nothing of her thoughts.

"Yes," she said, "I suppose it might as well be in the Serpentine." She turned again to the drawer.

"A knife will open it easily, Harry."

Harry Rames moved uncomfortably.

"It had better be left alone, Cynthia," he said. But she insisted and, opening a blade of his knife, he went reluctantly across the room to her side.

"It is your wish, Cynthia. You will remember that?" he said gravely. "For myself I would much rather that it should never be unlocked until both of us are dead."

Cynthia showed no surprise at the gravity of his voice. But now she too paused. "There is still time," she was saying to herself in feverish trouble of mind, though her face was calm. "There is still time. He is giving me my chance--my last chance." Her eyelids were lowered over her eyes and she glanced at him under the thick lashes.

"You are afraid to open it, Harry?"

"Yes, I am afraid."

It was not merely the outrush of old and overwhelming memories which he dreaded. But that locked drawer had become to him a symbol of his own self-mastery. So long as it remained locked, and no longer, he would dominate his torments and be the captain of his soul. For so long he would keep locked a frail door against his yearnings. Cynthia, in a voice so faltering and low that it was hardly audible, said:

"Still I should like it opened."

"Very well."

She stood with her fingers clenched upon her palms whilst Harry inserted the blade of his knife in the chink of the drawer, ran it along until it touched the lock, and then forced apart the fastenings. There was a crack as of splintering wood. Harry Rames replaced his knife in his pocket, pulled out the drawer, and carried it over to his writing-table.

"There it is," he said, moving away from it to the fireplace. Cynthia bent over the drawer and turned on the light of a reading lamp which stood upon the table.

"This is your own chart upon the top, Harry?"

"Yes. It is the last one, you see. Hemming may be bringing back another."

"Will you show me exactly the point you reached?"

It seemed to Harry as if she was bent on trying him to the last point of endurance.

"It is marked there quite plainly, Cynthia," he said.

Cynthia leaned over the drawer--for a long time. Harry Rames was quite surprised at the closeness of her scrutiny. It was so long since she had shown any interest in his journey or indeed in anything except his political career. As a matter of fact, Cynthia saw of that map nothing but a blur: for her eyes were dim with tears, and she bent so low over its configurations simply because in that attitude her face was hidden.

She moved.

"What is this?"

She took up a brown package, tied up with string, which lay in a corner of the drawer.

"I don't know," said Rames with a puzzled face. "I have forgotten."

"May I open it?"

"Of course."

Cynthia cut the string and, one after another, perhaps a score of brown telegraph envelopes slipped out in a cascade and fell upon the table in front of her.

"Telegrams," she said curiously. "Unopened, too! Oh, Harry!" this with a mocking laugh of reproach. Then she looked at the address of one of the telegrams. It ran:

RAMES,

S. S. PERHAPS,

TILBURY DOCKS.

As she read her face changed. There came a look of introspection in her dark, wide-open eyes. She swept back in her thoughts over the course of years and took note of the irony of things and of the surprising changes in a life like hers which, to all the world, was uneventful and prescribed.

"I remember," she said. "These are the good wishes sent to you when you started. You once told me that you never opened them."

"I hadn't the time. We had to catch the tide out of London. We were late getting away. I had forgotten that I had kept them all."

"I am going to open them."

"It is too late to answer them."

"I wonder."

Cynthia opened the telegrams until she came upon one about half through the number which arrested her attention. This she spread out before her and smiled at its phrasing.

"Harry!" she said.

Rames turned about.

"Yes?"

"Come and read this."

He stood behind Cynthia's chair and read aloud the message still legible upon the form.

"Every heart-felt wish for a triumphant journey from an unknown friend in--;" and then he stopped with an intake of his breath. "In South America," he resumed, and so stood quite still for the space of a few seconds. Then he leaned forward and looked at the name of the telegraph office from which the message had been sent.

"Daventry," he cried.

"Yes," said Cynthia with a little laugh upon which her voice broke. "We had a telegraph office on the estancia. We were very proud of it, I can tell you"; and then the amusement died away from her voice, and "oh!" she whispered in a long sigh, as she felt his arm about her.

"You sent that! You! Cynthia! Before I knew you, before we met."

"Yes, dear, I sent it."

"Just think," he cried. "It reached me at Tilbury. It travelled out with me to the South. It was in the desk in my cabin for three long dark winters. It came back with me to England. By chance I met you----"

"No, not by chance, Harry," Cynthia interrupted. "I sent Mr. Benoliel to fetch you."

"Yes, you did," he agreed, with a laugh. "We met, and we married, and through all these changes it has lain here unopened. Why didn't I open it? That was conceit, Cynthia. I was haughty. I was going out to discover the South Pole. I didn't open my telegrams."

"But if you had opened it, Harry, you would only have laughed. For it's just the message of a schoolgirl, isn't it? You were one of my heroes--oh, not the only one but the latest one--I had just let you in past the turnstile to my enchanted garden. I was seventeen on the very day I sent it. I drove down to the office--oh in such a condition of importance. I pictured to myself you, the unknown you, sitting in your cabin and wondering and wondering and wondering who your little friend was in South America. Then I drove back and"--she stopped and went on again slowly--"yes, other things happened to me that day." She looked down again at the telegram. "Yes, the message of a foolish and romantic school-girl."

"I should like to be able to think, Cynthia," said her husband, "that I had opened it when it came."

"But you didn't," said Cynthia, "and so--" she broke off her sentence. She took the telegram form, folded it, and replaced it in its envelope. She took a brush from a little bottle of gum which stood ready upon the table by the inkstand and, smearing the inner border of the envelope, stuck it down again. Then she stood up and turned to her husband. "And so," she continued, "you must take it, Harry, as though it were despatched to you by me only to-day for the first time and delivered to you here now at midnight."

She held out to him the telegram and he took it, gazing at her with a look of wonder. And then hope flamed in his eyes. Cynthia turned away abruptly. To her that swift flame of hope, of life, was almost intolerable.

"Then you knew," he cried.

Cynthia nodded her head, but she kept her face averted.

"I have known a long time," she answered in a low voice. "Ever since the letter came to you with the Rexland stamp."

The sound of her voice and her attitude pierced to Rames's heart. His exultation gave way to concern.

"I am very sorry, Cynthia," he said gently. "I tried to hide it."

"Oh, my dear, I know you did. With all your strength you tried to hide it. You watched yourself each minute. But," and she turned to him with a little smile of tenderness, "I watched you closer still, and the longing grew too big to be hidden."

Harry Rames made no pretence to deny the truth of her words, knowing full well that all denial would be vain. The screen was down between them.

"Yes," he said; "but Cynthia, I keep my bargain."

"My dear, there is no longer any bargain between us," she answered, "for on both sides there is love. Of that I am very sure."

She held out her hands to him and he caught them and held her against his breast.

"You said you had rather that drawer was not unlocked until both of us were dead," she whispered. "My dear, if that drawer was not to be unlocked, we might both of us be dead at once for all the value our lives were going to be. So you will go, you must, unless we are to be wrecked altogether. We have been most unhappy, both of us. I, because I thought of the dangers," and she suddenly caught him close as though even now she dared not let him go, "and could not bring myself to make the sacrifice and let you run the risk-- you, because the call was always in your ears. It couldn't go on. That's the truth, Harry. Especially now that you know that your secret's no longer a secret to me. We should grow estranged, embittered, each one thinking the other horribly selfish. Perhaps, even hatred might come."

"No," protested Harry.

"Oh, yes, yes. It has come from smaller causes often enough. It might come, Harry, and that would be terrible. I have thought it out, my dear. All the time we were cruising down in the West I was thinking our position over and over and over. And it seemed to me that you must win this Hickleton election first--and then I would tell you that I understood your great trouble and let you go. But you had to win first. I couldn't let you go while people might be able to say that you had gone because you had been beaten in your political ambitions. I was too proud of you, my dear, to allow that. You must lay down your career at a moment of success, leaving behind you a good name amongst your colleagues and perhaps a great many regrets. But you have won the election now, you have made good, as they say, and so, for both our sakes, you must go."

She drew herself out of his arms and moved away to the fire.

"Of course it's just what I wanted when I first met you, isn't it?" she said with a wavering effort of a laugh. "I urged you to go back and finish your work the first time I met you--one night at the Admiralty. Only things have changed a good deal since then, haven't they?"

Her voice, which had been steady up till now, broke, and with a sob she suddenly hid her face in her hands. "Oh, Harry," she cried as though her heart was breaking, and he hurried to her, exclaiming:

"Cynthia, I am a brute. I can't leave you here for three years alone."

She held him off with her arm outstretched, dreading lest she should weaken and take her advantage of his remorse and so have to go through all this heart-rending renunciation again at some future time.

"You won't, Harry," she said, drying her eyes with her handkerchief. "I have thought it all out. My father asked me on his death-bed not to desert the Daventry estancia altogether. He loved it so himself that he did not wish to think that he would die and that no one of his own people would ever see it again and make sure that all was going well with it. And here's the opportunity. While you go down to the Antarctic I will go back to the Daventry estancia. I couldn't live here day after day with you away amidst the storms and the snow. There I shall be able to. I will have the estancia to look after. When will you go?"

"Not so very soon, Cynthia, after all," he said. "It will take me a year before the preparations are complete. Besides, there's the money to be raised."

Cynthia raised her shoulders in a gesture of reproach.

"Oh, Harry! There's no trouble about the money, of course."

Rames stared at her. "Cynthia," he cried. "You'll help?"

"More than help, Harry," she answered. "You see I let you go--yes. I even bid you go--yes. But I mean to have my share, my dear, in whatever you do. I mean that you shall carry something of me, something more than a telegram this time, to your farthest South."

Rames sat down in a chair by the side of the fire close to where she stood. He gazed into the flames in silence. With all gentleness and love she was heaping coals of fire upon his head. Every look, every word she spoke, confessed the deep pain which he was causing her. She was brave, but through the curtain of her bravery her fear and anguish shone. He spoke as a man will who is smitten by his conscience.

"I am very sorry, Cynthia. When I asked you to marry me I had no suspicion that any longing could get so strong a hold on me. I once told you carelessly that men were driven out upon these expeditions by the torment of their souls. I said that knowing it only by hearsay and by the plain proof of it which they show in what they have written. Now I know it--here," and he struck his breast above his heart. "Yes, I have got to go if I am ever to have peace. But I am sorry, Cynthia."

His voice trailed off into silence and Cynthia laid a hand upon his head and stroked his hair. "I know," she said, "I know."

"All that I thought so fine, so well worth having--the fight with other men for mastery, the conquest with what conquest would bring--power and rule and governing--it's extraordinary how completely all desire for it has vanished out of me!" he continued. "Do you remember the account I gave you of my maiden speech?"

"Yes."

Cynthia's hand had gone to her breast, but her voice was steady.

"There was a fragment of time when the world went blank, when I lost the thread of my speech, and stood dumb. A fragment of time so short that it wasn't noticeable to any one in the House except myself."

"Yes."

"Well, these three years of politics seem to me just such an unnoticeable interruption of my real life. The fight which I revelled in appears to me now a squabble made ignoble with intrigues, bitter with mean disappointments, the victory not worth the fight. No doubt I am wrong. I went into the House of Commons, you see, without ideas," and Cynthia started at the word so familiar to her fancies. "Now I have one, a big one, and it has mastered me."

And so Harry Rames passed at last through the turnstile into Cynthia's private garden. But it was in accordance with the irony of their lives that she wished with every drop of her blood that he had remained outside.

"I long for simple things, not shifts and intrigues and bitterness; the gray mists on glaciers; the day's journey over the snow, with its wind ridges and its storms; the hard, lean life of it all; the fight, not with men, but with enormous things of nature, some dangerous, some serene, but, whether dangerous or serene, wholly indifferent." He gazed for a little while into the fire, seeking in the analysis of his emotions his apologia.

"I think, Cynthia," he continued, "that once a man has gone far into the empty spaces of the earth, he has the mark of them upon him. Voices call from them over all the leagues of all the seas and need no receivers at the end."

"Yes," said Cynthia, and once more her memories travelled back to the death-bed of old Daventry in the dark room of the white house. He had given her reasons for his great love of his estancia on the wide plains of Argentina. But there had been another reason, she remembered, which his failing wits had not allowed his tongue to formulate. Cynthia had often wondered what that reason was. She had no doubt that her husband had explained it now. "Yes, my father also heard those voices."

After a short silence Harry Rames reached out his hand and took hers.

"I think, my dear," he said gently, "that things would have been different, that I should not have wanted to go, had we been fortunate enough to have children--" and with a cry Cynthia turned to him fiercely.

"No, no!" she exclaimed. "During this hour, for the first time, I have been thanking God we had no children. For if we had, you would still have wanted to go just as much as you do now, and that I could not have borne."

Harry had no answer for her outburst. In his heart he knew that what she had said was true. He sat in silence, his eyes upon the fire and her hand in his; and a moment or two later she dropped upon her knees at his side.

"But oh, Harry, come back to me!" she cried. "You must go I know. That's the way things happen. But oh, come back to me."

CHAPTER XXXVII

THE LAST

At nine o'clock on a morning of July during the next year an auxiliary barquentine of four hundred and fifty tons steamed westward with the tide past the Isle of Wight. Besides the helmsman, Cynthia and Harry Rames were upon the bridge. They stood side by side, Cynthia gripping the rail in front of her with both of her hands. They did not speak. The ship glided past Cowes gay with its white yachts and crowded esplanade and rounded Gurnard Point into Newtown Bay. Cynthia looked ahead through a blur of tears, watching for and yet dreading to see a low square church tower stand out against the sky close to the water in a dip of the coast-line hills. Opposite to that church the ship was stopped and a boat was lowered. Cynthia, with Robert Brook to look after her, was put ashore on Yarmouth pier; and the barquentine dipped her flag and steamed on to the Needles and the open sea on its three years' voyage.

Robert Brook escorted Cynthia across the water to Southampton, and the next day witnessed her departure from the docks on a steamer of the Royal Mail for Buenos Ayres. He returned to London that afternoon, took a solitary dinner at his club, and walked afterward to Curzon Street. The Rames's house was all lit up, and from the open windows music drifted out upon the summer night. Harry and Cynthia had let their house a week before, and to-night the new residents were giving a party. Robert Brook had an invitation and went in. He listened for half an hour to a party of coons and then could endure no more. The comic songs and the laughter seemed to him that night in this house a desecration. For in the characters of Harry Rames and his wife he chose to see something of greatness, in their lives something of achievement. He looked about the walls. Some dark and terrible hours must needs have been passed by both Harry and Cynthia within them before the great resolution had been taken which had condemned her to three years of loneliness on an estancia in South America and had stripped him of a sure career in politics.

Robert Brook fell into a black mood and an utter weariness with his own life. For him season was to follow season and to find him still a guest at the parties and the entertainments until he became old and a bore. He envied Harry his expedition, Cynthia her sorrow. He went out wretched and walked by instinct down Whitehall. On his way to his club he passed the windows of the Board of Trade. These, too, were brilliantly lit; for within the building a Cabinet Minister was endeavoring to compose an acute struggle between artisans and their employers. Robert Brook watched those windows; and his disgust with his own life increased. Here again was achievement for others, not for himself. There would never be room for him within that building, nor within any other where the nation's administration was being done. And his life was going; indeed, the best part of it was done. He walked on to his own small house and let himself in with his key. The passage was dark and the house quite silent. He stood for a while alone in the darkness and the silence. He thought of Cynthia and Harry, of Devenish and his colleagues, of others without eminence, but, at all events, with wives and children. He had given up his life to the House of Commons and the House of Commons repaid him by barely knowing his name. There was probably no man in London more wretched that night than Robert Brook.

THE END

ks.

Milton Keynes UK
Ingram Content Group UK Ltd.
UKHW042143281024
450365UK00010B/579

9 789362 518491